A GRAMMAR OF UGARITIC

RESOURCES FOR BIBLICAL STUDY

Editor
Hyun Chul Paul Kim, Old Testament/Hebrew Bible

Number 102

SBL PRESS

A GRAMMAR OF UGARITIC

John Screnock

with Vladimir Olivero

SBL PRESS

SBL PRESS

Atlanta

Library of Congress Control Number: 2022947945

For Walter

Contents

Acknowledgements xi
Abbreviations xiii

Introduction 1

Lesson 1 13
1.1. The Ugaritic Abjad 13
1.2. Vowels in Ugaritic 14
1.3. Noun Declension 15
1.4. Articulation and Definiteness in Ugaritic 17
1.5. Copular ("to be") Clauses 17
1.6. Verbal Stems 17
1.7. G-Stem QATALA Verbs 17
1.8. QATALA *yadaʿa*, "to know" 19
1.9. Verb-Subject Agreement 19
1.10. Vocabulary 19
1.11. Exercises 20

Lesson 2 23
2.1. Dual and Plural Nouns 23
2.2. Adjectives 24
2.3. Prepositions 25
2.4. G-Stem QATALA Dual and Plural 26
2.5. Tri-radical Roots 27
2.6. Theme Vowels 28
2.7. Weak Consonants and Vowel Contraction 29
2.8. Weak Verbs: Hollow 30
2.9. Vocabulary 31
2.10. Exercises 32

Lesson 3 35
3.1. Independent Pronouns 35
3.2. Genitive Phrases 36
3.3. Pattern and Theme Vowels of YAQTULU Verbs 37
3.4. G-Stem YAQTULU Verbs 38
3.5. Weak Verbs: Hollow Verbs in YAQTULU 39
3.6. Consonant Cluster ṣt → št 40
3.7. *Kalīlu* and *kullu* 40
3.8. Ugaritic Cuneiform 41
3.9. Vocabulary 43
3.10. Exercises 44

Short Story 1: Baʿlu, ʾilu, wa ʿanatu 47

Lesson 4 49
4.1. Suffixed Pronouns 49
4.2. Valency and Verb Argument Structures 51
4.3. D-Stem Verbs: QATALA and YAQTULU 52
4.4. N-Stem Verbs: QATALA and YAQTULU 53
4.5. Weak Verbs: I-n 55
4.6. Weak Verbs: I-ʾ 57
4.7. Function and Meaning of *wa* 57
4.8. Vocabulary 58
4.9. Exercises 59

Short Story 2: Rigamū Bêti 61

Lesson 5 63
5.1. Relative Words and Demonstrative Pronouns 63
5.2. Enclitic Particles 65
5.3. Irrealis Mood 65
5.4. G-Stem Jussive, Volitive, and Imperative Verbs 66
5.5. N-Stem and D-Stem Jussive, Volitive, and Imperative Verbs 69
5.6. Geminate Roots 71
5.7. Stative Verbs 73
5.8. *Bi* of Exchange 73
5.9. Vocabulary 74
5.10. Exercises 75

Short Story 3: ʾaklu Luki wa Rani 77

Lesson 6 79
6.1. Weak Verbs: Hollow Verbs in the Jussive, Volitive, and Imperative 79
6.2. Weak Verbs: I-ʾ Verbs in the Jussive, Volitive, and Imperative 81
6.3. Weak Verbs: I-n Verbs and LQḤ in the Jussive, Volitive, and Imperative 81
6.4. Weak Verbs: III-y/w 83
6.5. Š-Stem Verbs 88
6.6. Questions 90
6.7. Vocabulary 90
6.8. Exercises 91

Short Story 4: Ṯalāṯu ʾalapūma Qaṭanūma 93

Lesson 7 95
7.1. Participles 95
7.2. Infinitives 98
7.3. Cardinal Numerals 100
7.4. Weak Verbs in the Š-Stem 103
7.5. Š-Stem ṮB, "to return" 104
7.6. Weak Verbs: I-y/w 104
7.7. Weak Verbs: HLK and HLM 108
7.8. YAQTULU in Past-Tense Contexts 108
7.9. Locative Accusatives 109
7.10. Vocabulary 109
7.11. Exercises 110

Short Story 5: Šaʿrūḫurāṣitu 113

Lesson 8 115
8.1. Weak Verbs: YTN and III-n 115
8.2. Passive Stem Verbs: Gp, Dp, and Šp 116
8.3. Stems with Affixed *t*: Gt, tD, and Št 121
8.4. L-Stem Verbs 124
8.5. R-Stem Verbs 124
8.6. YAQTULU 3md and 3mp Prefix *y*- 125

Acknowledgments

A large number of people contributed to the making of this grammar. First and foremost, I thank Vladimir Olivero. He was a student in the Ugaritic class that used my initial drafts of the first two chapters. He soon became a co-instructor and has now taught the class with me for several years. Along the way, he contributed in many ways to refining and improving the class—its aims, structure, and materials. In the particular iteration of our materials presented in the pages of this grammar, he drafted large portions of the introduction, lesson five, and lesson eight, and he contributed significantly to the revision of other lessons, exercises, and supplementary material. In the final stages of editing and proofing, he continued to play an essential role in bringing the grammar to completion. He has been a crucial source of encouragement and knowledge.

I am also very grateful to Robert Holmstedt, who has shaped me as a scholar, linguist, and teacher, including (among other things) in my approach to Ugaritic. He taught me the language at the University of Toronto, served as a sounding-board as I worked on the grammar, and used an early draft of it as a textbook for his Ugaritic class—providing valuable feedback. His passion for pedagogy is infectious and in many ways stands behind my instinct to create a grammar of Ugaritic in the first place.

Jacob Thomas and BanglaTypeFoundry did me a great service in creating Oxford Ugaritic, the font used to represent cuneiform in this publication. I thank Jacob for the excellence and care that he put into the font. And I am thankful for his collegiality and patience in working with me, a true neophyte when it comes to the technology of fonts. I am grateful to the John Fell Oxford University Press Research Fund for financially supporting the creation of the font. I also thank Valérie Matoïan for her assistance and the Mission archéologique syro-française de Ras Shamra-Ougarit for providing images for the introduction.

Jordan Maly-Preuss, an advanced DPhil student in Classics at Oxford, proofread the antepenultimate draft. Because she was a student in an earlier Ugaritic class—who gave valuable feedback on how to improve the lessons and other materials—she was able to engage not just the quality of the English in this grammar, but also the precision of our grammatical descriptions and the accuracy of our Ugaritic. Besides catching mistakes, Jordan also suggested a number of improvements. Sincere thanks also to Nicole Tilford and Bob Buller of SBL Press and RBS series editor Paul Kim for their work transforming my manuscript into a book.

A number of other individuals have helped along the way. John Cook used a draft of the grammar at Asbury Theological Seminary and provided helpful feedback. The people who took Ugaritic from 2016 to 2021 pointed out typos, suggested improvements, and gave encouraging positive reviews to the lessons as I developed them. A few that stand out—though I thank all of them, and I doubtless am forgetting some important ones—include Hannah Bash, Michele Bianconi, Parsa Daneshmand, Andrew Daniel, David Forward, Ryan Francis, Sebastien Kenny, Simone Landman, Benjamin Lucas, Jesse Lundquist, Alexander McCarron, Serena Millen, Josiah Peeler, Trevor Pomeroy, Susy Rees, Ellen Ryan, Robert Simpson, Edward Tolmie, Kieran Vernon, Cale Waress, and Jason Webber. I am also very grateful to senior colleagues at Oxford who encouraged me to teach Ugaritic and who supported the endeavor of teaching and grammar-writing. The Centre for Hebrew and Jewish Studies, the Faculty of Asian and Middle Eastern Studies, and the Hebrew, Jewish, and early Christian subject group have supported and made space for the way in which I teach Ugaritic at Oxford, while Martine Smith-Huvers and Sue Forteath helped with advertising, room booking, and countless other practical but essential matters for the running of this class.

I dedicate the book to Walter Schultz, a long-time friend, teacher, and mentor who has always encouraged me in my life's pursuits. In the summer of 2003, after the first year of my undergraduate degree, I was excited about ancient languages and eager to teach. In response to my overzealous attempts to make him my first student, Walter went out of his way not to stifle this inclination, and let me try to teach him Koine Greek. As with every other good passion he observed in me, he encouraged it without reserve. For him, and others in my life (Dad, Mom, Sarah, Ethan, Charlotte, Fred, Berta) who always support me, I have much gratitude.

John Screnock
Kidlington, UK
20 April 2021

Abbreviations

Grammatical Number

1	first person
2	second person
3	third person
d	dual
p/pl	plural
s/sg	singular

Grammatical Case

acc	accusative
gen	genitive
nom	nominative
obl	oblique
voc	vocative

Grammatical Gender

c/com	common
f/fem	feminine
m/masc	masculine

Stems

D	*Doppelungsstamm* (doubled stem)
Dp	passive of D-stem
G	*Grundstamm* (basic stem)
Gp	passive of G-stem
Gt	G-stem with infixed t

L	lengthened stem
N	stem with affixed n, passive of G-stem
R	reduplicated stem
Rt	R-stem with infixed t
Š	stem with affixed š, causative of G-stem
Šp	passive of Š-stem
Št	Š-stem with infixed t
tD	D-stem with infixed t

Additional Grammatical Abbreviations

TAM	tense, aspect, mood

Other Abbreviations

AfO	*Archiv für Orientforschung*
AOAT	Alter Orient und Altes Testament
ANEM	Ancient Near East Monographs
BibOr	*Bibliotheca Orientalis*
HdO	Handbuch der Orientalistik
HSS	Harvard Semitic Studies
JSNL	*Journal of Northwest Semitic Languages*
KTU	Dietrich, Manfried, Oswald Loretz, and Joaquín Sanmartín, eds. *Die keilalphabetischen Texte aus Ugarit*. Münster: Ugarit-Verlag, 2013. 3rd enl. ed. of *KTU: The Cuneiform Alphabetic Texts from Ugarit, Ras Ibn Hani, and Other Places*. Edited by Manfried Dietrich, Oswald Loretz, and Joaquín Sanmartín. Münster: Ugarit-Verlag, 1995.
LSAWS	Linguistic Studies in Ancient West Semitic
Or	*Orientalia*
RS	Ras Shamra
SAOC	Studies in Ancient Oriental Civilization
UF	*Ugarit-Forschungen*
WAWSup	Writings from the Ancient World Supplement series

Introduction

This textbook grew out of our experience teaching Ugaritic at the University of Oxford. When I (John Screnock) learned Ugaritic during my PhD, as part of a minor in Northwest Semitic languages at the University of Toronto, I had a number of years of Hebrew and Aramaic under my belt. I was not, however, a comparative Semiticist. Nor did I have extensive knowledge of Akkadian and Arabic like some of my classmates, for whom the existing textbooks on Ugaritic seemed to be designed. The learning curve felt steep at times.

When I began to teach at Oxford in 2015, I used an approach commonly employed in Ugaritic classes: we started reading texts from the first day, learning the grammar inductively. Only the seasoned Hebraists and Assyriologists survived to the end of the first eight-week term. I realized early on during that first term that my students needed a better resource for their first engagement with the language—a first-year grammar of Ugaritic suitable for a wider audience. Over the following years, I developed the present grammar, with the aim of retaining all of the students at Oxford who wanted to learn Ugaritic—graduates and undergraduates, Egyptologists, classicists, archaeologists, linguists, Arabists, Hebraists, Assyriologists, theologians, and even students studying subjects like philosophy and economics. Vladimir Olivero was a student in the class where I trialed the initial chapters; he soon became a trusted coteacher and collaborator, who helped hone the lessons and exercises.

To be clear, our grammar is not meant to be easy. It is intended for students who are serious about studying language in the context of university education. However, the grammar is accessible. We make every effort not to assume background knowledge and concepts from northwest Semitic, Hebrew, Akkadian, or Arabic—none of which should be assumed in an elementary grammar. In our experience of teaching Ugaritic, we have seen massive improvements as a result of using this grammar. Students finish the course and learn the grammar well. After eight lessons, students are able to read tablets and texts in cuneiform. Many of them go on to learn Ugaritic in greater depth—including questioning the reconstruction of Ugaritic presented here.

In short, if you are a student or are teaching students who do not already know Akkadian, Hebrew, or Arabic, then this is the right place to start. Even if you already have one of these languages, you will learn Ugaritic better by going through our full grammar. In our experience, only students with a strong understanding of comparative Semitics will be better off starting with a grammatical précis and moving straight into texts.

The goal of the textbook is to lead students through the grammar of Ugaritic at a steady pace, giving grammatical information in digestible blocks rather than a single outline. All parts of speech, syntax, and vocabulary are taught gradually from the first lesson. Cuneiform is introduced in lesson 3 and used for exercises throughout the remainder of the lessons. Exercises focus equally on translation from Ugaritic and composition into Ugaritic—using vocalized Ugaritic, unvocalized transcription, and cuneiform. Short stories provide further exposure to the Ugaritic language in narrative contexts, providing repetition of common forms and vocabulary. The range of delivery helps students to fully develop their language skills and provides a good basis for classroom teaching, which can also involve listening and speaking in Ugaritic.

Instructors should, of course, be flexible in the speed at which they move through the textbook, depending on the linguistic experience and time commitments of their students. We cover the eight lessons and five short stories in eight–nine weeks, with one two-hour session per week. The material could be covered more rapidly with multiple sessions per week, or, conversely, instructors can stretch a single lesson over multiple sessions or weeks. Finally, the exercises at the end of each lesson are evenly distributed in terms of difficulty and the grammar and vocabulary that are covered; as a result, instructors can choose to assign only the odd numbered exercises if desired.

Students will learn a reconstruction of Ugaritic that they can use to read texts with fluency. This is not a new reconstruction of Ugaritic, but rather follows current scholarship—in particular, Dennis Pardee and John Huehnergard, whose reconstructions of Ugaritic are similar to one another. This grammar prepares students to use intermediate-level resources such as Pierre Bordreuil and Dennis Pardee's *A Manual of Ugaritic* and John

Huehnergard's *An Introduction to Ugaritic*.[1] Because the *Manual of Ugaritic* in particular contains an excellent collection of texts—including images, line drawings, transcriptions, and vocalizations—this grammar makes an effort to prepare students to read from that corpus. As a result, we tend to follow Pardee's version of Ugaritic the most, and where there is indeterminate evidence about vocalization, we opt for vocalization that aligns with the *Manual of Ugaritic*.

Ugarit

The ancient city-state of Ugarit was located near the coast of the Mediterranean in present-day Syria, near Latakia.[2] The site was inhabited as far back as the eighth millennium, though most of our textual knowledge of Ugarit—thanks to the discovery of thousands of clay tablets, mainly in Akkadian and Ugaritic—comes from the end of the Bronze Age (fourteenth–twelfth centuries BCE). During the Bronze Age, Ugarit was strategically located at the crossroads of ancient Near Eastern civilizations in Mesopotamia, Egypt, the Levant, and Asia Minor. The territory of Ugarit extended from Mount Ṣaphon in the north to as far south as Siyannu, bounded on the east by the Jabal al-Ansariyeh mountain range and on the west by the Mediterranean Sea. Ugarit also controlled an important port and kept close relations with communities on the island of Cyprus, just across the Mediterranean from Ugarit. Cyprus was a significant source of copper, the main ingredient (with tin) for the valuable metal bronze. Ugarit's location made it an important economic hub. It thrived at the end of the Bronze Age, occupying a pivotal role between the great powers of the time—the Egyptian and the Hittite kingdoms—and functioning as a major link in trade between the Eastern Mediterranean, Mesopotamia, Asia Minor, and Egypt.

---

1. Pierre Bordreuil and Dennis Pardee, *A Manual of Ugaritic*, LSAWS 3 (Winona Lake, IN: Eisenbrauns, 2009); John Huehnergard, *An Introduction to Ugaritic* (Peabody, MA: Hendrickson, 2012).

2. See the overviews of the city and its history in Itamar Singer, *The Calm before the Storm: Selected Writings of Itamar Singer on the Late Bronze Age in Anatolia and the Levant*, WAWSup 1 (Atlanta: Society of Biblical Literature, 2011), 19–146; and Marguerite Yon, *The City of Ugarit at Tell Ras Shamra* (Winona Lake, IN: Eisenbrauns, 2006), 7–26.

Fig. 1. Quadrilingual vocabulary written in Sumerian, Akkadian, Hurrian, and Ugaritic (RS 20.149; the column with the Sumerian lexical entry is broken off). Image courtesy of Mission archéologique syro-française de Ras Shamra-Ougarit.

Evidence of Ugarit's international status can be seen in the range of languages attested at Ugarit. Textual artifacts written in nine languages have been unearthed at Ugarit: Ugaritic, Akkadian, Hurrian, Sumerian, Hittite, Egyptian, Cypro-Minoan, Phoenician, and Luwian.[3] Texts in Akkadian outnumber texts in any other language, including Ugaritic. Polyglot vocabularies were part of the Ugaritic scribal curriculum based on Mesopotamian education, and today they give scholars a helpful tool for understanding Ugaritic and Hurrian. There are eight copies of a quadrilingual

3. For a good discussion of the social and linguistic situation to which these artifacts point, see Philip J. Boyes, *Script and Society: The Social Context of Writing Practices in Late Bronze Age Ugarit* (Oxford: Oxbow, 2021), 197–224.

vocabulary written in Sumerian, Akkadian, Hurrian, and Ugaritic. All the columns are written in syllabic cuneiform, which means that the Ugaritic words appearing in the right column are fully vocalized. Figure 1 shows a fragment of one of these quadrilingual vocabularies.

Interestingly, there is a series of Akkadian and Hurrian texts written in the Ugaritic consonantal alphabet rather than in syllabic cuneiform. Hurrian tablets include eleven texts written only in Hurrian and five texts written both in Ugaritic and Hurrian. The genre of the texts of both categories belongs to the religious sphere. Cypro-Minoan, which remains undeciphered, is attested on seven items (four clay tablets, two clay labels, and one silver bowl), whereas Hieroglyphic Luwian occurs in impressions of digraphic seals (Akkadian and Luwian). Hieroglyphic Egyptian is also attested on various items, such as the scarab belonging to Amenophis III or the vase celebrating the wedding of King Niqmaddu. See figure 2 for examples of tablets in Cypro-Minoan, Luwian, and Hieroglyphic Egyptian.

To reconstruct the history of the city, we only have sources found in situ from the second half of the fourteenth century BCE onward (from the reign of Niqmaddu II). The following eight kings have been identified in the texts and in the impressions of seals (as presented by Yon[4]):

Ammistamru I (?–ca. 1370)
Niqmaddu II (ca. 1370–1340/35)
Arhalbu (ca. 1340/35–1332)
Niqmepa (ca. 1332–1260)
Ammistamru II (ca. 1260–1230)
Ibiranu (ca. 1230–1210)
Niqmaddu III (ca. 1210–1200)
Ammurapi (ca. 1200–1190/85)

Ammistamru I was probably in a subordinate position to Amenophis III of Egypt. Around 1360, Ugarit moved from the Egyptian to the Hittite sphere of control, after Suppiluliuma attacked Mitanni and expanded his dominion in the area; around the same time, the royal palace of Ugarit was destroyed by a fire.

---

4. Yon, *City of Ugarit*, 24.

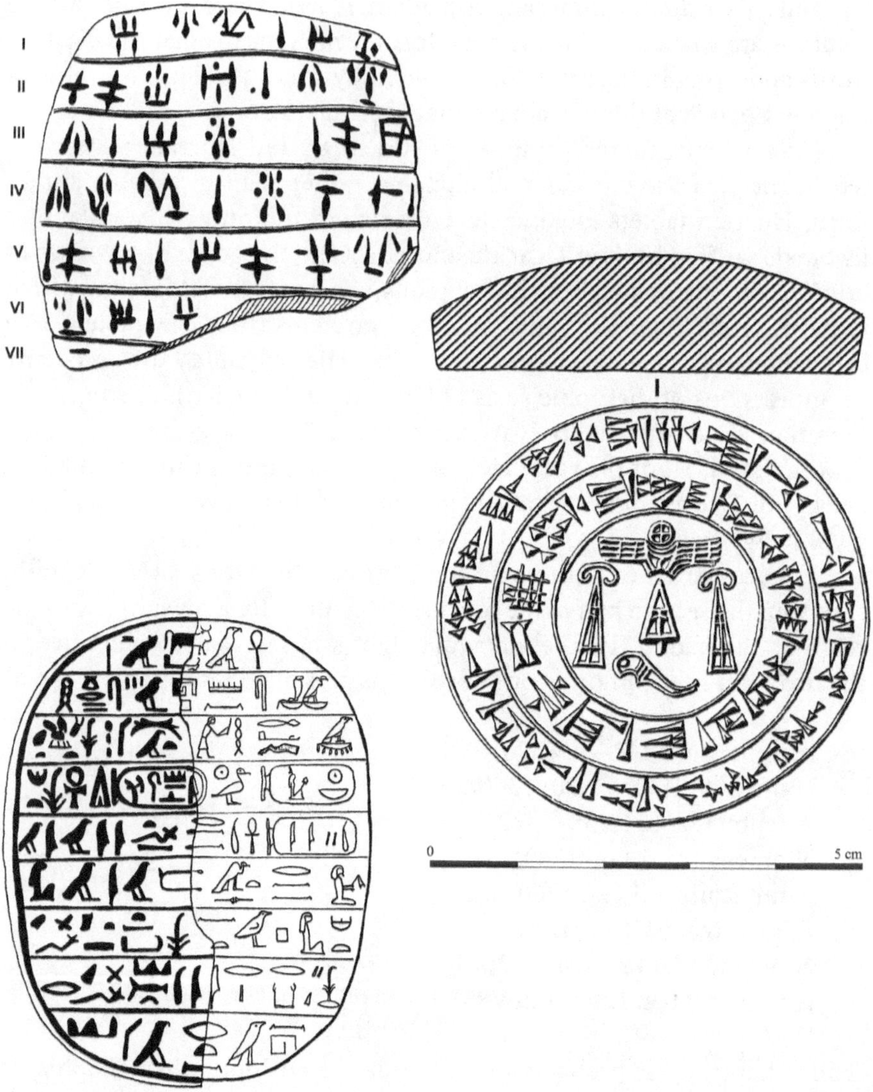

Fig. 2, from top to bottom: (1) Cypro-Minoan tablet (RS 17.006). Source: Olivier Masson in Claude F. A. Schaeffer, *Ugaritica III: Sceaux et cylindres hittites, épée gravée du cartouche de Mineptah, tablettes chypro-minoennes et autres découvertes nouvelles de Ras Shamra* (Paris: Geuthner, 1956), pl. IX b. (2) Seal of Muršili II in Luwian and Akkadian (RS 14.202). Source: Wolfgang Forrer in Schaeffer, *Ugaritica III*, 89, fig. 109. (3) Scarab of Amenophis III (RS 16.094). Source: Paule Krieger in Schaeffer, *Ugaritica III*, 223, fig. 204. Images courtesy of Mission archéologique syro-française de Ras Shamra-Ougarit.

The city of Ugarit was seized and destroyed around 1190–1185 BCE during the Bronze Age collapse.[5] Most ancient sources blame the Bronze Age collapse on invasion by the Sea Peoples, and Ugaritic tablets themselves allude to an impending threat from the sea. The last king of Ugarit, Ammurapi, was unable to stand his ground against these invasions.

The Discovery of Ugarit

The Ugaritic civilization was discovered by accident, when a farmer found that his plow did not penetrate the soil properly in a certain location.[6] Upon further investigation, he found the top stone of a tomb. He had discovered the city's cemetery, near modern day Al-Beida, the bay to the northwest of Ugarit.

The area was under French control at the time, under a mandate of the League of Nations. Soon after the farmer's discovery, news of the find reached the local governor, who contacted the Antiquities Department for Lebanon and Syria. Soon enough, the Louvre museum in Paris became involved and sent an excavation team led by Claude Schaeffer. René Dussaud, curator of the Department of Near Eastern Antiquities at the Louvre, suggested to Shaeffer that he move his attention from the initial site to a hill to the east—Ras Shamra. It was a well-informed suggestion: Ras Shamra is where the ancient city itself was discovered and along with it the majority of texts and other artifacts.

Excavations of Ugarit started in 1929 and have carried on almost uninterrupted since then. Besides Ugarit itself, other important archaeological sites have enhanced our knowledge of the history and social life of the Levantine city. These include Minet el-Beida (ancient Mahadu)—the seaport of Ugarit which was excavated between 1929 and 1935—and Ras Ibn Ḥani, founded by the king of Ugarit in the thirteenth century BCE and situated on a promontory southwest of Ugarit.

5. On the Bronze Age collapse—the history, events, and cause(s) of which are heavily debated—see, e.g., Eric H. Cline, *1177 B.C.: The Year Civilization Collapsed* (Princeton: Princeton University Press, 2014).

6. On the discovery of Ugarit, see the summary of Bordreuil and Pardee, *Manual of Ugaritic*, 1–6.

Ugaritic Cuneiform and Language

Ugaritic literature is somewhat unique in the ancient Near East, insofar as it is written using an alphabetic cuneiform system. In the late Bronze Age, the lingua franca, Akkadian, was written using Mesopotamian writing technology: cuneiform on clay tablets and stone. The Egyptian and Hittite Empires, as well as city-states in the Levant, used Akkadian for administration and foreign relations. In the Iron Age, writing technology changed as Aramaic became the lingua franca: the Phoenician alphabet—a linear script whose characters were inspired by Egyptian hieroglyphs, and suitable for writing with ink on material such as papyrus (writing technology from Egypt)—became the preferred writing system.

Ugaritic stands somewhere in between these two eras with their respective linguae franca and writing technologies.[7] Ugaritic uses cuneiform writing technology together with an alphabet. Their scribal curriculum was Mesopotamian,[8] but the influence of the Phoenician alphabet can also be perceived (e.g., in the character for *ś*). The testimony of the textual artifacts through time shows that, for a long time, Ugarit primarily used Akkadian; toward the end of the Bronze Age, however, they began to use a unique cuneiform system to represent their own language.[9] The writing system and writing technology of Ugarit, then, exemplify its geographic, economic, and political position: at the crossroads of different cultures, dependent on other civilizations yet powerful in its own way. Just as Ugarit was at the hinge of several empires geopolitically, Ugaritic was at the hinge of Late Bronze and Early Iron Age writing systems.

When modern scholars first encountered Ugaritic tablets, they did not know how to read Ugaritic cuneiform. The system, though technologically the same as Akkadian cuneiform, apparently did not derive its characters from Akkadian or Sumerian cuneiform. At the time, no one had unearthed multilingual texts that could help in deciphering Ugaritic cuneiform and understanding the language itself, like the Rosetta Stone had done for the decipherment of hieroglyphs. One thing, however, was clear

7. For a nuanced overview of the developments in writing technologies during this period and the emergence of alphabetic cuneiform, see Boyes, *Script and Society*, 43–84.

8. See above on the many word lists that use Akkadian and Ugaritic.

9. See Robert Hawley, Dennis Pardee, and Carole Roche-Hawley, "The Scribal Culture of Ugarit," *Journal of Ancient Near Eastern History* 2 (2015): 229–67.

enough: the writing system had around thirty total characters, which must make up an alphabet. Charles Virolleaud, the team member responsible for texts and language, identified one of these characters (a small, vertical wedge) as a word divider, rather than a letter (see §3.8). This suspicion turned out to be correct and crucial in the decipherment of Ugaritic. As more scholars attempted to decipher the script and the language, various theories emerged. Hans Bauer, a Semiticist, approached the task on the assumption that the language was Semitic. Using Virolleaud's idea that the small wedge was a word divider, Bauer started to identify characters that most commonly occur in Semitic languages at the beginnings and ends of words (e.g., *t*, often used in verbal prefixes and suffixes). Other scholars, including Virroleaud, joined in this promising approach. When an economic text containing words for numerals was discovered, Virolleaud was able to work out many more letters based on the widely attested common stock of words for numbers in Semitic languages. By 1931, the alphabet had essentially been deciphered. When multilingual vocabulary lists (see above) were later discovered, they confirmed the initial decipherment.

The thirty-letter cuneiform alphabet is attested in numerous abecedaries (cf. *KTU* 5.4; 5.5; 5.6; 5.8; 5.9 i.17–18; 5.12; 5.13; 5.14; 5.16; 5.17; 5.20; 5.21; 5.28; 5.32).[10] In one of these witnesses, *KTU* 5.14, the alphabet is preserved along with the syllabic transcription of each letter (A, BE, GA, ḪA, etc.). Unfortunately, the two columns are fragmentary, and only the first ten and the last ten letters are preserved (i.e., two-thirds of the alphabet). The tablet, discovered in 1955, was a further confirmation of the correct decipherment of the Ugaritic language. Besides the abecedaries containing the so-called long alphabet, two more abecedaries have been discovered. These tablets, *KTU* 5.24 and 5.27, both preserve a cuneiform alphabet in a different order (*ḥ l h m q w ṯ r* etc.), corresponding in many ways to southern Semitic order. The former was discovered in Beth Shemesh in 1987 and contains twenty-three signs, whereas the latter, found in Ugarit in 1988, has twenty-seven signs. They constitute the earliest witnesses of an order later attested for Old South Arabian.[11]

---

10. Text references are given according to the standard edition, abbreviated *KTU*: Manfried Dietrich, Oswald Loretz, and Joaquín Sanmartín, eds., *Die keilalphabetischen Texte aus Ugarit* (Münster: Ugarit-Verlag, 2013), 3rd enl. ed. of *KTU: The Cuneiform Alphabetic Texts from Ugarit, Ras Ibn Hani, and Other Places*, ed. Manfried Dietrich, Oswald Loretz, and Joaquín Sanmartín (Münster: Ugarit-Verlag, 1995).

11. Cf. A. G. Loundine, "L'abécédaire de Beth Shemesh," *Le Muséon* 100 (1987):

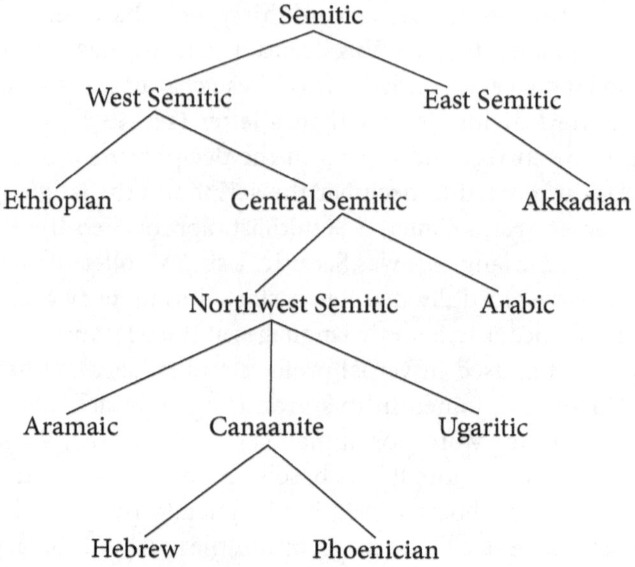

Fig. 3. Ugaritic in the Semitic Language Family

There are also ten tablets that make use of a short alphabet of twenty-two letters. Often, these texts run from right to left, as in Phoenician, and are likely to represent a cuneiform version of the linear alphabet. No short-alphabet abecedary has been preserved. The tablets come from Ugarit (*KTU* 4.31; 4.710), Minet el-Beida (*KTU* 1.77), Tell Ta'anakh (*KTU* 4.767), Tabor (*KTU* 6.1), Kamid el-Loz (*KTU* 6.2; 6.67), Hala Sultan Tekke (*KTU* 6.68), Sarepta (*KTU* 6.70), and Tell Nebi Mend (*KTU* 6.71).[12]

Ugaritic is a Northwest Semitic language, similar to Phoenician, Hebrew, and Aramaic (see fig. 3). Though it shares many features with both Phoenician and Hebrew, it does not belong to the Canaanite sub-branch of Northwest Semitic (*contra* some scholars). There is a set of distinctive characteristics that keeps Ugaritic apart from the Canaanite subgroup, such as the absence of the Canaanite shift (*ā* > *ō*), the (near?)

243–50; Pierre Bordreuil and Dennis Pardee, "Un abécédaire du type sud-sémitique découvert en 1988 dans les fouilles archéologiques françaises de Ras Shamra-Ougarit," *Comptes rendus des séances de l'Académie des Inscriptions et Belles-Lettres* 139 (1995): 855–60.

12. For a thorough discussion, see Josef Tropper, *Ugaritische Grammatik*, 2nd ed., AOAT 273 (Münster: Ugarit-Verlag, 2012), 73–80.

absence of a determinative article (which may nonetheless be due to the early attestation of the language); the occurrence of the relative pronoun *d* instead of *š-*, *ʾš*, or *ʾašer*; the prefix *ša* in the causative stem (compare *ha* in Hebrew and *ya* [< *ha*] in Phoenician); and the presence of independent pronouns for the accusative and genitive case.[13]

What is known about Ugaritic reflects the very final stages of the documentation in this language and hails from the last century in the life of the city (ca. 1300–1190 BCE). The texts in which Ugaritic has been preserved belong to different genres and speak to the thriving intellectual and economic environment that the community of the city enjoyed. Besides the most famous poetic and religious texts, there are also letters, legal texts, economic and administrative texts, and scribal exercises.

---

13. Though outdated, see Daniel Sivan, *A Grammar of the Ugaritic Language* (Leiden: Brill, 2001), 3. Several occurrences of *h* before a noun can be understood as an article, e.g., *habbêta* (*KTU* 2.70), "the house," and *hayyêna* (RS 94.2284), "the wine." It is also possible to analyze these cases as a previous phase in the grammaticalization of *hanna*, where *han-* is cliticized to the beginning of a noun but has a more deictic function, i.e., *habbêtu*, "this house," and *hayyênu*, "this wine." See Aaron D. Rubin, *Studies in Semitic Grammaticalization* (Winona Lake, IN: Eisenbrauns, 2005), 76; Bordreuil and Pardee, *Manual of Ugaritic*, 57. Note also the phonological change from (proto-Semitic) *ḏ* to *d*, not uncommon in Ugaritic, rather than *ḏ* > *z* as in Phoenician and Hebrew.

Lesson 1

1.1. The Ugaritic Abjad
1.2. Vowels in Ugaritic
1.3. Noun Declension
1.4. Articulation and Definiteness in Ugaritic
1.5. Copular ("to be") Clauses
1.6. Verbal Stems
1.7. G-Stem QATALA Verbs
1.8. QATALA *yadaʿa*, "to know"
1.9. Verb-Subject Agreement
1.10. Vocabulary
1.11. Exercises

1.1. The Ugaritic Abjad

The Ugaritic abjad (an abjad is an alphabet without vowels) and the sounds they reflect are similar to what is found in other Semitic languages:

ʾ ʿ b d ḏ g ǵ h ḥ ḫ k l m n p q r s ś ṣ š t ṭ ṯ w y z ẓ

Vowels were, with one exception discussed below, never written. The letters with correspondents in English make the same sound as their English counterparts, for example, *b* as in "boy." We can refer to the letters by their English names or their names in other Semitic languages such as Hebrew or Arabic—for example, *d* is "dee" or "dalet" or "dal." The letters that do not correspond to English are as follows:

ʾ (alef)	glottal stop (brief absence of sound), as in "uh-oh"
ʿ (ayin)	like *alef*, but voiced
ḏ (D line)	as in "th̲e"
ǵ (hard G)	emphatic *g*
ḥ (H dot or het)	like English *h*, but harsher
ḫ (H rocker)	like English *h*, but harsher
ś (S two)	same as *s* (alternative sign for the same phoneme)
ṣ (S dot or tsade)	as in "it's a girl"
š (esh or shin)	as in "shark"
ṭ (T dot)	emphatic *t*

ṯ (T line) as in "<u>th</u>in"
ẓ (Z dot) same as ṣ

The first letter of the abjad, *alef*, is actually never written in Ugaritic; instead, three different forms of *alef* appear, depending on the vowel that follows *alef*. These are ả, ỉ, and ủ, which we call alef-a, alef-i, and alef-u, respectively. For example, the word *ʾummu*, "mother," is written /ủm/ in Ugaritic characters. Note that ả, ỉ, and ủ are each one character (not two); our transcriptions of these characters are formed by placing an *alef* sign (which is ʾ on its own) above the associated vowel.

Despite the names and the use of a primary associated vowel, it is crucial to learn that each *alef* can be used before multiple types of vowel. ả is used when *alef* is followed by an *a*-vowel, whether short or long. ủ is used for *alef* followed by short or long *u* (including long *u* resulting from contraction, i.e., *û*); ủ is also used, however, for *alef* followed by *ô*. ỉ is used for *alef* followed by short or long *i* (including contracted *î*) and for *alef* followed by *ê*. Finally, when *alef* is syllable-closing and thus not followed by a vowel—*alef* before a consonant or at the end of a word—the sign ỉ is used.

Sign	Phonological Possibilities	Examples
ả	ʾa, ʾā	ảb = *ʾabû*, "father"
ỉ	ʾi, ʾī, ʾî, ʾê, ʾø	ỉl = *ʾilu*, "god"
		ỉb = *ʾêbu*, "enemy"
		mỉd = *maʾda*, "very"
ủ	ʾu, ʾū, ʾû, ʾô	ksủ = *kussaʾu*, "chair"
		ủ = *ʾô*, "or"

1.2. Vowels in Ugaritic

Although vowels were typically not indicated in the Ugaritic writing system, we have a good idea of what the vowels are because of (1) the use of ả, ỉ, and ủ; (2) the existence of a number of Ugaritic word lists written using Akkadian cuneiform symbols (which indicate vowels); and (3) comparative Semitic evidence. Ugaritic has the basic Semitic vowels *a*, *i*, *u*, *ā*, *ī*, and *ū*. Two additional long vowels, *ê* and *ô*, are present due to vowel contraction. Long vowels are indicated by a macron (¯) or, when the vowel is a result of contraction, by a circumflex (ˆ).

The full list of vowels is: *a i u ā ī ū â ê î ô û*. Long vowels have the same quality as short vowels; they are merely held longer.

a, ā, â	as in "f<u>a</u>ther"
i, ī, î	as in "<u>ea</u>ts"
u, ū, û	as in "sc<u>oo</u>ps"
ê	as in "m<u>ay</u>"
ô	as in "<u>o</u>nly"

Circumflex (ˆ) simply indicates that the vowel results from contraction. For example, the word ʾaḫû, "brother," was originally ʾaḫawu; the triphthong *awu* has contracted to *û* (see §2.7). The sound quality and length of *û* is identical to *ū*. Similarly, in some verbs a triphthong might reduce to a contracted vowel, as in ʿanaya (3ms QATALA ʿNY "he answered"), which might appear as ʿanâ (see §6.4).

1.3. Noun Declension

Ugaritic nouns are declined for case (nominative, genitive, vocative, and accusative) and number (singular, dual, and plural) and carry morphological features indicating gender (masculine or feminine).

In the singular, feminine nouns have the infix *-at-* before the case ending. Though some nouns use the infix *-t-* instead, these occur less often and can be memorized as part of the lexical form; for example, *miʾtu*, "hundred" (§7.10), and *bittu* (< *bintu*), "daughter" (§2.9). In some cases, a noun that is grammatically feminine—that is, taking feminine adjectives and verbs—takes masculine case endings and vice versa.

The case endings for the singular are *-u* for nominative, *-i* for genitive/vocative, and *-a* for accusative.

		Masc	Fem
	Nom	–*u*	–*atu*
Sg	Gen/Voc	–*i*	–*ati*
	Acc	–*a*	–*ata*

Using the noun *malku*, "king," and its feminine counterpart *malkatu*, "queen," the singular case endings combined with the root *malk** are realized as follows:

		Masc	Fem
Sg	Nom	*malku*	*malkatu*
	Gen/Voc	*malki*	*malkati*
	Acc	*malka*	*malkata*

Depending on their syntactic role in the phrase to which they belong, nouns take various cases. The nominative is used when the noun is the subject of the clause, the predicate complement of a copular ("to be") clause (i.e., a predicate nominative), or the head of a dislocated noun phrase (i.e., *casus pendens*).

*rabb**u** malk**u***, "the king is great" (nominative subject and nominative complement to copula)
*manna šalām**u** rigmahu ṯaṯib layya*, "whatever peace [there is]—send word of it to me" (nominative dislocated phrase)

The genitive is used when the noun is the complement of a preposition or when the noun modifies a preceding noun in a bound-phrase. The same case ending is used for vocatives.

*lê malk**i***, "to the king" (genitive complement to preposition)
*rigmu malk**i***, "a word of the king" (genitive free noun in bound phrase)
*malk**i** ʾatta rabbu*, "O king, you are great" (genitive vocative noun)

The accusative is used when the noun is the complement of a verb or when a bare noun phrase acts as an adverb.

*ragama malku rigm**a***, "the king said a word" (accusative complement to verb)
*šalima malku yôm**a** ʾaḥḥada*, "the king was well for one day" (accusative adverbial noun phrase)

Some nouns—proper nouns especially—are *diptotic*, which means they use only two of the three case endings: *-u* for the nominative and *-a* for genitive, vocative, and accusative. Other nouns, such as *ʾugārit*, "Ugarit," are indeclinable.

1.4. Articulation and Definiteness in Ugaritic

There is no article in Ugaritic. As such, only context determines whether a noun or noun phrase is definite or indefinite. Thus, *malkatu* could be "a queen" or "the queen."

1.5. Copular ("to be") Clauses

Ugaritic uses several copular words; similar to the English verb "is," these words link or connect the subject of a clause with the predicate. For example, *malku ʾiṯu ʿimma malkati* means "the king is with the queen." Unlike English, but like other Semitic languages, Ugaritic syntax does not require an overt (i.e., phonologically realized) copula. Thus *malku ʿimma malkati* also means "the king is with the queen," even though there is no explicit copular word. The copula is present syntactically but not represented phonetically.

1.6. Verbal Stems

The verbal systems of Semitic languages utilize various morphosyntactic features, such as conjugation (roughly equivalent to tense in English), gender, person, number, and *stem*. The same root can occur in different stems with changes to the basic meaning of the verb. The verbal root ṮB, for example, means "to return" in the G-stem and "to cause [someone] to return" in the Š-stem. Each stem is often associated with one or more typical semantic changes to the basic verbal idea; for example, the N stem is often passive, and the Š-stem is often causative. Some stems, however, were more productive than others at the stage of Ugaritic represented in our evidence, and one should never assume that the typical semantic change attributed to a particular stem in fact applies to the verbal root in question. Rather, lexicons should be consulted for the meaning of a verb in every stem in which it appears.

1.7. G-Stem QATALA Verbs

The stems will be introduced progressively throughout these lessons. In this lesson, we will introduce the G-stem, a term derived from the German *Grundstamm*, "basic stem." As the name implies, this is the basic form of the verb, both morphologically and semantically. If a given verbal root occurs in the G-stem, the first glosses and definition given for the verbal root in a lexicon will be for the G-stem. For the moment, every verbal form presented will be in the G-stem, and as such it will be impossible to identify what exactly makes the G-stem the G-stem. When other stems are introduced, students will have a better idea what G-stem refers to.

Ugaritic utilizes several conjugations, which also will be introduced progressively, beginning with the QATALA conjugation. Each conjugation can be used with a variety of *tense*, *aspect*, and *mood* features (TAM). However, the primary TAM feature of each conjugation is aspectual. The QATALA conjugation conveys *perfect* aspect—the speaker has the whole action in view. For translation into English, QATALA Ugaritic verbs often become past tense English verbs, because typically an action is seen as complete (and thus whole) *after* it has occurred. Students should take care, however, to remember that the QATALA conjugation is not always necessarily past tense; context is crucial for determining tense. For verbs that describe states rather than actions (often called "stative" verbs; e.g., *šalima*, "it is well"), the QATALA conjugation has present tense (all other things being equal contextually).

Morphologically, the QATALA conjugation utilizes suffixes to inflect for gender, person, and number. To the base form of the verb are appended the following suffixes:

Third masculine singular (3ms)	*–a*
Third feminine singular (3fs)	*–at*
Second masculine singular (2ms)	*–ta*
Second feminine singular (2fs)	*–ti*
First common singular (1cs)	*–tu*

Using the verb RGM, "to say," the singular forms of the G QATALA, with inflectional suffixes, are as follows:

3ms	*ragama*	"he said"
3fs	*ragamat*	"she said"
2ms	*ragamta*	"you said"
2fs	*ragamti*	"you said"
1cs	*ragamtu*	"I said"

1.8. QATALA *yadaʿa*, "to know"

The common verb YDʿ is introduced at this point only in the QATALA conjugation. The form of this verb in the other major conjugation, YAQTULU (cf. §3.3), is abnormal because it is a "weak verb" (cf. §7.6). For the sake of consistency, the YAQTULU form *yidaʿu* is also given in the vocabulary in §1.10, though it will not be explained or used in exercises until lesson 7. The meaning of YDʿ, like English "to know," involves perfect aspect: *knowing* involves past action (the process of acquiring knowledge) with present implications (the state of having knowledge). As such, YDʿ tends to appear in the QATALA conjugation and should be translated with English past tense "knew" or present tense "know" according to context.

1.9. Verb-Subject Agreement

As in English, the subject of a verb and the verb agree in number and person; additionally, as in other Semitic languages, the subject and verb agree in gender. Thus *ragama̱ malku*, "the king said," and *ragamat̲ malkatu*, "the queen said." Ugaritic is a *pro-drop* language: verbal clauses do not require overt subjects. Thus *ragama*, "he said," and *ragamti*, "you said." Second and first person verbs are very often found without overt subjects.

1.10. Vocabulary

The lists of vocabulary given at the end of each lesson are organized thematically, not alphabetically. The glosses provided are meant to aid in the acquisition of vocabulary. For a full account of any word's meaning, students should consult Gregorio del Olmo Lete and Joaquín Sanmartín, *A Dictionary of the Ugaritic Language in the Alphabetic Tradition.*

baʿlu	noun, masc., "master," "lord"; personal name "Baʿlu," "Baal"
ʿabdu	noun, masc., "servant"
ʾamatu	noun, fem., "servant," "maidservant"
bêtu	noun, masc., "house," "household" (pl. *bahatūma*)
ʾilu	noun, masc., "god"; personal name "Ilu," "El"
ḫaṭṭu	noun, masc., "staff," "rod"
malku	noun, masc., "king"
malkatu	noun, fem., "queen"

RGM	verb, "to say" (G QATALA *ragama*, YAQTULU *yargumu*)
rigmu	noun, masc., "word," "thing," "matter"
ŠLM	verb, "to be well" (G QATALA *šalima*, YAQTULU *yišlamu*)
šalāmu	noun, masc., "peace," "well-being"
šapšu	noun, fem., "sun"
QRʾ	verb, "to call" (G QATALA *qaraʾa*, YAQTULU *yiqraʾu*)
YDʿ	verb, "to know" (G QATALA *yadaʿa*, YAQTULU *yidaʿu*—cf. §7.6)
ʿRB	verb, "to enter" (G QATALA *ʿaraba*, YAQTULU *yiʿrabu*)
QRB	verb, "to approach" (G QATALA *qaraba*, YAQTULU *yiqrabu*)
ʾiṯu	indeclinable copula, "to be"
wa	coordinating particle and phrase-edge marker (see §4.7), "and"
lā	particle, "not," negation
lê, lêya	preposition, "to," "for," "from," "before"
bi, biya	preposition, "in," "on," "to," "by (=agent or instrument)," "from," "for (=exchange)" (cf. §5.8)
ʿimma, ʿimmānu	preposition, "with," "to"

1.11. Exercises

The exercises given at the end of each lesson involve translation from Ugaritic (whether vocalized, unvocalized, or cuneiform) into English, as well as translation from English into Ugaritic. Where an exercise is taken from a real Ugaritic text, the *KTU* reference is provided in parentheses (see further the chapter "Transitioning to Other Resources").

A. Translate into English.

1. *baʿlu bêti* (*KTU* 4.15:2)
2. *lā ʿarabat* (*KTU* 2.88:28)
3. *rigmu lê malki*
4. *malkatu wa malku*
5. *qaraba ḫaṭṭu* (*KTU* 1.169:5)
6. *ragamat ʾamatu*
7. *yadaʿta*

B. Write in Ugaritic.

1. in the house (*KTU* 5.11:6)
2. for the servant (*KTU* 4.313:19)
3. the god of the king (*KTU* 1.4 iv:38)
4. I entered (*KTU* 2.16:7–8)
5. the master called

C. Translate into English.

1. *baʿlu ʾiṯu bi bêti*
2. *ragamat malkatu rigma lê malki*
3. *ʿarabtu lê šapši* (adapted from *KTU* 2.16:7–8)
4. *qaraʾtu ʿabda lê bêti*
5. *ragama baʿlu, "ʿabdi," wa ʿaraba ʿabdu.*
6. *ʿabdu wa ʾamatu ʾiṯu ʿimma malki wa malkati, wa šalima bêtu.*

D. Write in Ugaritic.

1. I know the king and queen.
2. The maidservant entered with the master.
3. The king was well, and the queen was well.
4. Ilu said, "I called to the king," and the king knew.
5. You entered the house.

LESSON 2

2.1. Dual and Plural Nouns
2.2. Adjectives
2.3. Prepositions
2.4. G-Stem QATALA Dual and Plural
2.5. Tri-radical Roots
2.6. Theme Vowels
2.7. Weak Consonants and Vowel Contraction
2.8. Weak Verbs: Hollow
2.9. Vocabulary
2.10. Exercises

2.1. Dual and Plural Nouns

In addition to the singular, which was introduced in lesson 1, nouns can be dual or plural in number. Unlike English, where the plural is two or more, in Ugaritic the plural is three or more; the dual is used for two. And whereas the dual is only used in limited contexts in languages such as Hebrew, the dual is fully functional in Ugaritic: any noun can be found in the dual. For example, *malkatu* is "queen," *malkātu* is "queens," and *malkatāma* is "two queens."

In the dual and plural, all nouns are diptotic, taking one ending for nominative case and another ending for accusative, genitive, and vocative; often this case is called "oblique." The case endings are:

		Masc	Fem
Dual	Nom	*–āma*	*–atāma*
	Acc/Gen/Voc (Obl)	*–êma*	*–atêma*
Pl	Nom	*–ūma*	*–ātu*
	Acc/Gen/Voc (Obl)	*–īma*	*–āti*

The root *malk** with all of the forms we have learned so far is as follows:

		Masc	Fem
Sg	Nom	*malku*	*malkatu*
	Gen/Voc	*malki*	*malkati*
	Acc	*malka*	*malkata*
Dual	Nom	*malkāma*	*malkatāma*
	Acc/Gen/Voc (Obl)	*malkêma*	*malkatêma*
Pl	Nom	*malakūma*	*malakātu*
	Acc/Gen/Voc (Obl)	*malakīma*	*malakāti*

Nouns of the pattern *qitlu*, *qatlu*, and *qutlu*,[1] whose root forms are monosyllabic—such as our paradigm example *malku*—have bisyllabic roots in the plural, with the vowel *a* between the second and third radicals (*malakūma*).

For some nouns, the historical root is not apparent in the singular form, and as such the plural form needs to be memorized as well. For example, the plural of *bêtu*, "house, household," is *bahatūma*. Irregular plural forms will be listed in the vocabulary section.

2.2. Adjectives

As in other Semitic languages, adjectives in Ugaritic can function as attributives (modifying a noun), as complements to copulas (i.e., predicate adjectives), or be nominalized (substantivized) and function as nouns. Adjectives are declined for case, number, and gender, using the same case endings as nouns. When functioning as attributives, adjectives follow the noun they modify and agree with the noun in case, number, and gender. Adjectives do not necessarily follow their noun immediately; for example, an adjective will never split a noun bound to a genitive—for example, *binu malki ṭābu*, "the king's good son." When an adjective is nominalized or the complement of a copula, it takes its case based on its syntactic role and its gender and number according to its referent. The adjective *ṭābu*, "good," is declined as follows in the singular:

1. On the use of the root QTL for verbal and nominal patterns, see §2.5.

		Masc	Fem
Sg	Nom	*ṭābu*	*ṭābatu*
	Gen/Voc	*ṭābi*	*ṭābati*
	Acc	*ṭāba*	*ṭābata*
Dual	Nom	*ṭābāma*	*ṭābatāma*
	Acc/Gen/Voc (Obl)	*ṭābêma*	*ṭābatêma*
Pl	Nom	*ṭābūma*	*ṭābātu*
	Acc/Gen/Voc (Obl)	*ṭābīma*	*ṭābāti*

One common way in which adjectives are formed is using the infix *-iyy-* between the base of a noun (or a nominal pattern built on a verbal root) and its case vowel. For example, *qadmiyyu*, "ancient," is built on the root QDM, "to go before."

2.3. Prepositions

As in any language, prepositions in Ugaritic are capable of communicating a wide range of meaning. The initial glosses provided in the vocabulary sections are a helpful start, but the best way to get a feel for the semantic range of each preposition is by reading texts. Three of the most common prepositions are *bi*, "in," *lê*, "to," and *ʿimma*, "with." Ugaritic has no preposition whose primary or basic sense has to do with *motion away* from something, that is, "from" (e.g., Hebrew *min*). This sense can instead be communicated by various prepositions, primarily *bi* and *lê*. Prepositions are heads of prepositional phrases and require complements—noun phrases or infinitive phrases that complete the prepositional phrase. In other words, a preposition cannot stand on its own but requires a word that it governs.

lê malki	"to a/the king"
bi bêti	"in a/the house"
ʿimma ʾili	"with Ilu"

Some prepositional phrases in Ugaritic are compound, requiring two prepositions; for example, ***bêna*** *ʾili wa* ***bêna*** *baʿli*, "between Ilu and Baʿlu."

Some nouns are used frequently with prepositions to the extent that they (nearly) become lexicalized; in these cases, the lexicalized noun is bound to the following noun. *Panûma*, "face," for example, is often used with a preposition to indicate the location "before": *lê panî baʿli*, "before Baʿlu" (woodenly, "at the face of Baʿlu"). Another example involving triphthong reduction (see §2.7 below) is *bîdi* (contracted from *bi yadi*), "in the hand of" (and dual *bîdê*, "in the hands of").

With a copula (whether overt or null, positive or negative), the preposition *lê* usually connotes possession; for example, *binu ʾiṯu lê baʿli*, "Baʿlu has a son" (woodenly, "there is a son for/belonging to Baʿlu").

With verbs of movement (e.g., ʿRB, "to enter," QRB, "to approach," and YṢʾ, "to go out"), Ugaritic prepositions sometimes describe a different *part* of the verbal process than is natural in English. For example, in the phrase *ṯaṯib rigma* ***ʿimma*** *ʿabdika*, "return a word **to** your servant," the preposition *ʿimma* describes the location of the thing sent (*rigma*, "a word") *after* it has moved from the sender to the recipient: at that point, it is "with" the servant. In English, however, "with" would describe a different part of the process of returning. The English translation "return a word *with* your servant" connotes that the servant is the instrument of delivery or that the servant accompanies the "word." In such cases we cannot translate the Ugaritic preposition literally but must attend to context and correct English idiom.

2.4. G-Stem QATALA Dual and Plural

We learned in the previous lesson that the QATALA conjugation uses suffixes to inflect for gender, person, and number. The following suffixes are used for the dual and plural:

Third masculine dual (3md)	*–ā*
Third feminine dual (3fd)	*–atā*
Second common dual (2cd)	*–tumā*
First common dual (1cd)	*–nāyā*
Third masculine plural (3mp)	*–ū*
Third feminine plural (3fp)	*–ā*
Second masculine plural (2mp)	*–tumu*
Second feminine plural (2fp)	*–tina*
First common plural (1cp)	*–nū*

There may have been distinct second-person masculine and feminine dual endings, but it seems more likely that there was a common form for second-person dual. The combined forms of RGM in the singular, dual, and plural are:

3ms	*ragama*	"he said"
3fs	*ragamat*	"she said"
2ms	*ragamta*	"you said"
2fs	*ragamti*	"you said"
1cs	*ragamtu*	"I said"
3md	*ragamā*	"the two of them said"
3fd	*ragamatā*	"the two of them said"
2cd	*ragamtumā*	"the two of you said"
1cd	*ragamnāyā*	"the two of us said"
3mp	*ragamū*	"they said"
3fp	*ragamā*	"they said"
2mp	*ragamtumu*	"you said"
2fp	*ragamtina*	"you said"
1cp	*ragamnū*	"we said"

Just as the person and gender of the verb needs to agree with the person and gender of the subject, the number must agree:

ragamā malkāma	"two kings said"
ragamū malakūma	"kings said"

2.5. Tri-radical Roots

Most lexemes in Ugaritic—whether noun, verb, or adjective—are built on a tri-radical (three-letter) root. The verb *ragama*, "he said," and *rigmu*, "word," both derive from the same root made of the three letters *r*, *g*, and *m*. These letters are referred to as "radicals." The root QTL or QṬL ("to kill" in other Semitic languages)—which does not exist in Ugaritic as far as we know—is often used in Semitic grammar to refer to verbal forms and noun patterns generally (note our use of QATALA and YAQTULU to refer to conjugations). Specific forms of verbs can be written using QTL to distinguish the root from the inflectional vowels and affixes: the third feminine dual QATALA, for example, could be written q*a*t*a*l*atā*.

2.6. Theme Vowels

In the G-stem, each verbal root takes a particular "theme vowel" appearing between the second and third radical. The theme vowel of RGM in QATALA is *a*; thus we have learned the verb as *ragama*. The theme vowel of ŠLM in QATALA, however, is *i*; the third masculine singular is thus *šalima*.

3ms	*šalima*	"he is well"
3fs	*šalimat*	"she is well"
2ms	*šalimta*	"you are well"
2fs	*šalimti*	"you are well"
1cs	*šalimtu*	"I am well"
3md	*šalimā*	"the two of them are well"
3fd	*šalimatā*	"the two of them are well"
2cd	*šalimtumā*	"the two of you are well"
1cd	*šalimnāyā*	"the two of us are well"
3mp	*šalimū*	"they are well"
3fp	*šalimā*	"they are well"
2mp	*šalimtumu*	"you are well"
2fp	*šalimtina*	"you are well"
1cp	*šalimnū*	"we are well"

In this grammar we will not encounter any verbs with a *u* theme vowel in the QATALA conjugation; the form is *qatula* (3ms), *qatulat* (3fs), et cetera.

Theme vowels differ between lexemes only in the G-stem; in other stems, there is one consistent theme vowel for all lexemes (e.g., *a* for all D-stem QATALA verbs; cf. §4.3). Some further complexities involving theme vowels, which occur in weak verbs, will be explained as the weak verbs are introduced; the theme vowel of a hollow verb, for example, is lengthened (cf. §§2.8 and 3.5).

Theme vowels in the G-stem YAQTULU conjugation are introduced in §§3.3–4. In the vocabulary section of each lesson, the QATALA and YAQTULU forms of each verb—showing the theme vowels of the verb in the G-stem—will be listed alongside its meaning.

2.7. Weak Consonants and Contraction

Some consonants are prone to elide or contract in Ugaritic. These are the glides *w* and *y*, which are our primary concern when thinking about contraction in Ugaritic. The letters ʾ and *h* also cause some abnormalities. It should be noted that many of the ways in which weak consonants and vowels contract are unknown given the limitations of the data. Moreover, it is not uncommon in the corpus of Ugaritic texts for a weak consonant to remain without contraction or elision.

When *y* or *w* appear in a diphthong, they contract: *aw* becomes *ô*, *ay* becomes *ê*, *iy* becomes *î*, and *uw* becomes *û*.

When *y* or *w* appear in triphthongs, they can contract: for example, *awu* and *ayu* become *û*, *aya* becomes *â*, and *ayi* becomes *î*. The triphthong *iyi* always contracts to *î*. Contraction of *y* occurs most often in III-y/w verbs (see §6.4). The following table summarizes possible contractions for triphthongs:

	-a	*-i*	*-u*
ay/w-	*â*	*î*	*û*
iy/w-	*î*	*î*	*û*
uy/w-	no contraction	no contraction	*û*

Triphthongs can also reduce via an intermediate step where the final vowel is dropped: the triphthong *uya*, created when the 1cs suffixed pronoun is used, often becomes *î* via the diphthong *uy* (i.e., not directly from the triphthong *uya*: *uya* > *uy* > *î*; see §4.1).

The triphthong *iya* always contracts in the collocation *bi* plus *yad-* ("in the hand/s of"). For example, *bîdê* (< *bi yadê*) *šamumānu*, "in the hands of Shamumanu."

There are numerous contexts where *y* might be retained in a triphthong, such as with the suffixed pronoun *-ya* (see §4.1) and with III-y/w verbs (see §6.4). The triphthong *iya* always contracts in *bîdê* (see above) but remains in other contexts. This evidence shows fairly clearly the inconsistency of contraction versus noncontraction. What we see in the written texts is a language in flux. Either we are seeing the very period of time when Ugaritic lost *y* in these contexts, or (more likely) the scribes (and other text-producers) are inconsistent in rendering an old form (with *y*) or a form consistent with their own living language (with contraction of *y*).

There is some evidence that ʾ sometimes assimilated or perhaps elided in combination with the gutturals ʿ, *h*, *ḫ*, and *ḥ* (e.g., ʾ*ḫ* > *ḫḫ*; ʾʿ > ʿ). However, it is much more common to find *alef* behaving as a strong consonant, with the exception of typical I-ʾ verb irregularities (see §4.6).

Verbs ending with ʾ, ʿ, *ḥ*, *ḫ*, and *ǵ* are strong, showing no abnormalities.

Historically, *h* sometimes contracted or shifted to *y* or *w*, which subsequently contracted (e.g., *bahtu* > *baytu* > *bêtu*, "house"). None of these shifts occur synchronically within the stage of the language we are learning; any resulting abnormalities (e.g., plural *bahatūma*, "houses") are indicated in the vocabulary listing and can be memorized. However, there are some indications that the letter *h* may not have been phonologically distinct: there is at least one text where *w* occurs everywhere we would expect *h*. This is anomalous, however, and there is evidence that *h* did not contract in verbs.

When a weak consonant is doubled, it does not elide or contract.

2.8. Weak Verbs: Hollow

Weak verbs are verbs that contain one or more weak consonants as radicals and, as a result, do not follow the typical pattern found in strong verbs (verbs with no weak consonants). Hollow verbs originally had *w* or *y* as the second radical (i.e., II-w or II-y). Because there is no trace of the middle radical remaining in the period of Ugaritic to which we have access, the root of hollow verbs is listed in lexicons as a biradical. In the QATALA conjugation, the theme vowel, found between radicals one and two (since there are only two radicals), is long instead of short. Moreover, when an inflectional suffix is added that begins with a consonant, a helping vowel *ā* (regardless of the theme vowel) is added before the suffix. Whereas the 3fs, for example, is *qāl* plus suffix *-at* (*qālat*), the 2ms is *qāl* plus *-ā-* plus *-ta* (*qālāta*). G QATALA QL, "to fall," is conjugated as follows:

3ms	*qāla*	"he fell"
3fs	*qālat*	"she fell"
2ms	*qālāta*	"you fell"
2fs	*qālāti*	"you fell"
1cs	*qālātu*	"I fell"

3md	*qālā*	"the two of them fell"
3fd	*qālatā*	"the two of them fell"
2cd	*qālātumā*	"the two of you fell"
1cd	*qālānāyā*	"the two of us fell"
3mp	*qālū*	"they fell"
3fp	*qālā*	"they fell"
2mp	*qālātumu*	"you fell"
2fp	*qālātina*	"you fell"
1cp	*qālānū*	"we fell"

2.9. Vocabulary

ʾaḫâtu	noun, fem., "sister" (pl. *ʾaḫḫâtu*)
ʾaḫû	noun, masc., "brother" (pl. *ʾaḫḫûma*)
ʾabû	noun, masc., "father"
ʾummu	noun, fem., "mother" (pl. *ʾummahātu*)
binu	noun, masc., "son" (pl. *banūma*)
bittu	noun, fem., "daughter" (pl. *banātu*)
rapaʾu	noun, masc., "ancestral being," "shade"
ʾaklu	noun, masc., "food"
ʾalpu	noun, masc., "bovid," "ox"
LḤM	verb, "to eat" (G QATALA *laḥama*, YAQTULU *yilḥamu*)
naharu	noun, masc., "river"
panûma	pl. noun, masc., "face" (always plural)
yadu	noun, masc. or fem., "hand" (du. *yadāma*; pl. *yadātu*); preposition, "together with"
taḥmu	noun, masc., "message," "word"
NR	verb, "to shine" (G QATALA *nāra*, YAQTULU *yanūru*)
yômu	noun, masc., "day"
YṢʾ	verb, "to go out, depart" (G QATALA *yaṣaʾa*, YAQTULU *yaṣiʾu*—cf. §7.6)
ʿazzu	adjective, "strong"
ʿuzzu	noun, masc., "strength"
MT	verb, "to die" (G QATALA *mīta*, YAQTULU *yamūtu*)
QL	verb, "to fall" (G QATALA *qāla*, YAQTULU *yaqīlu*)

RM	verb, "to be/become high" (G QATALA *rāma*, YAQTULU *yarīmu*)
ṭābu	adjective, "good"
ʾênu, ʾênuna	indeclinable negated copula, "there is not"
bêna	preposition, "between"
bîdi, bîdê	complex preposition, "in the hand(s) of," "in the authority of"
lê panî	complex preposition, "before"

2.10. Exercises

A. Translate into English.

1. *laḥamū ʾakla ṭāba*
2. *qarabū banūma wa banātu*
3. *ʾummu wa ʾabû*
4. *yaṣaʾat malkatu* (adapted from *KTU* 2.88:38)
5. *ʾaḫû ʿimma ʾaḫâti*
6. *ḫaṭṭu bîdi malkati*

B. Write in Ugaritic.

1. message of the queen (*KTU* 2.88:1)
2. with the daughter of the king
3. We did not fall.
4. an ox for food (*KTU* 6.13:3)
5. the brother of the king's mother
6. You have been well, strong father.
7. You said, "I have become high."

C. Translate into English.

1. *nārū panûma ṭābūma biya malki*
2. *qālā ʿabdāma lê baʿli*
3. *qaraʾū rapaʾīma ṭābīma* (adapted from *KTU* 1.161:8)
4. *ragamat ʾaḫâtu, "ʾaḫî, yômu qaraba. lā qālānāyā."*
5. *ʾaḫḫûma ʾiṯu lê malki wa ʾênu banūma*

6. *naharu ʾiṯu bêna ʾamati wa bêna bêti*
7. *malki wa malkati rāmātumā*
8. *ʾanayyu* (fem. noun, "fleet of ships") *malki bi ṣurri* ("Tyre") *mītat* (adapted from *KTU* 2.38:10–13)

D. Write in Ugaritic.

1. The king has a mother and father and brothers and sisters.
2. The servants fell before the master, the king entered, and the master fell.
3. O sister, you have been exalted ("become high"), and you know the queen.
4. There is no food and we did not eat.
5. The king called the queen to the house of Ilu, and they did not enter.

Lesson 3

3.1. Independent Pronouns
3.2. Genitive Phrases
3.3. Pattern and Theme Vowels of YAQTULU Verbs
3.4. G-Stem YAQTULU Verbs
3.5. Weak Verbs: Hollow Verbs in YAQTULU
3.6. Consonant Cluster ṣt → št
3.7. *Kalīlu* and *kullu*
3.8. Ugaritic Cuneiform
3.9. Vocabulary
3.10. Exercises

3.1. Independent Pronouns

Ugaritic uses a range of independent pronouns. First- and second-person pronouns begin with *ʾa-*, while third-person pronouns begin with *h-*. In some cases, feminine and masculine forms are distinguished, while in others (e.g., the 1cs), one form is used for either gender—the gender is referred to as *common*. There are no attested second- or third-person feminine pronouns in the dual and plural; this may be an accident of history, or the masculine forms may in fact be common forms. The **nominative** pronouns are as follows:

1cs	*ʾanāku* / *ʾanā*	"I"
2ms	*ʾatta*	"you"
2fs	*ʾatti*	"you"
2cd	*ʾattumā*	"(the two of) you"
2cp	*ʾattumu*	"you," "y'all"
3ms	*huwa*	"he"
3fs	*hiya*	"she"
3cd	*humā*	"they," "the two of them"
3cp	*humū*	"they"

There are distinct **oblique** forms of the pronouns, formed by adding *-ti* to the nominative forms. The attested oblique pronouns are:

3ms	*huwati*	"him"
3fs	*hiyati*	"her"
3cd	*humāti*	"them," "the two of them"
3cp	*humūti*	"them"

The nominative pronouns are used when the pronoun is the subject of the clause (or takes any of the other roles requiring the nominative), while the oblique pronouns are used in all other instances.

3.2. Genitive Phrases

A noun can be modified by another noun in the genitive, resulting in a semantic relationship roughly translatable by English "of." For example, *binu malki* is "son of the king." In Ugaritic and other Semitic languages, the first word in such a phrase is *bound* (oftentimes referred to as "construct state") to the following word—like a prefix or an article, it depends on the following word and cannot occur without it. Sometimes the bound and free ("absolute") forms of a word are indistinguishable; in other cases, the bound form is phonologically shorter. The distinct bound forms in Ugaritic occur in the dual (masculine and feminine) and in the plural masculine (bolded in the table below). Forms of the root **malk* are:

		Free	Bound
Sg Masc	Nom	*malku*	
	Gen	*malki*	
	Acc	*malka*	
Sg Fem	Nom	*malkatu*	
	Gen	*malkati*	
	Acc	*malkata*	
Dual Masc	Nom	***malkāma***	***malkā***
	Acc/Gen/Voc	***malkêma***	***malkê***
Dual Fem	Nom	***malkatāma***	***malkatā***
	Acc/Gen/Voc	***malkatêma***	***malkatê***

Pl Masc	Nom	***malakūma***	***malakū***
	Acc/Gen/Voc	***malakīma***	***malakī***
Pl Fem	Nom	*malakātu*	
	Acc/Gen/Voc	*malakāti*	

Bound nouns in Ugaritic are fully inflected for case. The only difference between the distinct bound and free forms above is the presence or absence of *-ma* at the end of the word. All of the singular forms, as well as the feminine plural forms, are the same whether bound or free.

Genitive phrases can communicate a range of relationships between the bound word and modifying genitive. For example, there are genitives of possession, of kind, of material, of respect ("about/concerning"), and objective and subjective genitives. The English gloss "of" is often sufficient, but context may indicate something more specific.

3.3. Pattern and Theme Vowels of YAQTULU Verbs

As the name suggests, YAQTULU verbs follow the pattern *yaqtulu*. The use of various theme vowels (see below) results in two other patterns, *yaqtilu* and *yiqtalu*.

The theme vowel of a verb in the YAQTULU conjugation will typically differ from its theme vowel in the QATALA conjugation. For example, the root ŠLM, "to be well," has an *i* theme vowel in QATALA (*šal**i**ma*) and an *a* theme vowel in YAQTULU (*yišl**a**mu*). The prefix vowel of YAQTULU is *a* (*y**a**qtulu* and *y**a**qtilu*) except when the theme vowel is *a*, in which case the prefix vowel is *i* (*yiqtalu*). Active verbs often take an *a* theme vowel in QATALA and *u* theme vowel in YAQTULU (*qatala* and *yaqtulu*), while stative verbs often use *u* and *i* (*qatula* and *yaqtilu*) or *i* and *a* (*qatila* and *yiqtalu*).

Theme vowels differ between lexemes only in the G-stem; in other stems, there is one consistent theme vowel for all lexemes (e.g., *i* for all D-stem YAQTULU verbs; cf. §4.3). Some further complexities involving theme vowels, which occur in weak verbs, will be explained as the weak verbs are introduced. The theme vowel of a hollow verb, for example, is lengthened (cf. §§2.8 and 3.5), while the theme vowel of a geminate verb drops altogether (cf. §5.6).

3.4. G-Stem YAQTULU Verbs

The YAQTULU conjugation primarily conveys *imperfect* aspect: the action is in progress from the perspective of the speaker or part of the process is in view. Imperfect aspect includes iterative action (to do something again and again) and habitual action (e.g., "Baʿlu rides on the clouds"). For translation into English, YAQTULU Ugaritic verbs often become present or future tense English verbs. The YAQTULU conjugation can also occur in clearly past tense contexts, however, as in the mythic poetry of Ugarit (see §7.8). Finally, the YAQTULU verb can be used for irrealis mood (introduced in §5.3).

The YAQTULU conjugation uses prefixes and suffixes to inflect for gender, person, and number. To the base form of the verb are appended the following affixes:

	prefix	suffix
Third masculine singular (3ms)	*y–*	*–u*
Third feminine singular (3fs)	*t–*	*–u*
Second masculine singular (2ms)	*t–*	*–u*
Second feminine singular (2fs)	*t–*	*–īna*
First common singular (1cs)	*ʾ–*	*–u*
Third masculine dual (3md)	*t–*	*–ā(na)*
Third feminine dual (3fd)	*t–*	*–ā(na)*
Second masculine dual (2cd)	*t–*	*–ā(na)*
First common dual (1cd)	*n–*	*–ā*
Third masculine plural (3mp)	*t–*	*–ū(na)*
Third feminine plural (3fp)	*t–*	*–na*
Second masculine plural (2mp)	*t–*	*–ū(na)*
Second feminine plural (2fp)	*t–*	*–na*
First common plural (1cp)	*n–*	*–u*

Note that in most of the dual and some of the plural forms, the final *-na* is optional.

The forms of the G YAQTULU verb for the root RGM are:

3ms	*yargumu*	"he says"
3fs	*targumu*	"she says"
2ms	*targumu*	"you say"
2fs	*targumīna*	"you say"
1cs	*ʾargumu*	"I say"
3md	*targumā(na)*	"the two of them say"
3fd	*targumā(na)*	"the two of them say"
2cd	*targumā(na)*	"the two of you say"
1cd	*nargumā*	"the two of us say"
3mp	*targumū(na)*	"they say"
3fp	*targumna*	"they say"
2mp	*targumū(na)*	"you say"
2fp	*targumna*	"you say"
1cp	*nargumu*	"we say"

3.5. Weak Verbs: Hollow Verbs in YAQTULU

When the theme vowel of a hollow verb is in a closed syllable, rather than an open syllable, the vowel is short, because long vowels tend to reduce in closed syllables. Whereas the QATALA form avoids closed syllables by using a helping vowel—preserving the long theme vowel—in the YAQTULU conjugation (and related conjugations; cf. §6.1) closed syllables occur. For example, G-stem YAQTULU of the verb QL:

3ms	*yaqīlu*	"he falls"
3fs	*taqīlu*	"she falls"
2ms	*taqīlu*	"you fall"
2fs	*taqīlīna*	"you fall"
1cs	*ʾaqīlu*	"I fall"
3md	*taqīlā(na)*	"the two of them fall"
3fd	*taqīlā(na)*	"the two of them fall"
2cd	*taqīlā(na)*	"the two of you fall"
1cd	*naqīlā*	"the two of us fall"

3mp	*taqīlū(na)*	"they fall"
3fp	***taqilna***	"they fall"
2mp	*taqīlū(na)*	"you fall"
2fp	***taqilna***	"you fall"
1cp	*naqīlu*	"we fall"

3.6. Consonant Cluster ṣt → št

The consonant cluster *ṣt*, given the difficulty of its pronunciation, changes to *št*, as in *maḫaštu* (< *maḫaṣtu*), "I struck." The phenomenon applies mainly to III-ṣ verbs in the QATALA conjugation.

G QATALA MḪṢ

3ms	*maḫaṣa*	"he struck"
3fs	*maḫaṣat*	"she struck"
2ms	*maḫašta*	"you struck"
2fs	*maḫašti*	"you struck"
1cs	*maḫaštu*	"I struck"
3md	*maḫaṣā*	"the two of them struck"
3fd	*maḫaṣatā*	"the two of them struck"
2cd	*maḫaštumā*	"the two of you struck"
1cd	*maḫaṣnāyā*	"the two of us struck"
3mp	*maḫaṣū*	"they struck"
3fp	*maḫaṣā*	"they struck"
2mp	*maḫaštumu*	"you struck"
2fp	*maḫaština*	"you struck"
1cp	*maḫaṣnū*	"we struck"

3.7. *Kalīlu* and *kullu*

The related words *kalīlu* and *kullu* have different uses. *Kalīlu* is a noun meaning "everything," whereas *kullu* is a quantifier meaning "each, every, all." *Kullu* follows nominal syntax: to quantify a noun, it is bound to that noun. *Kullu* is *not* an adjective; it always appears *before* the word it quantifies, and it is always singular—regardless of the number of the word it quantifies. It may be helpful to think of *kullu* using the English gloss "all of," because it must be bound to a genitive noun. For example, *kullu malki*, "every king," and *kullu malakīma*, "every king" or "all kings." Similarly, *kullu* can be bound to suffixed pronouns (see §4.1): *kulluna*, "each of us," "all of us" (*-na* means "us"). As a nominal, *kullu* also takes case depending on its syntactic role in the clause: *laḥamtu ʿimma kulli baʿalīma*, "I ate with all the masters," with singular *kulli* (despite plural *baʿalīma*) in the genitive as the complement to *ʿimma*.

Unlike *kullu*, *kalīlu* is never bound to a genitive or a pronoun, and as such is simply a noun meaning "everything"; it does not quantify other nouns. *Kalīlu* is always singular.

When *kullu* is used alone (without an overt quantified noun) it may appear to have a sense similar to *kalīlu*; we understand a different underlying syntax, however, that of quantification (with a covert quantified noun). For example, *šalimū kullu*, "all [of them] are well," where the referent of "them" is understood in context, versus *šalimu kalīlu*, "everything is well."

3.8. Ugaritic Cuneiform

Although there can be some variation in how each letter is written, the cuneiform of Ugaritic is fairly regular, especially when compared to Akkadian cuneiform. When students begin to read from line drawings, they should be aware that slight variations can occur; working with line drawings or the images themselves is the best way to become acquainted with such variation.

ả	𐎀	ḫ	𐎃	ṣ	𐎕
ỉ	𐎛	k	𐎋	š	𐎌
ủ	𐎜	l	𐎍	t	𐎚
ʿ	𐎓	m	𐎎	ṭ	𐎉
b	𐎁	n	𐎐	ṯ	𐎘
d	𐎄	p	𐎔	w	𐎆
ḏ	𐎏	q	𐎖	y	𐎊
g	𐎂	r	𐎗	z	𐎇
ġ	𐎙	s	𐎒	ẓ	𐎑
h	𐎅	ś	𐎝	word divider	𐎟
ḥ	𐎈				

Students may consult the work of John Ellison for a more in-depth description of Ugaritic cuneiform.[1]

Before this point, we have only encountered vocalized Ugaritic. Now that we have introduced the writing system, we will also see Ugaritic in cuneiform and in transcription. There are three ways to represent Ugaritic, corresponding to different aspects of the language and its writing: we can represent the *cuneiform* itself, using line drawings or fonts; we can *transcribe*, using Latin characters to represent cuneiform characters; and we can *vocalize*, using Latin characters to represent how the language would have been read aloud and spoken.

> Cuneiform: 𐎁𐎓𐎇
> Transcription: bʿz (within English prose, slashes are used: /bʿz/)
> Vocalization: *bi ʿuzzi*
> Translation: "with strength"

The distinction between vocalization and the other two types of representation is critical. Vocalization corresponds to the phonological realities of the language, whereas representation of cuneiform characters (by line-drawings, fonts, or transcription) corresponds to what is written on a textual artifact. In the exercises at the end of each lesson, students will be asked to transcribe and vocalize, in addition to translating.

As noted in §1.1, there are three different forms of *alef*, depending on the vowel that follows *alef* (or the lack of a vowel, in the case of syllable-closing *alef*). Doubled consonants are only written once in Ugaritic cuneiform. See the following examples:

Cuneiform	Transcription	Vocalization	Meaning
𐎀𐎁	ảb	*ʾabû*	father
𐎜𐎎	ủm	*ʾummu*	mother

1. Appendix A of Huehnergard, *Introduction to Ugaritic*, 179–88, is the most accessible for beginning students; cf. 19–20. For more depth, see John L. Ellison, "The Scribal Art at Ugarit," in *Epigraphy, Philology, and the Hebrew Bible: Methodological Perspectives on Philological and Comparative Study of the Hebrew Bible in Honor of Jo Ann Hackett*, ed. Jeremy M. Hutton and Aaron D. Rubin, ANEM 12 (Atlanta: SBL Press, 2015), 157–90; Ellison, "A Paleographic Study of the Alphabetic Cuneiform Texts from Ras Shamra-Ugarit" (PhD diss., Harvard University, 2002).

Take note, in particular, of how *alef* and following vowels are treated in transcription and vocalization. In transcription, there is one character to represent the cuneiform character (å for 𐎀, ỉ for 𐎛, ủ for 𐎜); in vocalization, however, *alef* and the following vowel are distinct characters: *ʾummu*, not *ủmmu*.

The word divider character (𐎟) is typically, though not always, used to divide words (like a space in English). The period (.) character can be used to transcribe the word divider, though this grammar does not follow that practice. There is fluidity in the use of the word divider particularly when short particles, prepositions, and conjunctions are involved; for example:

Cuneiform	Transcription	Vocalization	Meaning
𐎆𐎐𐎗𐎚	wnrt	*wa nārat*	"and she shone"
𐎆𐎟𐎐𐎗𐎚	w . nrt (w nrt)	*wa nārat*	"and she shone"

In exercises involving cuneiform, we typically use word dividers; in some places, however, we have omitted word dividers to mimic what is found in actual cuneiform texts.

3.9. Vocabulary

ʾêbu	noun, masc., "enemy"
GRŠ	verb, "to drive away" (G QATALA *garaša*, YAQTULU *yagrušu*)
ǵazru	noun, masc., "young man," "hero"
kirta	personal name, masc., "Kirta" (indeclinable)
MḪṢ	verb, "to strike, smite" (G QATALA *maḫaṣa*, YAQTULU *yimḫaṣu*)
qibūṣu	noun, masc., "assembly," "clan"
ṮPṬ	verb, "to rule, judge" (G QATALA *ṯapaṭa*, YAQTULU *yaṯpuṭu*)
ʿuṣṣūru	noun, fem., "bird"
dabḥu	noun, masc., "sacrifice"
DBḤ	verb, "to sacrifice, slaughter" (G QATALA *dabaḥa*, YAQTULU *yidbaḥu*)
ʿālamu	noun, masc., "long duration of time"

kalīlu	noun, masc., only sg., "all, entirety, everything"
kullu	quantifier, masc., only sg., "each, every, all"
maʾadu	adjective, "much"
maʾda	adverb, "very" (acc. of noun maʾdu, "muchness")
Š'L	verb, "to request" (G QATALA *šaʾila*, YAQTULU *yišʾalu*)
ŠT	verb, "to put, place" (G QATALA *šāta*, YAQTULU *yašītu*)
ŠKB	verb, "to lie down" (G QATALA *šakaba*, YAQTULU *yiškabu*)
ŠMʿ	verb, "to hear" (G QATALA *šamaʿa*, YAQTULU *yišmaʿu*)
ṮB	verb, "to return" (G QATALA *ṯāba*, YAQTULU *yaṯūbu*)
ʾaṯra	preposition, "after, behind"
ʿadê	preposition, "up to"
ḥadaṯu	adjective, "new"
qadmiyyu	adjective, "ancient"
taḥta	preposition, "under"

3.10. Exercises

A. Transcribe (but do not vocalize or translate).

1. 𐎓𐎁𐎄 𐎟 𐎎𐎍𐎋
2. 𐎌𐎍𐎎 𐎟 𐎊𐎎
3. 𐎁 𐎟 𐎌𐎍𐎎 𐎟 𐎎𐎀𐎄
4. 𐎛𐎍𐎎 𐎟 𐎚𐎙𐎗𐎋 𐎟 𐎚𐎌𐎍𐎎𐎋 (*KTU* 2.34:3–4)
5. 𐎍𐎎𐎍𐎋 𐎟 𐎁𐎓𐎍𐎊 𐎟 𐎗𐎂𐎎 (*KTU* 2.40:1–2)

B. Translate into English.

1. *taṯūbu šapšu lê humūti bi rigamīma ṭābīma*
2. *ǵazru yidbaḥu lê ʾilīma wa yiškabu ʿadê yômi* (adapted from *KTU* 1.17 i:1–4)
3. *ʾattumā yaṣaʾtumā wa šaʾiltumā ʾalpa bi bêti malki*
4. *tišmaʿūna rapaʾūma ʿālama*
5. *ʾaṯra yômi ṯābat ʿuṣṣūru*

6. *wa ʾatta yadaʿta libba* (“heart”) *ʾaḫâti* (adapted from *KTU* 2.87:26)

C. Write in vocalized Ugaritic.

1. The hero will drive away all enemies.
2. You will return and you will place peace in the hands (dual) of the gods of the king.
3. The king’s son, hero of the gods, lay down in the house under an ox.
4. They have good sons and good daughters, and after a day there will be a message of a new son.
5. They smote the assembly of the gods and all of them fell under the sun.

D. Vocalize and translate into English.

1. ỉb qdmy
2. ỉl kll
3. ṯbt špš
4. mlk št ảkl b bt
5. yqrb ỉl w yšảl krt (adapted from *KTU* 1.14 i:37–38)
6. ảt ṯbt w tṯpṭn ʿlm

E. Transcribe, vocalize, and translate the following cuneiform.

1. 
2. 
 (*KTU* 2.11:11–12)

Short Story 1
Baʿlu, ʾilu, wa ʿanatu

The short stories presented between lessons 3–8 are meant to help students consolidate their knowledge and bolster recognition of forms. Each story uses only grammar and vocabulary that has been learned up to that point in the lessons, with a few additional words defined in the vocabulary section following each story. The stories are vocalized to enable rapid reading and maximize exposure to the Ugaritic language.

Baʿlu wa ʾilu ʾiṯu ʾêbūma. Baʿlu ragama lê ʾili, "malkatu ʿarabat bêta malki." ʾilu ragama, "ʾênu. Lā ʿarabat malkatu." "ʾiṯu," baʿlu ragama. "Yadaʿtu. ʿarabat malkatu bêta malki," ragama baʿlu. "Lā yadaʿta," ragama ʾilu, "Lā ʿarabat malkatu bêta malki. Malku ʿaraba bêta malki. Yadaʿtu." Baʿlu ragama "malkatu ʿarabat," wa ʾilu ragama "malku ʿaraba." Lā šalima. Wa baʿlu maḫaṣa ʾila lê panîma. ʾilu ragama, "Maḫašta panîma!" Wa ʾilu maḫaṣa baʿla lê panîma. Lā šalima. Wa **ʿanatu** qarabat wa ragamat, "Lā yadaʿtumā. Malkatu lā ʿarabat bêta malki, wa malku lā ʿaraba bêta malki. ʾalpu malki ʿaraba. ʾiṯu ʾalpu malki." Wa rigmu ʿanati ṭābu, wa šalima bi ʾilīma.

Vocabulary

ʿanatu—personal name, fem., "Anat"

Lesson 4

4.1. Suffixed Pronouns
4.2. Valency and Verb Argument Structures
4.3. D-Stem Verbs: QATALA and YAQTULU
4.4. N-Stem Verbs: QATALA and YAQTULU
4.5. Weak Verbs: I-n
4.6. Weak Verbs: I-ʾ
4.7. Function and Meaning of *wa*
4.8. Vocabulary
4.9. Exercises

4.1. Suffixed Pronouns

In addition to the independent pronouns learned in lesson 3, Ugaritic uses suffixed pronouns (sometimes called "pronominal suffixes" or "enclitic pronouns"). Ugaritic's suffixed pronouns can appear with nouns, prepositions, and verbs. With nouns, the sense is the same as a genitive construction; for example, *dabḥuka* (*-ka* = 2ms) is "your sacrifice." With prepositions, the suffixed pronoun is the complement of the preposition; for example, *lêka* is "to you." With verbs, the suffixed pronoun is a complement of the verb; for example, *maḫaṣaka* is "he struck you."

The suffixed pronouns are mostly the same whether they appear with nouns, prepositions, or verbs, but there is some variation. The suffixed pronouns found with **verbs**, and in most cases with prepositions and nouns, are as follows:

1cs	*-nī*	1cd	*-nāyā*	1cp	*-na*
2ms	*-ka*	2cd	*-kumā*	2mp	*-kumu*
2fs	*-ki*			2fp	*-kuna*
3ms	*-hu*	3cd	*-humā*	3mp	*-humu*
	-annu				
	-annannu				
3fs	*-ha*			3fp	*-huna*

Verbs use three different 3ms suffixed pronouns, all with the same sense: *-hu*, *-annu* and *-annannu*. If the verb ends with a short vowel, the vowel is dropped for the initial *a* of *-annu* or *-annannu* (e.g., *tišmaʿu*, "she hears," *tišmaʿannu*, "she hears him"). If the verb ends with a long vowel, the initial *a* of *-annu* or *-annannu* is dropped (e.g., *tišmaʿū*, "they hear," *tišmaʿūnnu*, "they hear him").

The suffixed pronouns with prepositions and nouns vary slightly from those used with verbs. The suffixed pronouns found with **prepositions** are as follows:

1cs	*-ya*	1cd	*-nāyā*	1cp	*-na*
	-î				
2ms	*-ka*	2cd	*-kumā*	2mp	*-kumu*
2fs	*-ki*			2fp	*-kuna*
3ms	*-hu*	3cd	*-humā*	3mp	*-humu*
3fs	*-ha*			3fp	*-huna*

Prepositions take the 1cs suffixed pronoun *-ya* instead of *-nī*. In some cases, there is contraction of *y* so that the final form of the pronoun is *-î*: for example, *ʿimmānuya*, "with me," can also appear as *ʿimmānî* (*ʿimmānuya* > *ʿimmānuy* > *ʿimmānî*).

An earlier form of the preposition *lê* is preserved with the 1cs pronoun. The earlier form **laya* typically reduces to *lê* via the intermediate form **lay*. With the 1cs pronoun, however, *y* doubles and does not contract: *layya*, "to me."

The suffixed pronouns found with **nouns** are as follows:

1cs	*-ya*	1cd	*-nāyā*	1cp	*-na*
	-î				
2ms	*-ka*	2cd	*-kumā*	2mp	*-kumu*
2fs	*-ki*			2fp	*-kuna*
3ms	*-hu*	3cd	*-humā*	3mp	*-humu*
3fs	*-ha*			3fp	*-huna*

Nouns use *-ya* for the 1cs pronoun, but when the noun is nominative the pronoun can contract to *-î* (as with *ʿimmānuya*). For example, *dabḥuya* and *dabḥî* (*-î* < *-uy* < *uya*) are both possible for "my sacrifice" (nominative).

4.2. Valency and Verb Argument Structures

Verbs in all languages have argument structures: the number and type of constituents that the verb requires to be complete. In English, the verb "to hit," for example, requires two constituents: an agent that performs the action and a patient on which the action is performed—*Sue hit the ball.* For this verb, the agent takes the syntactic role of subject, while the patient takes the syntactic role of object. The utterance *Sue hit*, while grammatical and plausible in a variety of scenarios, is nevertheless markedly incomplete for a native English speaker. Because "to hit" takes two arguments, we say that it is bivalent.

While we often cannot come to firm conclusions about the valency of an Ugaritic verb—because we have no access to native speakers of Ugaritic and because of the paucity of our written evidence—the concept of argument structure is important nevertheless. The Ugaritic verb MLʾ, "to fill," is trivalent; the meaning is not as in "the bowl filled with water" but "I filled the bowl with water."[1]

Valency and argument structure are helpful concepts to use when thinking about one verb's meaning in various stems. Speakers are able to shift the valency of a verb; at one point in English, there was productive morphology (the use of ablaut) to accomplish this, as evidenced in "to rise" (monovalent) and "to raise" ([causative] bivalent). In today's English, verbs like "to walk" can be used with secondary senses, achieved by a transformation of argument structure: "I walked to school" is bivalent with a location argument, whereas "I walked the dog" is (causative) bivalent with a patient argument.

Semitic languages have extremely productive systems for valency transformation, through the use of different stems. The N-stem in Ugaritic, for example, is typically the passive of the G-stem, downgrading one level of valency by removing the agent from its argument structure; the

1. Two related terms, "transitive" and "intransitive," refer to whether or not a verb takes an accusative complement (i.e., a "direct object"). We avoid the use of these terms when describing Ugaritic verbs, though we use them to clarify the meaning of some English glosses (e.g., transitive versus intransitive "to burn").

Š-stem, similarly, is often the causative of the G-stem, upgrading one level of valency by adding a *causer* that makes an agent perform an action.

4.3. D-Stem Verbs: QATALA and YAQTULU

The D-stem (from German *Doppelungsstamm*, "doubled stem") is characterized by the doubling of the middle radical. Historically, the semantics of the D-stem have to do with intensification of the G-stem meaning. This can be an intensification of sense, as with ʾHB—G-stem "to love," and D-stem "to love strongly"—or an intensification of valency, as with ŠLM—G-stem "to be well," and D-stem "to make someone/thing well." In the case of the former, the D-stem can lose its distinctiveness from the G-stem over time, and the two become synonymous. In practice, we often do not have access to both the G- and D-stem senses of a word in Ugaritic, and moreover in any Semitic language the core semantics of a stem often do not play out neatly in the meaning of each individual lexeme (see §1.6). For example, LḤM, "to eat," is "to serve someone food" in the D-stem and "to cause someone to eat" in the Š-stem—both are causative, but with different nuances. Or, again, G-stem TRḪ is "to marry," that is, the groom marrying the bride, while D-stem TRḪ is "to marry" or perhaps "cause/allow to marry," said of the bride's father giving his daughter in marriage. Students should always consult a lexicon for the sense of any verb in any stem, rather than assuming that the D-stem (or Š-stem, etc.) will relate in a certain way to the G-stem.

Taking ŠLM as an example, the D QATALA is *šillama* ("he made [someone/thing] well") and the D YAQTULU is *yašallimu* ("he makes [someone/thing] well"). The prefix and theme vowels of the D-stem are constant for all verbs. The morphology marking person, gender, and number are the same as in the G-stem. Using the root ŠLM, the forms are as follows:

D QATALA

3ms	*šillama*	"he made __ well"
3fs	*šillamat*	"she made __ well"
2ms	*šillamta*	"you made __ well"
2fs	*šillamti*	"you made __ well"
1cs	*šillamtu*	"I made __ well"
3md	*šillamā*	"the two of them made __ well"
3fd	*šillamatā*	"the two of them made __ well"

2cd	*šillamtumā*	"the two of you made __ well"
1cd	*šillamnāyā*	"the two of us made __ well"
3mp	*šillamū*	"they made __ well"
3fp	*šillamā*	"they made __ well"
2mp	*šillamtumu*	"you made __ well"
2fp	*šillamtina*	"you made __ well"
1cp	*šillamnū*	"we made __ well"

D YAQTULU

3ms	*yašallimu*	"he makes __ well"
3fs	*tašallimu*	"she makes __ well"
2ms	*tašallimu*	"you make __ well"
2fs	*tašallimīna*	"you make __ well"
1cs	*ʾašallimu*	"I make __ well"
3md	*tašallimā*(*na*)	"the two of them make __ well"
3fd	*tašallimā*(*na*)	"the two of them make __ well"
2cd	*tašallimā*(*na*)	"the two of you make __ well"
1cd	*našallimā*	"the two of us make __ well"
3mp	*tašallimū*(*na*)	"they make __ well"
3fp	*tašallimna*	"they make __ well"
2mp	*tašallimū*(*na*)	"you make __ well"
2fp	*tašallimna*	"you make __ well"
1cp	*našallimu*	"we make __ well"

Hollow verbs, which have no middle radical to double, are typically not found in the D-stem. Instead, the L-stem or R-stem is used (cf. §§8.4, 5). One exception is the abnormal root ḤWY, which uses the D-stem (e.g., *ḥiwwâ* < *ḥiwwaya*).

4.4. N-Stem Verbs: QATALA and YAQTULU

The N-stem is characterized by a prefixed *n*. The meaning of the N-stem is usually passive of the G-stem, though there are exceptions. The prefixed *n* is evident in the QATALA form, while in the YAQTULU form *n* assimilates to the first radical of the root. For example, MḪṢ in the N QATALA is *namḫaṣa* ("he was struck"), and the N YAQTULU is *yimmaḫiṣu* ("he is struck"; *yinmaḫiṣu* > *yimmaḫiṣu*). The theme vowels in the N-stem, both QATALA and YAQTULU, are constant for all roots.

The morphology marking person, gender, and number is the same as in the G-stem. Here are the forms, using the root MḪṢ (note the distinct issue *ṣt* → *št* in this root; cf. §3.6).

N QATALA		
3ms	*namḫaṣa*	"he was struck"
3fs	*namḫaṣat*	"she was struck"
2ms	*namḫašta*	"you were struck"
2fs	*namḫašti*	"you were struck"
1cs	*namḫaštu*	"I was struck"
3md	*namḫaṣā*	"the two of them were struck"
3fd	*namḫaṣatā*	"the two of them were struck"
2cd	*namḫaštumā*	"the two of you were struck"
1cd	*namḫaṣnāyā*	"the two of us were struck"
3mp	*namḫaṣū*	"they were struck"
3fp	*namḫaṣā*	"they were struck"
2mp	*namḫaštumu*	"you were struck"
2fp	*namḫaština*	"you were struck"
1cp	*namḫaṣnū*	"we were struck"

N YAQTULU		
3ms	*yimmaḫiṣu*	"he is struck"
3fs	*timmaḫiṣu*	"she is struck"
2ms	*timmaḫiṣu*	"you are struck"
2fs	*timmaḫiṣīna*	"you are struck"
1cs	*ʾimmaḫiṣu*	"I am struck"
3md	*timmaḫiṣā(na)*	"the two of them are struck"
3fd	*timmaḫiṣā(na)*	"the two of them are struck"
2cd	*timmaḫiṣā(na)*	"the two of you are struck"
1cd	*nimmaḫiṣā*	"the two of us are struck"
3mp	*timmaḫiṣū(na)*	"they are struck"
3fp	*timmaḫiṣna*	"they are struck"
2mp	*timmaḫiṣū(na)*	"you are struck"

2fp	*timmaḫiṣna*	"you are struck"
1cp	*nimmaḫiṣu*	"we are struck"

Hollow verbs in the N-stem take as their middle vowel a lengthened version of the N-stem theme vowel; for example, N QATALA ŠT is *našāta* ("he was placed") and N YAQTULU is *yiššītu* ("he is placed"). When the theme vowel is in a closed syllable, however, it is short; for example, *našatnu* ("we were placed").

4.5. Weak Verbs: I-n

The first radical *n* of I-n verbs assimilates to the second radical whenever the verb is inflected with a prefix. At this point in the grammar, we have only learned one conjugation that uses prefixes, the YAQTULU conjugation; the rule also applies to other conjugations that utilize prefixes (the jussive and volitive) and to stems we have not yet learned (Š, Gt) in both prefix- and suffix-based conjugations. For example, G YAQTULU 3ms NDR, "to make a vow," has the form *yadduru* (*yanduru* > *yadduru*).

3ms	*yadduru*	"he vows"
3fs	*tadduru*	"she vows"
2ms	*tadduru*	"you vow"
2fs	*taddurīna*	"you vow"
1cs	*ʾadduru*	"I vow"
3md	*taddurā(na)*	"the two of them vow"
3fd	*taddurā(na)*	"the two of them vow"
2cd	*taddurā(na)*	"the two of you vow"
1cd	*naddurā*	"the two of us vow"
3mp	*taddurū(na)*	"they vow"
3fp	*tadduma*	"they vow"
2mp	*taddurū(na)*	"you vow"
2fp	*tadduma*	"you vow"
1cp	*nadduru*	"we vow"

The verb LQḤ, "to take," behaves like a I-n verb in the G-stem (e.g., *yilqaḥu* > *yiqqaḥu*), but not in the other stems.

3ms	*yiqqaḥu*	"he takes"
3fs	*tiqqaḥu*	"she takes"
2ms	*tiqqaḥu*	"you take"
2fs	*tiqqaḥīna*	"you take"
1cs	*ʾiqqaḥu*	"I take"

In the N-stem QATALA, the morphological prefix *na-* results in a consonant cluster analogous to the G YAQTULU, and thus the *n* of the root assimilates with the second radical; for example, 3ms N-stem QATALA NDR *naddara* (< *nandara*), "he was vowed."

3ms	*naddara*	"he was vowed"
3fs	*naddarat*	"she was vowed"
2ms	*naddarta*	"you were vowed"
2fs	*naddarti*	"you were vowed"
1cs	*naddartu*	"I was vowed"
3md	*naddarā*	"the two of them were vowed"
3fd	*naddaratā*	"the two of them were vowed"
2cd	*naddartumā*	"the two of you were vowed"
1cd	*naddarnāyā*	"the two of us were vowed"
3mp	*naddarū*	"they were vowed"
3fp	*naddarā*	"they were vowed"
2mp	*naddartumu*	"you were vowed"
2fp	*naddartina*	"you were vowed"
1cp	*naddarnū*	"we were vowed"

In the N YAQTULU, the consonant cluster is *n* + *n*, resulting in, simply, a doubled *n*; for example, *yinnadiru*, "it is vowed." In the D-stem, neither the QATALA nor the YAQTULU forms entail a consonant cluster with the first radical, and as such I-n verbs retain *n* in the D-stem; for example, *yanaḥḥitu*, "he prepares" (3ms NḤT, "to prepare [something]; cf. §5.10). When reading a consonantal (unvocalized) text, the presence of cuneiform /n/ in a YAQTULU I-n verb form therefore indicates that the verb is D- or N-stem. For example, the 2ms YAQTULU of NDR would be written /tdr/ in the G-stem (*tadduru*), but /t**n**dr/ in the N-stem (*ti**nn**adiru*) or D-stem (*ta**n**addiru*).

4.6. Weak Verbs: I-ʾ

Alef is a strong consonant in Ugaritic, and therefore I-ʾ verbs do not have many irregularities. In the G YAQTULU, the *alef* of the root always drops in the 1cs, because of the presence of *alef* in the prefix morphology (e.g., *ʾaʾḫudu* > *ʾaḫudu*, "I seize"). Moreover, G YAQTULU I-ʾ verbs sometimes use a helping vowel rather than closing the first syllable with *alef*; for example, G YAQTULU ʾḪD can be *yaʾḫudu* or *yaʾuḫudu*, both meaning "he seizes"; the helping vowel takes the same quality as the theme vowel, in this case *u*. G YAQTULU ʾḪD is conjugated as follows:

3ms	*yaʾḫudu* / *yaʾuḫudu*	"he seizes"
3fs	*taʾḫudu* / *taʾuḫudu*	"she seizes"
2ms	*taʾḫudu* / *taʾuḫudu*	"you seize"
2fs	*taʾḫudīna* / *taʾuḫudīna*	"you seize"
1cs	*ʾaḫudu*	"I seize"
3md	*taʾḫudā(na)* / *taʾuḫudā(na)*	"the two of them seize"
3fd	*taʾḫudā(na)* / *taʾuḫudā(na)*	"the two of them seize"
2cd	*taʾḫudā(na)* / *taʾuḫudā(na)*	"the two of you seize"
1cd	*naʾḫudā* / *naʾuḫudā*	"the two of us seize"
3mp	*taʾḫudū(na)* / *taʾuḫudū(na)*	"they seize"
3fp	*taʾḫudna* / *taʾuḫudna*	"they seize"
2mp	*taʾḫudū(na)* / *taʾuḫudū(na)*	"you seize"
2fp	*taʾḫudna* / *taʾuḫudna*	"you seize"
1cp	*naʾḫudu* / *naʾuḫudu*	"we seize"

Similarly, in the N-stem QATALA form, a helping vowel may be used to split the initial consonant cluster, for example, *naʾḫada* or *naʾaḫada*, "he was seized."

4.7. Function and Meaning of *wa*

The word *wa*, often translated "and," is not strictly a conjunction and should not always be translated using a conjunction (whether "and," "but," etc.). Rather, *wa* marks the edge of a phrase, often in order to coordinate it with a preceding phrase on the same syntactic level (e.g., *malku wa mal-katu*, "the king and queen"). Sometimes, however, *wa* marks the edge of a phrase that is not parallel to the preceding phrase(s). For example, *wa* sometimes distinguishes the main predication from the subordinate temporal or circumstantial clause: *kīma napaltu wa ʾibbadūnī*, "when I fell, they destroyed me."

4.8. Vocabulary

ʾBD	verb, D "to destroy," Gt "to perish" (no G-stem)
ʾaduru	adjective, "powerful," "magnificent," "worthy"
rabbu	adjective, "great"
qarnu	noun, fem., "horn"
ʾḪD	verb, "to seize, take, hold" (G QATALA *ʾaḫada*, YAQTULU *yaʾḫudu* or *yaʾuḫudu*)
BʿR	verb, D "to burn [something]," Š "to illuminate" (no G-stem)
NǴR	verb, "to guard" (G QATALA *naǵara*, YAQTULU *yaǵǵuru*)
NPL	verb, "to fall" (G QATALA *napala*, YAQTULU *yappulu*)
ʾHB	verb, "to love" (G QATALA *ʾahiba*, YAQTULU *yaʾhubu* or *yaʾuhubu*); D "to love strongly"
TRḪ	verb, "to marry" (G QATALA *taraḫa*, YAQTULU *yitraḫu*)
ʾaṯṯatu	noun, fem., "woman"
mutu	noun, masc., "man"
naʿīmu	adjective, "pleasant," "gracious"
BRK	verb, D "to bless" (no G-stem)
šamnu	noun, masc., "oil"
LQḤ	verb, "to take" (G QATALA *laqaḥa*, YAQTULU *yiqqaḥu*)
NDR	verb, "to make a vow" (G QATALA *nadara*, YAQTULU *yadduru*)
kaspu	noun, masc., "silver"
ṯiqlu	noun, masc., "shekel"
NGŠ	verb, "to approach" (G QATALA *nagaša*, YAQTULU *yiggašu*)
ʾappu	noun, masc., "nose" (dual "nostrils"), "anger"
ʾišdu	noun, fem., "leg"
ʾudnu	noun, fem., "ear"

gû	noun, masc., "voice"
paʿnu	noun, fem., "foot" (dl. *paʿnāma*)
pû	noun, masc., "mouth"
ʾimma, himma	particle, "if"; conjunction, "or"
ʾêka, ʾêkaya	interrogative particle, "how?"
ka, kama	preposition, "like, as"

4.9. Exercises

A. Translate into English.

1. *naʾḫadū bi yadi ʾaduri*
2. *bittî yaṣaʾat wa ʾibbadat bêta malki. ʾibbadatannannu bi ʾappi rabbi.*
3. *ʾahubu ʿuṣṣūraya naʿīmata wa ʾudnêha*
4. *ʾilūki taǵǵurūki wa tašallimūki* (adapted from *KTU* 2.11:7–8)
5. *himma ʾagrušukumu bi bêtiya, kaspa ṯiqla ʾašītu bîdêkumu*
6. *laqaḥtu kulla muti wa ʾaṯṯati bîdê rabbi tamūtati* ("shipwreck") (adapted from *KTU* 2.38:20–22)
7. *ṯāba binu-ʿayāna* (proper name, nominative) *wa laqaḥa ṯiqlêma kaspa bîdê ʾamatika* (*KTU* 2.70:16–19)

B. Write in vocalized Ugaritic.

1. You will not be guarded by me.
2. The bird was vowed as a sacrifice to the gods.
3. If the two of them approach, the (male) servants will seize the two of them.
4. If you (fem. pl.) take my food, I will not bless you.
5. I do not know the house of my son, and there is no son in the house of my brother.
6. The hero enters, he sacrifices a bull, and he feeds the gods. He calls out with his voice and requests a great house from them.

C. Vocalize and translate into English.

1. qrbt ảnk l qbṣ ỉlm qdmy

2. ỉm ymḫṣ ảb bn wtgršn ủm
3. yndr kspk lmlk
4. ỉn ksp ảp mlk yảbd kl ʿbd bth
5. hm trḫth tảhbh mỉd

D. Transcribe, vocalize, and translate the following cuneiform.

1. 
2. 
3. 
 (*KTU* 2.72:29–30)
4. 
5. 
6.  (adapted from *KTU* 2.14:12–13)

Short Story 2
Rigamū Bêti

Yôma qarabtu bêta. Wa ʾalpu nagašanī, wa ʾaṯra ʾalpi ʾiṯu **mutu**. "**Yišlam lêki**," qaraʾa mutu. "Wa yišlam lêka," ʾanāku qaraʾtu. "**Mī** ʾatta?" ʾanāku ragamtu. "ʾanāku **šapšîʾilu**," ragama huwa, "wa ʾanāku baʿlu bêti." **ʾaṯṯatu** nagašat wa mutu ragama, "Hiya ʾummu banīya." "Yišlam lêki," hiya ragamat. "Mī ʾatti?" ʾanāku ragamtu. "ʾanāku ʾadattu bêti," ragamat. **Ǵalmu** nagaša. "Mī huwa?" ragamtu. "Huwa," ragamat ʾaṯṯatu, "huwa binuya—binunāyā." Šapšîʾilu ragama, "Huwa ǵazru bêti. Wa ʾaḫâtuhu tiggašu." "Yišlam lêki," ʾaḫâtu ragamat. "Mī ʾatti?" ʾanāku ragamtu. "Mī ʾanāku?" ragamat, "ʾanāku ʾêbu ʾaḫîya ʾaduru. ʾanāku ʾaḫuduhu wa ʾimḫaṣuhu wa ʾagrušuhu. ʾaḫûya huwa ʾênu ǵazru." "Ṭābu," ragamtu, "yadaʿtu kullukumu. Yišlam lêkumu!" Humū ragamū, "yišlam lêki!"

Vocabulary

mutu—noun, "man"
yišlam lêka/ki—"may it be well for you" (i.e., "hello" and "goodbye")
mī—interrogative pronoun, "who?"
šapšîʾilu—personal name, masc., "Shapshiʾilu" (unattested)
ʾaṯṯatu—noun, "woman"
ǵalmu—noun, "boy"

Lesson 5

5.1. Relative Words and Demonstrative Pronouns
5.2. Enclitic Particles
5.3. Irrealis Mood
5.4. G-Stem Jussive, Volitive, and Imperative Verbs
5.5. N-Stem and D-Stem Jussive, Volitive, and Imperative Verbs
5.6. Geminate Roots
5.7. Stative Verbs
5.8. *Bi* of Exchange
5.9. Vocabulary
5.10. Exercises

5.1. Relative Words and Demonstrative Pronouns

There are two types of relative words (similar to English "who," "whom," "which") in Ugaritic: relative markers and the relative particle. Ugaritic does not use relative pronouns (see below).

Relative markers appear after the constituent they modify (the "pivot" or "head" or the relative), whether immediately following or modifying from a distance. The relative markers are not as heavily inflected as other nominal elements in Ugaritic: there are fully inflected forms for the masculine and feminine singular, nominative and oblique forms for the plural (with no distinction in gender), and no dual forms (as far as we know).

<table>
<tr><th></th><th>Masc Sg</th><th>Fem Sg</th><th>Com Pl</th></tr>
<tr><td>Nom</td><td>dū</td><td>dātu</td><td>dūtu</td></tr>
<tr><td>Gen/Voc</td><td>dī</td><td>dāti</td><td rowspan="2">dūti</td></tr>
<tr><td>Acc</td><td>dā</td><td>dāta</td></tr>
</table>

The gender, number, and case of the relative marker are determined by the gender, number, and case of the relative head. Unlike relative pronouns in languages like English (e.g., "the man **to whom** I gave the note"), the relative marker's case is not determined by the role of the pivot inside the relative clause. This is the basis of the distinction between a relative marker (as we find in Ugaritic) and a relative pronoun (as we find in English). "To the queen who fell" is thus *lê malkati* ***dāti*** *qālat* with dative case, not **lê malkati* ***dātu*** *qālat* with nominative case (as subject of *qālat*).

The relative particle *du* coexisted with relative markers during our period of Ugaritic. The relative particle was uninflected and simply signaled the start of a relative clause. The same sentence, "to the queen who fell," could be written using the relative particle: *lê malkati* ***du*** *qālat*.

With both relative markers and the relative particle, the syntactic role of the relative head inside the relative clause is often determined on the basis of context alone (as in the examples in the preceding two paragraphs). However, *resumptive pronouns* may be used to clarify the syntactic role of the relative head, as in the following:

> *maḫaṣa ʾalpa dā yaǵǵuru****hu*** *ǵazru*, "he struck the ox that the young man was guarding **it**" (= "he struck the ox **whom** the young man was guarding")
> *maḫaṣa ʾalpa du* ***huwa*** *ʾiṯu lê ǵazri*, "he struck the ox that **it** belonged to the young man" (= "he struck the ox **who** belonged to the young man")
> *bêtu dū dabaḥat ʾaṯṯatu* ***ṯamma***, "the house that the woman sacrificed **there**" (= "the house **where** the woman sacrificed")

When working with unvocalized texts, there is ambiguity between the relative markers *dū, dī, dā*—which only modify masculine singular nouns—and the relative particle *du*—which can modify nouns of any gender and number. Both are written 𐎄 (/d/). Sensitivity to context is crucial in distinguishing the two. Where a masculine singular noun is the relative head, /d/ could indicate a relative marker or the relative particle. If a plural or feminine singular noun is more likely the relative head, /d/ can be taken as the relative particle.

Where an unvocalized text has 𐎄𐎚 (/dt/), the form must be a relative marker, either plural or feminine singular.

Demonstrative pronouns ("this," "these") are formed by the combination of the deictic pointer *hanna* ("here [is]," "behold") and the relative marker.

<table>
<tr><th></th><th>Masc Sg</th><th>Fem Sg</th><th>Com Pl</th></tr>
<tr><td>Nom</td><td>hannadū</td><td>hannadātu</td><td>hannadūtu</td></tr>
<tr><td>Gen/Voc</td><td>hannadī</td><td>hannadāti</td><td rowspan="2">hannadūti</td></tr>
<tr><td>Acc</td><td>hannadā</td><td>hannadāta</td></tr>
</table>

Like adjectives, demonstratives follow the nouns they modify. "To this queen," for example, is *lê malkati hannadāti*. The demonstratives are sometimes extended by enclitic particles (on which, see below) which do not change the sense of the demonstrative; for example, *hannadū**na***, "this."

5.2. Enclitic Particles

Ugaritic employs many enclitic particles about which we know little. While scholars have suggested various uses of some of these particles, there is not enough evidence to establish any of the theories. These particles are best treated, then, as not changing the sense or syntax of the words with which they are used.

The most common enclitic particles are ***-ma***, ***-ya***, ***-na***, and ***-ni***; less common particles are ***-ka***, ***-li***, and ***-ti***. More than one particle can be used at the end of a word; for example, *hannaniya*, "behold" (*hanna* + *ni* + *ya*).

Because of the widespread use of enclitic *-ma*, the presence of *-ma* at the end of a word does not always clearly indicate that the word is plural or, if it is plural, that the plural is the free form. For example, nominative /mlkm/ is most likely *malakūma*, "kings" (plural free state) but could, if context demands, be analyzed as *malakūma*, "kings of" (plural bound state with enclitic *-ma*), or *malkuma*, "king" (singular with enclitic *-ma*).

5.3. Irrealis Mood

In addition to aspect and tense, verbs can communicate mood. The mood of a verb involves the existential quality of the action described; actions are either *real*—actually existing in the real world—or *irreal*—not existing in the real world, that is, hypothetical or desired, et cetera.

We divide irrealis mood into four primary categories: deontic, epistemic, contingent, and dynamic. Deontic irreality deals with the attitude of the speaker toward the action, for example, if the speaker thinks something *should* or *ought* to happen ("let him return tomorrow") or states that something is *allowed* to happen ("you may have a chocolate"). Epistemic irreality deals with the speaker's knowledge of an action and its *potential* to occur ("she might bring a friend to dinner tonight"). Contingent irreality deals with actions whose reality depends on other actions ("if you build it, they will come"). Dynamic irreality has to do with someone's *ability* to do something ("she can juggle").

The QATALA conjugation interacts primarily with aspect and tense (it is primarily aspectual but also defaults to past tense; cf. §1.7); it is always real, unless some other contextual indicator (e.g., a conditional clause) overrides QATALA's default realis mood. The YAQTULU conjugation, on the other hand, can be used for irreal or real actions; context is crucial in determining which is intended, and students should always be aware of either possibility. When a YAQTULU follows a clause with an imperative verb, for example, it often should be understood as irreal.

5.4. G-Stem Jussive, Volitive, and Imperative Verbs

In this grammar we use the terms *volitive* and *jussive* to refer to particular verb forms in Ugaritic, not to subcategories of irrealis semantics defined in some linguistic literature. The jussive, volitive, and imperative forms flag particular irrealis semantics by their morphology. In contrast to the YAQTULU form—which can be taken as realis or irrealis—the jussive, volitive, and imperative must be taken as irrealis, and deontic irrealis in particular.

As deontic irreal verb-forms, the jussive, volitive, and imperative conjugation present what the speaker desires to happen. The imperative is the most forceful; the speaker *commands* that something happen: *dabaḥ*, "sacrifice." The volitive and jussive are less forceful than the imperative: *yidbaḥ* and *yidbaḥa*, "may he (or *let him*) sacrifice." The semantic distinction between volitive and jussive forms in Ugaritic is not entirely clear. The jussive is possibly stronger in its force.

The jussive and volitive are both negated by *ʾal* rather than *lā*. Negative commands are stated using negated jussives rather than imperatives.

Jussive form. The jussive, volitive, and imperative forms can be helpfully described in relationship to the YAQTULU form. The jussive is a shortened version of YAQTULU, dropping the last syllable, except in a few forms where it is identical to the YAQTULU form (see the paradigms below); for example, YAQTULU *yidbaḥu*, "he sacrifices," becomes jussive *yidbaḥ*, "may he sacrifice." If there is an optional final syllable, the jussive drops the optional syllable but not the required suffix; for example, YAQ-

TULU *tidbaḥū(na)*, "they sacrifice," becomes jussive *tidbaḥū*, "may they sacrifice."

Volitive form. The form of the volitive is identical to the jussive when the jussive ends with an open syllable/vowel; for example, jussive *tidbaḥī* and volitive *tidbaḥī* (both meaning "may you [fem. sg.] sacrifice"). When the jussive ends with a consonant/closed syllable, the volitive is jussive plus an *a* vowel at the end; for example, jussive *yidbaḥ* versus volitive *yidbaḥa* (both meaning "may he sacrifice").

Imperative form. The imperative uses the same theme vowel as the prefix conjugations YAQTULU, jussive, and volitive. However, the imperative drops the prefix syllable, and adds a helping vowel in the first syllable in harmony with the theme vowel. The imperative, like the jussive, does not retain the final *u* of the YAQTULU form. For example, YAQTULU *tidbaḥū* ("you [masc. pl.] will sacrifice") versus imperative *dabaḥū* ("sacrifice [masc. pl.]"); YAQTULU *tidbaḥu* ("you sacrifice [masc. sg.]") versus *dabaḥ* ("sacrifice [masc. sg.]"); YAQTULU *targumīna* ("you say [fem. sg.]") versus *rugumī* ("say [fem. sg.]"). The second feminine plural imperative is *dabaḥā*, "sacrifice (fem. pl.)," compared to YAQTULU *tidbaḥna* ("you [fem. pl.] will sacrifice").[1]

The jussive, volitive, and imperative of the G-stem are conjugated as follows:

DBḤ, "to sacrifice" – *a* theme vowel

G Jussive		G Volitive		G Imperative	
3ms	*yidbaḥ*	3ms	*yidbaḥa*		
3fs	*tidbaḥ*	3fs	*tidbaḥa*		
2ms	*tidbaḥ*	2ms	*tidbaḥa*	2ms	*dabaḥ*
2fs	*tidbaḥī*	2fs	*tidbaḥī*	2fs	*dabaḥī*
1cs	*ʾidbaḥ*	1cs	*ʾidbaḥa*		

1. The 2fp imperative may be unattested (see *KTU* 1.24:11 for one possible occurrence), but here we follow Bordreuil and Pardee, *Manual of Ugaritic*, 51.

G Jussive		G Volitive		G Imperative	
3md	*tidbaḥā*	3md	*tidbaḥā*		
3fd	*tidbaḥā*	3fd	*tidbaḥā*		
2cd	*tidbaḥā*	2cd	*tidbaḥā*	2cd	*dabaḥā*
1cd	*nidbaḥā*	1cd	*nidbaḥā*		
3mp	*tidbaḥū*	3mp	*tidbaḥū*		
3fp	*tidbaḥna*	3fp	*tidbaḥna*		
2mp	*tidbaḥū*	2mp	*tidbaḥū*	2mp	*dabaḥū*
2fp	*tidbaḥna*	2fp	*tidbaḥna*	2fp	*dabaḥā*
1cp	*nidbaḥ*	1cp	*nidbaḥa*		

QBʾ, "to invoke" – *i* theme vowel

G Jussive		G Volitive		G Imperative	
3ms	*yaqbiʾ*	3ms	*yaqbiʾa*		
3fs	*taqbiʾ*	3fs	*taqbiʾa*		
2ms	*taqbiʾ*	2ms	*taqbiʾa*	2ms	*qibiʾ*
2fs	*taqbiʾī*	2fs	*taqbiʾī*	2fs	*qibiʾī*
1cs	*ʾaqbiʾ*	1cs	*ʾaqbiʾa*		
3md	*taqbiʾā*	3md	*taqbiʾā*		
3fd	*taqbiʾā*	3fd	*taqbiʾā*		
2cd	*taqbiʾā*	2cd	*taqbiʾā*	2cd	*qibiʾā*
1cd	*naqbiʾā*	1cd	*naqbiʾā*		
3mp	*taqbiʾū*	3mp	*taqbiʾū*		
3fp	*taqbiʾna*	3fp	*taqbiʾna*		
2mp	*taqbiʾū*	2mp	*taqbiʾū*	2mp	*qibiʾū*
2fp	*taqbiʾna*	2fp	*taqbiʾna*	2fp	*qibiʾā*
1cp	*naqbiʾ*	1cp	*naqbiʾa*		

RGM, "to say" – *u* theme vowel

G Jussive		G Volitive		G Imperative	
3ms	*yargum*	3ms	*yarguma*		
3fs	*targum*	3fs	*targuma*		
2ms	*targum*	2ms	*targuma*	2ms	*rugum*
2fs	*targumī*	2fs	*targumī*	2fs	*rugumī*
1cs	*ʾargum*	1cs	*ʾarguma*		
3md	*targumā*	3md	*targumā*		
3fd	*targumā*	3fd	*targumā*		
2cd	*targumā*	2cd	*targumā*	2cd	*rugumā*
1cd	*nargumā*	1cd	*nargumā*		
3mp	*targumū*	3mp	*targumū*		
3fp	*targumna*	3fp	*targumna*		
2mp	*targumū*	2mp	*targumū*	2mp	*rugumū*
2fp	*targumna*	2fp	*targumna*	2fp	*rugumā*
1cp	*nargum*	1cp	*narguma*		

5.5. N-Stem and D-Stem Jussive, Volitive, and Imperative Verbs

In the N- and D-stems, the forms of the jussive, volitive, and imperative are similar to those of the G-stem described in §5.4 above.

The **jussive** is a shortened form of the N- or D-stem YAQTULU. The N- and D-stem **volitive** adds *-a* to the jussive form. The N- and D-stem **imperative** drops the personal prefix and suffix. The N-stem imperative does not drop the prefixed *n*, and it uses a prosthetic *alef* with an *i* vowel to enable pronunciation of the initial consonant cluster. For example, N-stem YAQTULU *tiddabiḥu* (< *tindabiḥu*), "you (masc. sg.) will be sacrificed," versus imperative *ʾiddabiḥ* (< *ʾindabiḥ*), "be sacrificed (masc. sg.)."

Using DBḤ, the forms of the N-stem jussive, volitive, and imperative are as follows:

N Jussive		N Volitive		N Imperative	
3ms	*yiddabiḥ*	3ms	*yiddabiḥa*		
3fs	*tiddabiḥ*	3fs	*tiddabiḥa*		
2ms	*tiddabiḥ*	2ms	*tiddabiḥa*	2ms	*ʾiddabiḥ*
2fs	*tiddabiḥī*	2fs	*tiddabiḥī*	2fs	*ʾiddabiḥī*
1cs	*ʾiddabiḥ*	1cs	*ʾiddabiḥa*		
3md	*tiddabiḥā*	3md	*tiddabiḥā*		
3fd	*tiddabiḥā*	3fd	*tiddabiḥā*		
2cd	*tiddabiḥā*	2cd	*tiddabiḥā*	2cd	*ʾiddabiḥā*
1cd	*niddabiḥā*	1cd	*niddabiḥā*		
3mp	*tiddabiḥū*	3mp	*tiddabiḥū*		
3fp	*tiddabiḥna*	3fp	*tiddabiḥna*		
2mp	*tiddabiḥū*	2mp	*tiddabiḥū*	2mp	*ʾiddabiḥū*
2fp	*tiddabiḥna*	2fp	*tiddabiḥna*	2fp	*ʾiddabiḥā*
1cp	*niddabiḥ*	1cp	*niddabiḥa*		

Using ŠLM, the forms of the D-stem jussive, volitive, and imperative are as follows:

D Jussive		D Volitive		D Imperative	
3ms	*yašallim*	3ms	*yašallima*		
3fs	*tašallim*	3fs	*tašallima*		
2ms	*tašallim*	2ms	*tašallima*	2ms	*šallim*
2fs	*tašallimī*	2fs	*tašallimī*	2fs	*šallimī*
1cs	*ʾašallim*	1cs	*ʾašallima*		
3md	*tašallimā*	3md	*tašallimā*		
3fd	*tašallimā*	3fd	*tašallimā*		
2cd	*tašallimā*	2cd	*tašallimā*	2cd	*šallimā*
1cd	*našallimā*	1cd	*našallimā*		

D Jussive		D Volitive		D Imperative	
3mp	*tašallimū*	3mp	*tašallimū*		
3fp	*tašallimna*	3fp	*tašallimna*		
2mp	*tašallimū*	2mp	*tašallimū*	2mp	*šallimū*
2fp	*tašallimna*	2fp	*tašallimna*	2fp	*šallimā*
1cp	*našallim*	1cp	*našallima*		

5.6. Geminate Roots

A geminate root is a root where the second and third radical are the same. Geminate roots in Ugaritic are not well understood, given the scant nature of our evidence. Usually, the theme vowel is dropped; for example, *rabba* (< *rababa*; G 3ms QATALA RBB), "he is great." Given the rules of Ugaritic cuneiform, the consonant cluster of the identical second and third radicals is written just once, making the written form similar to Hollow roots (e.g., compare /mt/, "he died," and /rb/, "he is great"). We know that geminate roots exist, however, because of deviant cases where the theme vowel is not dropped—and because of comparative evidence. In the QATALA conjugation, a helping vowel *ā* is inserted before suffixes beginning with a consonant (as with hollow verbs).

3ms	*rabba*	"he is great"
3fs	*rabbat*	"she is great"
2ms	*rabbāta*	"you are great"
2fs	*rabbāti*	"you are great"
1cs	*rabbātu*	"I am great"
3md	*rabbā*	"the two of them are great"
3fd	*rabbatā*	"the two of them are great"
2cd	*rabbātumā*	"the two of you are great"
1cd	*rabbānāyā*	"the two of us are great"
3mp	*rabbū*	"they are great"
3fp	*rabbā*	"they are great"
2mp	*rabbātumu*	"you are great"
2fp	*rabbātina*	"you are great"
1cp	*rabbānū*	"we are great"

The YAQTULU conjugation follows the pattern *yaqullu*. In the 3fp and 2fp forms, the impossible consonant cluster (e.g., -*bbn*- for RBB) is reduced; for example, *tarubna* (< **tarubbna*), "they (fem.) will become great." The paradigm, with RBB, is as follows:

3ms	*yarubbu*	"he will become great"
3fs	*tarubbu*	"she will become great"
2ms	*tarubbu*	"you will become great"
2fs	*tarubbīna*	"you will become great"
1cs	*ʾarubbu*	"I will become great"
3md	*tarubbā(na)*	"the two of them will become great"
3fd	*tarubbā(na)*	"the two of them will become great"
2cd	*tarubbā(na)*	"the two of you will become great"
1cd	*narubbā*	"the two of us will become great"
3mp	*tarubbū(na)*	"they will become great"
3fp	*tarubna*	"they will become great"
2mp	*tarubbū(na)*	"you will become great"
2fp	*tarubna*	"you will become great"
1cp	*narubbu*	"we will become great"

In the jussive and imperative, the loss of the theme vowel often entails a phonologically impossible consonant cluster at the end of the word, causing the third radical to drop.

G Jussive	G Volitive	G Imperative
3ms *yarub* (< *yarubb*)	3ms *yarubba*	
3fs *tarub* (< *tarubb*)	3fs *tarubba*	
2ms *tarub* (< *tarubb*)	2ms *tarubba*	2ms *rub* (< *rubb*)
2fs *tarubbī*	2fs *tarubbī*	2fs *rubbī*
1cs *ʾarub* (< *ʾarubb*)	1cs *ʾarubba*	
3md *tarubbā*	3md *tarubbā*	
3fd *tarubbā*	3fd *tarubbā*	
2cd *tarubbā*	2cd *tarubbā*	2cd *rubbā*
1cd *narubbā*	1cd *narubbā*	

G Jussive		G Volitive		G Imperative	
3mp	*tarubbū*	3mp	*tarubbū*		
3fp	*tarubna* (< *tarubbna*)	3fp	*tarubna* (< *tarubbna*)		
2mp	*tarubbū*	2mp	*tarubbū*	2mp	*rubbū*
2fp	*tarubna*	2fp	*tarubna*	2fp	*rubbā*
1cp	*narub* (< *narubb*)	1cp	*narubba*		

5.7. Stative Verbs

Most of the verbs we have covered so far indicate actions; for example, MḪṢ, "to strike," or LḤM, "to eat." *Stative* verbs are verbs that indicate states of being, rather than actions. Some examples include ŠLM, "to be well," RM, "to be high," and RBB, "to be great."

Because they indicate states of being, stative verbs should be translated somewhat differently. Similar to YDʿ (see §1.8), a stative verb in the QATALA conjugation typically indicates a *present* state with roots in the past: *rāma*, "he is high" or "he has become high." The distinction between "he is high" and "he has become high" depends on whether the moment of achieving the state is in view, and this depends on context. However, in either case the subject of the verb has taken on the state in the past and continues in that state in the present. If the context very clearly indicates as much, the QATALA conjugation may be used for *past* tense: for example, ***rāma*** *wa qāla*, "**he was high** but he fell."

The YAQTULU conjugation is used for future tense: *tarubbu*, "she will be great" or "she will become great." Again, the distinction between these two glosses depends on whether the moment of achieving the state, *greatness*, is in view—this depends on context.

5.8. *Bi* of Exchange

In economic settings, or any context where exchange might occur, *bi* is used to indicate how much was paid or given "for" something, or the thing "for" which an amount of money was paid. For example, "a sheep for (*bi*) two shekels," or "twenty shekels of silver for (*bi*) an ox."

5.9. Vocabulary

baraqu	noun, masc., "lightning"
ǵalmu	noun, masc., "boy"
ǵūru	noun, masc., "mountain"
kussaʾu	noun, fem., "chair," "throne"
lawasanda	proper noun, place, indeclinable "Lawasanda"
marḫaqtu	noun, fem., "distant place"; often adverbial "[from] far away"
ṣimdu	noun, masc., "mace"
šamumānu	personal name, masc., diptotic, "Shamumanu"
šumu	noun, masc., "name" (dual *šumatā*, pl. *šumātu*)
yammu	noun, masc., "sea"; personal name "Yam"
BN	verb, "to understand" (G QATALA *bāna*, YAQTULU *yabīnu*)
NḪT	verb, "to prepare [something]" (G QATALA *naḫata*, YAQTULU *yiḫḫatu*), D "to prepare [something]"
NSʿ	verb, "to pay" (G QATALA *nasaʿa*, YAQTULU *yissaʿu*)
PʿR	verb, "to proclaim" (G QATALA *paʿara*, YAQTULU *yipʿaru*)
RBB	verb, "to be great, become great" (G QATALA *rabba*, YAQTULU *yarubbu*)
ʾū	conjunction, "and"
ʾô	conjunction, "or"
kī, kīya, kīma	conjunction, circumstantial "when," "if," "because"; complementizer "that"; emphatic "indeed"
du	relative particle, "that, who, which"
dū	relative marker, "that, who, which"
hanna	interjection, "look, behold"; adverb, "here" (also *hannana*, *hannaniya*, *halli*, *hatti*, *halliha*, *hallima*, *hallina*, *halliniya*)
hannadū	demonstrative pronoun, "this"
kāma, kamāma	adverb, "thus"
ṯamma	adverb, "there" (also *ṯammāna*, *ṯammāniya*, *ṯammati*)

5.10. Exercises

A. Write in vocalized Ugaritic.

1. The queen said to the king, "I wish you would fall[2] (NPL)," and he went out.
2. Message of Shamumanu, your brother, who is lord of the household in Lawasanda.
3. On this day, Sigildu (personal name) paid a shekel for his words. (inspired by *KTU* 3.9)

B. Write in vocalized Ugaritic and cuneiform.

1. At the feet of my master, from far away, I have fallen. (adapted from *KTU* 2.86:6–9)
2. To the queen, my mother, say: May these gods guard you, may they make you well. (adapted from *KTU* 2.15:2–6)

C. What letters would you change in the cuneiform of B2 above to revise to the following: "To the queen, our mother, say (masc. pl.): May this god guard you, may he make you well"?

D. Vocalize and translate the following Ugaritic.

1. 
2. ndr ỉṯt (ʾiṯṯatu, "gift") ʿmn mlk (adapted from *KTU* 2.30:12–14)
3. rgmt ỉm ỉmḫṣk b ṣmdy w tql ky ʿzt ảnk

4a. ydʿt ky ngšt ảṯt nʿmt b ym … (continued in 4b)

4b. (continued from 4a)

… 

5.  (*KTU* 1.161:8)

2. Or in English more closely aligned to Ugaritic syntax, "may you fall."

E. Translate the following passages into English:

1. *kôṯaru* (personal name) *ṣimdêma yanaḫḫitu wa yipʿaru šumatêhumā: "šumuka ʾiṯu yagrušu. yagruši, guruš yamma! guruš yamma lê kussaʾihu."* (adapted from *KTU* 1.2 iv:11–12)
2. *rabbātu yôma hannadā, ʾanāku wa bêtî du ʿimmānuya. kī garaštu malka, wa laqaḥtu kaḥṯahu wa ʾaṯṯātihu layya.*

Short Story 3
ʾaklu Luki wa Rani

ʾiṯu ʾaḫâma—**luku** wa **ranu**. ʾaḫâma šamaʿā ʾummahumā bi bêti wa qaraʾat, "ʾabaʿʿiru ʾakla hannadā." "Tabaʿʿiru ʾakla?" ragamā ʾaḫâma. "ʾaklu hannadū ʾaklunāyā. ʾal tabaʿʿir! Himma tabaʿʿiru ʾaklanāyā wa lā nilḥamānnannu." Qarabā ʾaḫâma ʾummahumā. "Biʿʿarti ʾaklanāyā?" ragamā lêha. "Himma biʿʿarti ʾaklanāyā wa lā nilḥamānnannu." "Ǵalmêya!" ragamat ʾummuhumā, "Lā yadaʿtumā ʾakla, wa ʾênu ṭābāma ʾattumā. **Likā** lê marḥaqti, naḥḥitā ʾaklakumā lêkumā, wa ʾanāku šalimtu." Luku wa ranu **halakā** lê marḥaqti. Tiḥḥatāna ʾakla wa tabaʿʿirāhu. Lā šalima lêhumā. ʾummu ragamat lê ʾaḫâtihumā dāti ʿimma ʾummihumā, "lā biʿʿartu ʾaklahumā. Hanna, bittiya, nilḥamā."

Vocabulary

- luku—personal name, masc., "Luku" (unattested)
- ranu—personal name, masc., "Ranu" (unattested)
- likā—2nd dual imperative of HLK, "to go"
- HLK—verb, "to go"

Lesson 6

6.1. Weak Verbs: Hollow Verbs in the Jussive, Volitive, and Imperative
6.2. Weak Verbs: I-ʾ Verbs in the Jussive, Volitive, and Imperative
6.3. Weak Verbs: I-n Verbs and LQḤ in the Jussive, Volitive, and Imperative
6.4. Weak Verbs: III-y/w
6.5. Š-Stem Verbs
6.6. Questions
6.7. Vocabulary
6.8. Exercises

6.1. Weak Verbs: Hollow Verbs in the Jussive, Volitive, and Imperative

As is the case with the YAQTULU conjugation (see §3.5), the theme vowel of hollow verbs in the jussive, volitive, and imperative prefers to be long (e.g., G-stem 3ms volitive QL *yaqīla*, "may he fall") but is short in closed syllables (e.g., G-stem 3ms jussive QL *yaqil*, "let him fall").

Most of the imperative and volitive forms have open syllables and thus long vowels. The only **volitive** forms with a closed theme-vowel syllable are the 3fp and 2fp, which are identical to their respective YAQTULU forms (e.g., *taqilna*, "may you fall"). The forms are as follows:

3ms	*yaqīla*	"let him fall"
3fs	*taqīla*	"let her fall"
2ms	*taqīla*	"may you fall"
2fs	*taqīlī*	"may you fall"
1cs	*ʾaqīla*	"let me fall"
3md	*taqīlā*	"let the two of them fall"
3fd	*taqīlā*	"let the two of them fall"
2cd	*taqīlā*	"let the two of you fall"
1cd	*naqīlā*	"let the two of us fall"
3mp	*taqīlū*	"let them fall"
3fp	*taqilna*	"let them fall"

2mp	*taqīlū*	"may you fall"
2fp	*taqilna*	"may you fall"
1cp	*naqīla*	"let us fall"

The only **imperative** form with a closed theme-vowel syllable is the 2ms, for example, *qil*, "fall." The other imperative forms have the theme vowel in open syllables, and thus a long theme vowel. The forms are as follows:

2ms	*qil*	"fall"
2fs	*qīlī*	"fall"
2cd	*qīlā*	"fall"
2mp	*qīlū*	"fall"
2fp	*qīlā*	"fall"

The **jussive** has several forms with closed syllables—the 3ms, 3fs, 2ms, 1cs, 3fp, 2fp, and 1cp—where the theme vowels is therefore short. The forms are as follows:

3ms	*yaqil*	"let him fall"
3fs	*taqil*	"let her fall"
2ms	*taqil*	"may you fall"
2fs	*taqīlī*	"may you fall"
1cs	*ʾaqil*	"let me fall"
3md	*taqīlā*	"let the two of them fall"
3fd	*taqīlā*	"let the two of them fall"
2cd	*taqīlā*	"let the two of you fall"
1cd	*naqīlā*	"let the two of us fall"
3mp	*taqīlū*	"let them fall"
3fp	*taqilna*	"let them fall"
2mp	*taqīlū*	"may you fall"
2fp	*taqilna*	"may you fall"
1cp	*naqil*	"let us fall"

6.2. Weak Verbs: I-ʾ Verbs in the Jussive, Volitive, and Imperative

The G-stem jussive and volitive of I-ʾ verbs follow the same irregularities as the G-stem YAQTULU of I-ʾ verbs. The jussive and volitive sometimes use a helping vowel rather than closing the first syllable with *alef*; for example, G volitive ʾḪD can be *yaʾḫuda* or *yaʾuḫuda*, both meaning "let him seize." The *alef* of the root always drops in the 1cs jussive and volitive, because of the presence of *alef* in the prefix morphology (e.g., *ʾaʾḫud* > *ʾaḫud*, "let me seize").

I-ʾ imperatives are regular (e.g., *ʾuḫud*, "seize"). Forms of the jussive, volitive, and imperative for I-ʾ verbs are as follows:

G Jussive		G Volitive		G Imperative	
3ms	*yaʾḫud / yaʾuḫud*	3ms	*yaʾḫuda / yaʾuḫuda*		
3fs	*taʾḫud / taʾuḫud*	3fs	*taʾḫuda / taʾuḫuda*		
2ms	*taʾḫud / taʾuḫud*	2ms	*taʾḫuda / taʾuḫuda*	2ms	*ʾuḫud*
2fs	*taʾḫudī / taʾuḫudī*	2fs	*taʾḫudī / taʾuḫudī*	2fs	*ʾuḫudī*
1cs	*ʾaḫud*	1cs	*ʾaḫuda*		
3md	*taʾḫudā / taʾuḫudā*	3md	*taʾḫudā / taʾuḫudā*		
3fd	*taʾḫudā / taʾuḫudā*	3fd	*taʾḫudā / taʾuḫudā*		
2cd	*taʾḫudā / taʾuḫudā*	2cd	*taʾḫudā / taʾuḫudā*	2cd	*ʾuḫudā*
1cd	*naʾḫudā / naʾuḫudā*	1cd	*naʾḫudā / naʾuḫudā*		
3mp	*taʾḫudū / taʾuḫudū*	3mp	*taʾḫudū / taʾuḫudū*		
3fp	*taʾḫudna / taʾuḫudna*	3fp	*taʾḫudna / taʾuḫudna*		
2mp	*taʾḫudū / taʾuḫudū*	2mp	*taʾḫudū / taʾuḫudū*	2mp	*ʾuḫudū*
2fp	*taʾḫudna / taʾuḫudna*	2fp	*taʾḫudna / taʾuḫudna*	2fp	*ʾuḫudā*
1cp	*naʾḫud*	1cp	*naʾḫuda*		

6.3. Weak Verbs: I-n Verbs and LQḤ in the Jussive, Volitive, and Imperative

In the jussive and volitive, I-n verbs follow the same irregularities as in the YAQTULU conjugation (see §4.5): the root *n* assimilates to the second radical. For example, G jussive 3ms NDR has the form *yaddur* (< *yandur*), "let him vow." The 3ms volitive of NDR is, similarly, *yaddura* (< *yandura*), "I wish he would vow" (i.e., "may he vow").

The imperative forms of I-n verbs usually drop the first letter *n* of the root; for example, 2ms imperative NDR is *dur*, "vow." However, imperatives sometimes occur with *n*, using the regular pattern; for example, *nudur*, "vow."

Forms of the jussive, volitive, and imperative for I-n verbs are as follows:

G Jussive		G Volitive		G Imperative	
3ms	*yaddur*	3ms	*yaddura*		
3fs	*taddur*	3fs	*taddura*		
2ms	*taddur*	2ms	*taddura*	2ms	*dur*
2fs	*tadduri̅*	2fs	*tadduri̅*	2fs	*duri̅*
1cs	*ʾaddur*	1cs	*ʾaddura*		
3md	*taddurā*	3md	*taddurā*		
3fd	*taddurā*	3fd	*taddurā*		
2cd	*taddurā*	2cd	*taddurā*	2cd	*durā*
1cd	*naddurā*	1cd	*naddurā*		
3mp	*taddurū*	3mp	*taddurū*		
3fp	*taddurna*	3fp	*taddurna*		
2mp	*taddurū*	2mp	*taddurū*	2mp	*durū*
2fp	*taddurna*	2fp	*taddurna*	2fp	*durā*
1cp	*naddur*	1cp	*naddura*		

As with the YAQTULU conjugation, if the character *n* is written in cuneiform for a jussive or volitive I-n verb, this indicates that the verb is D- or N-stem (see §4.5) because *n* has not assimilated to a different consonant. For example, N-stem jussive 3ms NDR *yinnadir*, "let it be vowed."

The verb **LQḤ**, "to take," behaves like a I-n verb in the G-stem jussive (*yiqqaḥ*), volitive (*yiqqaḥa*), and imperative (*qaḥ*).

6.4. Weak Verbs: III-y/w

6.4.1. G-stem QATALA and YAQTULU

In the QATALA and YAQTULU conjugations, the final radical of III-y/w verbs sometimes contracts and sometimes does not. To take an example, the verb ʿNY ("to answer") could manifest without contraction in a form like *yaʿniyu* (G-stem 3ms YAQTULU "he answers"), or there could be contraction to the form *yaʿnû* (*iyu* > *û*; G-stem 3ms YAQTULU "he answers"). When contraction occurs, the resulting vowel depends on the theme vowel and the morphological suffix, according to the rules for contraction given in §2.7.

Most roots that were historically III-w have become III-y by the period of Ugaritic we are learning. One exception is ʾTY (often listed as ʾTW in lexicons), "to come." The original *w* is retained in the QATALA conjugation (e.g., *ʾatawa*, "he came"), while in the YAQTULU conjugation it has shifted to *y* (e.g., *yiʾtayu*, "he will come").

Where the diphthongs *ay*, *iy*, or *aw* close a nonfinal syllable (i.e., *ay*, *iy*, or *aw* followed by a consonant), they contract to *ê*, *î*, and *ô*, respectively (see §2.7; see §6.4.3 below for *ay*, *iy*, or *aw* in a final syllable). For example, G-stem 2fs QATALA *ʿanêti* (< *ʿanayti*; "you answered"); G-stem 1cp QATALA *šatînū* (< *šatiynū*); and G-stem 2ms QATALA *ʾatôta* (< *ʾatawta*; "you came").

Long vowels that are the result of contraction show the same tendency as other long vowels to reduce in closed syllables. Thus, if contraction occurs with a form like *ʿanayat* (G-stem 3fs QATALA "she answered"), the end result is not *ʿanât* but *ʿanat* (*ʿanayat* > *ʿanât* > *ʿanat*).

Examples of the G QATALA and YAQTULU in III-y/w roots, with various theme vowels, are given below, using the verbs ʿNY ("to answer"), ŠTY ("to drink"), BǴY ("to explain"), and ʾTY ("to come"). Where uncontracted forms are possible, they are given first, followed by forms with contraction. If contraction or vowel-shifting has occurred, the change is noted in parentheses (e.g., *ay* > *ê*, or *ayu* > *û*).

G QATALA ʿNY: *a* theme vowel

3ms	*ʿanaya* / *ʿanâ* (*aya* > *â*)
3fs	*ʿanayat* / *ʿanat* (*aya* > *â* > *a*)
2ms	*ʿanêta* (*ay* > *ê*)
2fs	*ʿanêti* (*ay* > *ê*)
1cs	*ʿanêtu* (*ay* > *ê*)

3md	*ʿanayā* / *ʿanâ* (*ayā* > *â*)
3fd	*ʿanayatā* / *ʿanâtā* (*aya* > *â*)
2cd	*ʿanêtumā* (*ay* > *ê*)
1cd	*ʿanênāyā* (*ay* > *ê*)
3mp	*ʿanayū* / *ʿanû* (*ayū* > *û*)
3fp	*ʿanayā* / *ʿanâ* (*ayā* > *â*)
2mp	*ʿanêtumu* (*ay* > ê)
2fp	*ʿanêtina* (*ay* > *ê*)
1cp	*ʿanênū* (*ay* > *ê*)

G QATALA ŠTY: *i* theme vowel

3ms	*šatiya* / *šatî* (*iya* > *î*)
3fs	*šatiyat* / *šatit* (*iya* > *î* > *i*)
2ms	*šatîta* (*iy* > *î*)
2fs	*šatîti* (*iy* > *î*)
1cs	*šatîtu* (*iy* > *î*)
3md	*šatiyā* / *šatî* (*iyā* > *î*)
3fd	*šatiyatā* / *šatîtā* (*iya* > *î*)
2cd	*šatîtumā* (*iy* > *î*)
1cd	*šatînāyā* (*iy* > *î*)
3mp	*šatiyū* / *šatû* (*iyū* > *û*)
3fp	*šatiyā* / *šatî* (*iyā* > *î*)
2mp	*šatîtumu* (*iy* > *î*)
2fp	*šatîtina* (*iy* > *î*)
1cp	*šatînū* (*iy* > *î*)

G QATALA ʾTY (ʾTW): *a* theme vowel, *w* third radical

3ms	*ʾatawa* / *ʾatâ* (*awa* > *â*)
3fs	*ʾatawat* / *ʾatat* (*awa* > *â* > *a*)
2ms	*ʾatôta* (*aw* > *ô*)
2fs	*ʾatôti* (*aw* > *ô*)
1cs	*ʾatôtu* (*aw* > *ô*)
3md	*ʾatawā* / *ʾatâ* (*awā* > *â*)

3fd	*ʾatawatā* / *ʾatâtā* (*awa* > *â*)
2cd	*ʾatôtumā* (*aw* > *ô*)
1cd	*ʾatônāyā* (*aw* > *ô*)
3mp	*ʾatawū* / *ʾatû* (*awū* > *û*)
3fp	*ʾatawā* / *ʾatâ* (*awā* > *â*)
2mp	*ʾatôtumu* (*aw* > *ô*)
2fp	*ʾatôtina* (*aw* > *ô*)
1cp	*ʾatônū* (*aw* > *ô*)

G YAQTULU ʿNY: *i* theme vowel

3ms	*yaʿniyu* / *yaʿnû* (*iyu* > *û*)
3fs	*taʿniyu* / *taʿnû* (*iyu* > *û*)
2ms	*taʿniyu* / *taʿnû* (*iyu* > *û*)
2fs	*taʿnîna* (*iyī* > *î*)
1cs	*ʾaʿniyu* / *ʾaʿnû* (*iyu* > *û*)
3md	*taʿniyā(na)* / *taʿnî(na)* (*iyā* > *î*)
3fd	*taʿniyā(na)* / *taʿnî(na)* (*iyā* > *î*)
2cd	*taʿniyā(na)* / *taʿnî(na)* (*iyā* > *î*)
1cd	*naʿniyā* / *naʿnî* (*iyā* > *î*)
3mp	*taʿniyū(na)* / *taʿnû(na)* (*iyū* > *û*)
3fp	*taʿnîna* (*iy* > *î*)
2mp	*taʿniyū(na)* / *taʿnû(na)* (*iyū* > *û*)
2fp	*taʿnîna* (*iy* > *î*)
1cp	*naʿniyu* / *naʿnû* (*iyu* > *û*)

G YAQTULU BǴY: *a* theme vowel

3ms	*yibǵayu* / *yibǵû* (*ayu* > *û*)
3fs	*tibǵayu* / *tibǵû* (*ayu* > *û*)
2ms	*tibǵayu* / *tibǵû* (*ayu* > *û*)
2fs	*tibǵayīna* / *tibǵîna* (*ayī* > *î*)
1cs	*ʾibǵayu* / *ʾibǵû* (*ayu* > *û*)
3md	*tibǵayā(na)* / *tibǵâ(na)* (*ayā* > *â*)
3fd	*tibǵayā(na)* / *tibǵâ(na)* (*ayā* > *â*)

2cd	*tibǵayā(na)* / *tibǵâ(na)* (*ayā > â*)
1cd	*nibǵayā* / *nibǵâ* (*ayā > â*)
3mp	*tibǵayū(na)* / *tibǵû(na)* (*ayū > û*)
3fp	*tibǵêna* (*ay > ê*)
2mp	*tibǵayū(na)* / *tibǵû(na)* (*ayū > û*)
2fp	*tibǵêna* (*ay > ê*)
1cp	*nibǵayu* / *nibǵû* (*ayu > û*)

6.4.2. N- and D-stem QATALA and YAQTULU

The abnormalities of III-y/w N- and D-stem verbs are the same as in the G-stem. At the end of the verb, the same conditions occur that can result in contraction: the sequence theme-vowel – *y* – verbal-suffix. The N- and D-stem QATALA will follow the same patterns as the G QATALA with *a* theme vowel, and the N- and D-stem YAQTULU will follow the same patterns as the G YAQTULU with *i* theme vowel. D YAQTULU ŠQY ("to give drink"), for example, is *yašaqq****iyu*** ("he gives drink") or, with contraction, *yašaqq****û***.

N-stem QATALA ŠTY		D-stem QATALA ŠQY		N-stem YAQTULU ŠTY		D-stem YAQTULU ŠQY	
3ms	*naštaya* or *naštâ*	3ms	*šiqqaya* or *šiqqâ*	3ms	*yiššatiyu* or *yiššatû*	3ms	*yašaqqiyu* or *yašaqqû*
3fs	*naštayat* or *naštat*	3fs	*šiqqayat* or *šiqqat*	3fs	*tiššatiyu* or *tiššatû*	3fs	*tašaqqiyu* or *tašaqqû*
2ms	*naštêta*	2ms	*šiqqêta*	2ms	*tiššatiyu* or *tiššatû*	2ms	*tašaqqiyu* or *tašaqqû*
2fs	*naštêti*	2fs	*šiqqêti*	2fs	*tiššatîna*	2fs	*tašaqqîna*
1cs	*naštêtu*	1cs	*šiqqêtu*	1cs	*ʾiššatiyu* or *ʾiššatû*	1cs	*ʾašaqqiyu* or *ʾašaqqû*
etc.		etc.		etc.		etc.	
cf. endings of the G-stem QATALA ʿNY above		cf. endings of the G-stem QATALA ʿNY above		cf. endings of the G-stem YAQTULU ʿNY above		cf. endings of the G-stem YAQTULU ʿNY above	

6.4.3. Jussive, Volitive, and Imperative

In III-y/w roots in all stems, forms of the jussive and imperative that normally end with closed syllables drop the final radical *y*. Taking ʿNY as an example, the 2ms imperative is *ʿini* (< *ʿiniy*; "answer"). Similarly, the 3fs jussive is *yaʿni* (< *yaʿniy*; "let her answer"). Where a III-y/w form in the jussive, volitive, or imperative ends with an open syllable with *y*, contraction may occur as in the YAQTULU form; for example, 3mp jussive *tibǵû* (< *tibǵayū*), "may they explain." Forms with *iyi* always result in contraction; for example, 2fs imperative *ʿinî* ("answer"; *ʿiniyī* > *ʿinî*).

Forms of the jussive, volitive, and imperative for III-y/w verbs are as follows:

ʿNY, "to answer": *i* theme vowel

G Jussive		G Volitive		G Imperative	
3ms	*yaʿni* (< *yaʿniy*)	3ms	*yaʿniya* / *yaʿnî*		
3fs	*taʿni* (< *taʿniy*)	3fs	*taʿniya* / *taʿnî*		
2ms	*taʿni* (< *taʿniy*)	2ms	*taʿniya* / *taʿnî*	2ms	*ʿini* (< *ʿiniy*)
2fs	*taʿnî* (< *taʿniyī*)	2fs	*taʿnî* (< *taʿniyī*)	2fs	*ʿinî* (< *ʿiniyī*)
1cs	*ʾaʿni* (< *ʾaʿniy*)	1cs	*ʾaʿniya* / *ʾaʿnî*		
3md	*taʿniyā* / *taʿnî*	3md	*taʿniyā* / *taʿnî*		
3fd	*taʿniyā* / *taʿnî*	3fd	*taʿniyā* / *taʿnî*		
2cd	*taʿniyā* / *taʿnî*	2cd	*taʿniyā* / *taʿnî*	2cd	*ʿiniyā* / *ʿinî*
1cd	*naʿniyā* / *naʿnî*	1cd	*naʿniyā* / *naʿnî*		
3mp	*taʿniyū* / *taʿnû*	3mp	*taʿniyū* / *taʿnû*		
3fp	*taʿnîna*	3fp	*taʿnîna*		
2mp	*taʿniyū* / *taʿnû*	2mp	*taʿniyū* / *taʿnû*	2mp	*ʿiniyū* / *ʿinû*
2fp	*taʿnîna*	2fp	*taʿnîna*	2fp	*ʿiniyā* / *ʿinî*
1cp	*naʿni* (< *naʿniy*)	1cp	*naʿniya* / *naʿnî*		

As with the YAQTULU conjugation, the jussive, volitive, and imperative forms of the N- and D-stem for III-y/w roots will follow the same patterns of contraction as the G jussive, volitive, and imperative with *i* theme vowel, given above.

6.5. Š-Stem Verbs

The Š-stem is formed using the prefix *ša-*. As with the N- and D-stems, the vocalization of the Š-stem is consistent for all lexemes—there are no theme vowel variations. The pattern for the QATALA conjugation is *šaqtila*. The pattern for the YAQTULU conjugation is *yašaqtilu*. Using Š-stem Bʿ R ("to illuminate") as an example, the paradigms are as follows:

Š QATALA

3ms	*šabʿira*	"he illuminated"
3fs	*šabʿirat*	"she illuminated"
2ms	*šabʿirta*	"you illuminated"
2fs	*šabʿirti*	"you illuminated"
1cs	*šabʿirtu*	"I illuminated"
3md	*šabʿirā*	"the two of them illuminated"
3fd	*šabʿiratā*	"the two of them illuminated"
2cd	*šabʿirtumā*	"the two of you illuminated"
1cd	*šabʿirnāyā*	"the two of us illuminated"
3mp	*šabʿirū*	"they illuminated"
3fp	*šabʿirā*	"they illuminated"
2mp	*šabʿirtumu*	"you illuminated"
2fp	*šabʿirtina*	"you illuminated"
1cp	*šabʿirnū*	"we illuminated"

Š YAQTULU

3ms	*yašabʿiru*	"he illuminates"
3fs	*tašabʿiru*	"she illuminates"
2ms	*tašabʿiru*	"you illuminate"
2fs	*tašabʿirīna*	"you illuminate"
1cs	*ʾašabʿiru*	"I illuminate"
3md	*tašabʿirā(na)*	"the two of them illuminate"
3fd	*tašabʿirā(na)*	"the two of them illuminate"
2cd	*tašabʿirā(na)*	"the two of you illuminate"

1cd	*našabʿirā*	"the two of us illuminate"
3mp	*tašabʿirū(na)*	"they illuminate"
3fp	*tašabʿirna*	"they illuminate"
2mp	*tašabʿirū(na)*	"you illuminate"
2fp	*tašabʿirna*	"you illuminate"
1cp	*našabʿiru*	"we illuminate"

Š Jussive		Š Volitive		Š Imperative	
3ms	*yašabʿir*	3ms	*yašabʿira*		
3fs	*tašabʿir*	3fs	*tašabʿira*		
2ms	*tašabʿir*	2ms	*tašabʿira*	2ms	*šabʿir*
2fs	*tašabʿirī*	2fs	*tašabʿirī*	2fs	*šabʿirī*
1cs	*ʾašabʿir*	1cs	*ʾašabʿira*		
3md	*tašabʿirā*	3md	*tašabʿirā*		
3fd	*tašabʿirā*	3fd	*tašabʿirā*		
2cd	*tašabʿirā*	2cd	*tašabʿirā*	2cd	*šabʿirā*
1cd	*našabʿirā*	1cd	*našabʿirā*		
3mp	*tašabʿirū*	3mp	*tašabʿirū*		
3fp	*tašabʿirna*	3fp	*tašabʿirna*		
2mp	*tašabʿirū*	2mp	*tašabʿirū*	2mp	*šabʿirū*
2fp	*tašabʿirna*	2fp	*tašabʿirna*	2fp	*šabʿirā*
1cp	*našabʿir*	1cp	*našabʿira*		

Š-stem verbs generally have causative semantics. For example, with G-stem LḤM, *mutu* ***laḥama*** *ʾakla* means "the man **ate** food," but with Š-stem LḤM, ***šalḥima*** *muta ʾakla* means "he **caused** the man **to eat** food." However, causative semantics should not always be assumed, and a lexicon should be consulted for each new word. Š-stem YTN, for example, means "to send" (G-stem "to give"; i.e., "to cause someone to deliver something"), and Š-stem KN is "to establish" (G-stem "to exist").

6.6. Questions

In Ugaritic, there are very few words that explicitly signal a question. One of these, *ʾêka* ("how?" and alternate form *ʾêkaya*), was introduced in lesson 4. Others include *ma*, "what?," and *mī*, "who?" Both of these can be used in conjunction with prepositions, for example, *lê ma*, "for what?" (="why?"), or *bi mī*, "with whom?" Such question words occur at the start of the clause. Yes/no questions are not explicitly marked in Ugaritic; context is our only guide in identifying such questions.

6.7. Vocabulary

ʾTY	verb, "to come" (G QATALA *ʾatawa* / *ʾatâ*, YAQTULU *yiʾtayu* / *yiʾatayu* / *yiʾtû* / *yiʾatû*)
ʿLY	verb, "to go up" (G QATALA *ʿalaya* / *ʿalâ*, YAQTULU *yaʿliyu* / *yaʿlû*)
ʿNY	verb, "to answer" (G QATALA *ʿanaya* / *ʿanâ*, YAQTULU *yaʿniyu* / *yaʿnû*)
BǴY	verb, "to explain" (G QATALA *baǵaya* / *baǵâ*, YAQTULU *yibǵayu* / *yibǵû*)
MT	verb, "to die" (G QATALA *mīta*, YAQTULU *yamūtu*)
NS	verb, "to flee" (G QATALA *nāsa*, YAQTULU *yanūsu*)
tamūtatu	noun, fem., "shipwreck"
ʾadānu	noun, masc., "lord"
ʾadattu	noun, fem., "lady" (pl *ʾadānātu*)
ʾarṣu	noun, fem., "earth, land"
hêkalu	noun, masc., "palace"
qirbu	noun, masc., "middle," "midst"
qudšu	noun, masc., "holiness"
šamûma	noun, masc., only pl., "heavens"
dānîʾilu	personal name, "Dani'ilu"
marziḥu	noun, masc., "drinking club"
sipru	noun, masc., "document," "account"
QNY	verb, "to acquire" (G QATALA *qanaya* / *qanâ*, YAQTULU *yaqniyu* / *yaqnû*)
ŠQY	verb, D "to give drink"

ŠTY	verb, "to drink" (G QATALA *šatiya* / *šatî* , YAQTULU *yištayu* / *yištû*)
ṯulḥanu	noun, masc., "table" (pl. *ṯulḥanātu*)
ʾal	particle, "not," negation with irrealis verbs
ma	pronoun, "what?" (only extant in *lê ma*, "why?")
manna	pronoun, "whatever" (also *mannaka*, *mannama*)
mī	pronoun, "who?"

6.8. Exercises

A. Write in vocalized Ugaritic and cuneiform.

1. When the man ate and drank at my table, he said, "I wish you would die."[1]
2. Let me explain this to you, boy: you should not acquire this bull. In a day, it will fall, its strength will flee, and it will not be well.
3. Look, there is food there, and you (sg.) must understand (*irrealis* YAQTULU) what the king proclaimed. Let us go up (du.) and pay (du.) a shekel for (*bi*) this food.
4. Who will illuminate my face if my sun flees (*irrealis* YAQTULU)? How will I feed ("cause to eat") my sons and my daughters?

B. Vocalize and translate the following Ugaritic.

1. w ảnk kl ḏrʿhm (ḏarʿi, "grain") … w ảklhm bd rb tmtt lqḥt (*KTU* 2.38:18–23)
2. ?
3. hn ỉšmʿ g b ủdny yrgm m b šmm ʿm šmmn
4. m hndt hnny ảḫty ảtyt tšʿrbh ʿbdm
5. 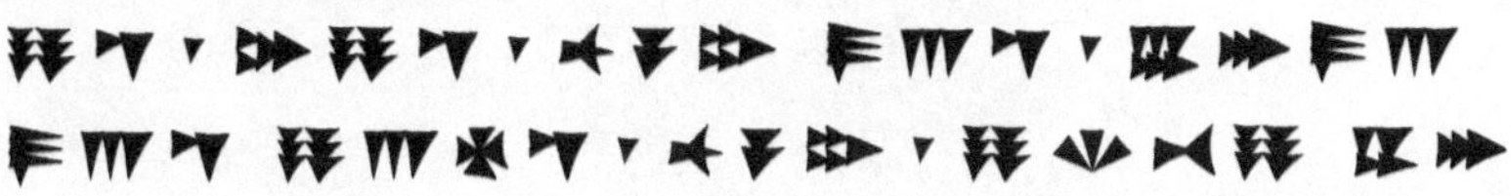

1. Or in English more closely aligned to Ugaritic syntax, "May you die."

 (adapted from *KTU* 1.17 i:5–8)

C. Translate the following passages into English.

1. *hannadū ʾiṯu sipru marziḥi dī qanaya šamumānu bi bêtihu. himma ʾagrušukumu bi bêtiya kaspa ḫamišīma* (*"fifty"*) *ṯiqla ʾissaʿu. wa šamumānu rabbu. ʾal yargum mutu marziḥi lê šamumāna, "ʾiš ʾala kaspaya dā ʿimmānuka." ṯiqlêma yissaʿu.* (adapted from *KTU* 3.9:1–17)
2. *ʾilu dabaḥa bi bêtihu maṣīda* ("game," i.e., meat from hunting) *ṣêda* ("quarry," i.e., meat from hunting) *bi qirbi hêkalihu* (*KTU* 1.114:1–2)
3. *ʾabīnu baraqa dā lā tabīnū šamûma, rigma dā lā tabīnū mutū ʾarṣi. ʾatî, wa ʾanāku ʾibǵayuhu lêki bi ǵūriya rabbi.* (adapted from *KTU* 1.3 iii:26–30)

Short Story 4
Ṯalāṯu ʾalapūma Qaṭanūma

Ṯalāṯu ʾalapūma **qaṭanūma** ʾiṯu bi ʾarṣi ʾugarit. **Banayū** ṯalāṯa bahatīma. ʾalpu qaṭanu ʾaḥḥadu banaya bêtahu bi yômi ʾaḥḥadi. Bêtu hannadū ʾênu naʿīmu, wa ʿazzu ʾênu. Wa ʾalpu qaṭanu hannadū ragama, "ʾanāku ʾênu **ḫarrāšu bahatīma**, wa lā yadaʿtu **ḫaršuta**. Himma bêtuya ʾênu ʿazzu, wa mī **yidaʿu**?" **Nabalu** ʾiṯu ʾalpu qaṭanu hannadū.

ʾalpu qaṭanu ʾaḥḥadu—ʾalpatu—banat bêtaha bi **yarḫi** ʾaḥḥadi. Tabniyu ʾalpatu qaṭanatu hannadāti yôma wa **lêla**, wa ḥarrāšu bahatīma ʾênu. Bêtu hannadū ʾiṯu naʿīmu, wa ʾênu ʿazzu. Wa ʾalpatu qaṭanatu hannadāti ragamat, "ʾanāku ʾênu ḥarrāšu bahatīma, wa banêtu yôma wa lêla. Ṭābu bêtuya." Nabalatu ʾiṯu ʾalpatu qaṭanatu hannadāti kama ʾaḫîha.

ʾalpu qaṭanu ʾaḥḥadu ragama bi **libbihu**, "Ḥarrāšu bahatīma ʾênu ʾanāku. **ʾiqqaḫ ḫarrāša bahatīma** ṭāba kama **kôṯari** wa huwa yabnû bêtaya." Banâ ḥarrāšu bahatīma bêta ṭāba bêta naʿīma wa ʿazza. ragama ʾalpu qaṭanu hannadū, "ʾanāku ʾênu nabalu. Bêtu hannadū ṭābu." ʾalpu qaṭanu hannadū ʾênu nabalu kama ʾaḫîhu wa ʾaḫâtihu.

ʾilu šamaʿa kīya taʾuhubu ʾaṯṯatuhu baʿla **rākiba ʾurpati** wa ʾappuhu **baʿara** maʾda. Baʿara ʾappuhu lê banī ʾalapī ʾugarit. ʾatâ lê ʾugarit lê bêti ʾalpi nabali. "Bêtu hannadū ʾênu ṭābu. ʿazzu ʾênu, naʿīmu ʾênu. ʾabbidannannu." ʾibbada ʾilu bêtahu. ʾatâ ʾilu lê bêti ʾalpati nabalati. "Bêtu hannadū ʾênu ṭābu. Naʿīmu ʾiṯu, wa ʾênu ʿazzu. ʾabbidannannu." ʾibbada ʾilu bêtaha.

ʾataya ʾilu lê bêti ʾalpi dī ʾênu nabalu. "Hannana, ṭābu bêtu hannadū. Naʿīmu ʾiṯu, wa ʿazzu. Nabalu lā banaya bêta hannadā. Ḥarrāšu bahatīma banâ." Bêtu ṭābu wa bêtu ʿazzu. wa ʾappu ʾili yabʿiru maʾda. "ʾabbidannannu."

Ṯalāṯu ʾalapūma qaṭanūma mītū ʿimmānu bahatīhumu, wa šalima kalīlu bi ʾugarit.

Vocabulary

qaṭanu—adj., "small"
BNY—verb, "to build" (G QATALA *banaya* / *banâ*, YAQTULU *yabniyu* / *yabnû*)
ḥarrāšu bahatīma—"house-builder"
ḥaršutu—noun, "manufacturing, tradesmanship" (not attested)
yidaʿu—3rd masculine singular YAQTULU of YDʿ, "to know"
nabalu—adj., "stupid," "foolish" (not attested)
yarḫu—noun, "moon," "month"
lêlu—noun, "night"
libbu—noun, "heart"
ʾiqqaḥ ḥarrāša bahatīma—"to take" a workman means "to hire" them
kôṯaru—personal name, masc., "Kotharu" (the artisan deity)
rākibu ʾurpati—"cloud-rider"
BʿR—verb, "to burn" (intransitive; not attested in the G-stem) (G QATALA *baʿara*, YAQTULU *yabʿiru*)

Lesson 7

7.1. Participles
7.2. Infinitives
7.3. Cardinal Numerals
7.4. Weak Verbs in the Š-Stem
7.5. Š-Stem ṮB, "to return"
7.6. Weak Verbs: I-y/w
7.7. Weak Verbs: HLK and HLM
7.8. YAQTULU in Past-Tense Contexts
7.9. Locative Accusatives
7.10. Vocabulary
7.11. Exercises

7.1. Participles

The Ugaritic participle is a verbal adjective. Like a regular adjective, it can be used to modify a noun ("attributive" use; e.g., *mutu* ***hāliku***, "walking man," i.e., "man who is walking"), or it can be a nominal ("substantive" use; e.g., ***rāgimu*** *rigma nāsa*, "the one who was saying a word fled").

The pattern for active **G-stem participles** is *qātilu*. The final *u* in this example is the nominative case ending. Participles are inflected for gender (e.g., fem. *rāgim****atu***, "one [fem.] saying"), case (e.g., accusative *rāgim****a***), and number (e.g., plural *rāgim****ūma***, "ones saying"), following the same rules as nouns and adjectives. Participles are not inflected for person. Using the verb RGM as an example, the G-stem participles are inflected as in the following chart.

G-stem RGM

		Masc	Fem
Sg	Nom	*rāgimu*	*rāgimatu*
	Gen	*rāgimi*	*rāgimati*
	Acc	*rāgima*	*rāgimata*

Dual	Nom	*rāgimāma* bound: *rāgimā*	*rāgimatāma* bound: *rāgimatā*
	Acc/Gen/Voc	*rāgimêma* bound: *rāgimê*	*rāgimatêma* bound: *rāgimatê*
Pl	Nom	*rāgimūma* bound: *rāgimū*	*rāgimātu*
	Acc/Gen/Voc (Obl)	*rāgimīma* bound: *rāgimī*	*rāgimāti*

Hollow verbs follow the pattern *qv̄lu*, where *v̄* is the theme vowel of the QATALA form. For example, for QL the form is *qālu* ("the one who is falling"; cf. the 3ms QATALA form *qāla*, with *ā* theme vowel). Using the verbs QL and MT as examples, hollow G-stem participles are inflected as in the following chart.

G-stem QL and MT

		Masc		Fem	
Sg	Nom	*qālu*	*mītu*	*qālatu*	*mītatu*
	Gen	*qāli*	*mīti*	*qālati*	*mītati*
	Acc	*qāla*	*mīta*	*qālata*	*mītata*
Dual	Nom	*qālāma* bound: *qālā*	*mītāma* bound: *mītā*	*qālatāma* bound: *qālatā*	*mītatāma* bound: *mītatā*
	Acc/Gen/Voc (Obl)	*qālêma* bound: *qālê*	*mītêma* bound: *mītê*	*qālatêma* bound: *qālatê*	*mītatêma* bound: *mītatê*
Pl	Nom	*qālūma* bound: *qālū*	*mītūma* bound: *mītū*	*qālātu*	*mītātu*
	Acc/Gen/Voc (Obl)	*qālīma* bound: *qālī*	*mītīma* bound: *mītī*	*qālāti*	*mītāti*

III-y participles sometimes have contraction of *y* and sometimes do not. For example, *šātiyu* or *šātû*, "one who drinks" (nom).

G-stem ŠTY

		Masc	Fem
Sg	Nom	*šātiyu* / *šātû*	*šātiyatu* / *šātîtu*
	Gen/Voc	*šātî* (< *šātiyi*)	*šātiyati* / *šātîti*
	Acc	*šātiya* / *šātî*	*šātiyata* / *šātîta*
Dual	Nom	*šātiyāma* / *šātîma* bound: *šātiyā* / *šātî*	*šātiyatāma* / *šātîtāma* bound: *šātiyatā* / *šātîtā*
	Acc/Gen/Voc (Obl)	*šātiyêma* / *šātêma* bound: *šātiyê* / *šātê*	*šātiyatêma* / *šātîtêma* bound: *šātiyatê* / *šātîtê*
Pl	Nom	*šātiyūma* / *šātûma* bound: *šātiyū* / *šātû*	*šātiyātu* / *šātîtu*
	Acc/Gen/Voc (Obl)	*šātîma* (< *šātiyīma*) bound: *šātî* (< *šātiyī*)	*šātiyāti* / *šātîti*

D-stem participles take the pattern *muqattilu*. Using the verb Bʿ R, for example, the D-stem participle is *mubaʿʿiru*, "one who burns [something]."

D-stem Bʿ R

		Masc	Fem
Sg	Nom	*mubaʿʿiru*	*mubaʿʿiratu*
	Gen/Voc	*mubaʿʿiri*	*mubaʿʿirati*
	Acc	*mubaʿʿira*	*mubaʿʿirata*
Dual	Nom	*mubaʿʿirāma* bound: *mubaʿʿirā*	*mubaʿʿiratāma* bound: *mubaʿʿiratā*
	Acc/Gen/Voc (Obl)	*mubaʿʿirêma* bound: *mubaʿʿirê*	*mubaʿʿiratêma* bound: *mubaʿʿiratê*
Pl	Nom	*mubaʿʿirūma* bound: *mubaʿʿirū*	*mubaʿʿirātu*
	Acc/Gen/Voc (Obl)	*mubaʿʿirīma* bound: *mubaʿʿirī*	*mubaʿʿirāti*

Š-stem participles take the pattern *mušaqtilu*. Using the verb Bʿ R, for example, the Š-stem participle is *mušabʿiru*, "one who illuminates [something]."

Š-stem Bʿ R

		Masc	Fem
Sg	Nom	*mušabʿiru*	*mušabʿiratu*
	Gen/Voc	*mušabʿiri*	*mušabʿirati*
	Acc	*mušabʿira*	*mušabʿirata*
Dual	Nom	*mušabʿirāma* bound: *mušabʿirā*	*mušabʿiratāma* bound: *mušabʿiratā*
	Acc/Gen/Voc (Obl)	*mušabʿirêma* bound: *mušabʿirê*	*mušabʿiratêma* bound: *mušabʿiratê*
Pl	Nom	*mušabʿirūma* bound: *mušabʿirū*	*mušabʿirātu*
	Acc/Gen/Voc (Obl)	*mušabʿirīma* bound: *mušabʿirī*	*mušabʿirāti*

When the verb's semantics require a complement—as in the examples *mušabʿiratu* and *mušabʿiru* above—the complement can be accusative (i.e., following verbal syntax) or genitive (i.e., following nominal syntax): *mubaʿʿirūma bêtahu*, "ones who burned his house," and *mubaʿʿirū bêtihu*, "burners of his house."

7.2. Infinitives

Infinitives are not used often in Ugaritic, as far as we can tell. It is also possible that many more cases occur, though we cannot know with certainty because unvocalized infinitives are usually identical to unvocalized QATALA verbs (e.g., infinitive *ragāmu*, "to say," and QATALA *ragama*, "he spoke," are both written /rgm/).

Most **G-stem infinitives** follow the pattern *qatālu* (e.g., *ragāmu*, "to say"), though other patterns (e.g., *qitlu*) also occur. The following paradigm of RGM illustrates the inflected forms.

Free use	*ragāmu*	"to say"
Nom	*ragāmu*	"to say," "saying"
Gen	*ragāmi*	"to say," "saying"
Acc	*ragāma*	"to say," "saying"

I-n infinitives behave like strong verbs. For example, *napālu*, "to fall."

Hollow verbs follow the pattern *qv̄lu*, where *v̄* is the theme vowel of the YAQTULU form; for example, *qīlu* (infinitive of QL; "falling," "to fall").

Free use	*qīlu*	"to fall"
Nom	*qīlu*	"to fall," "falling"
Gen	*qīli*	"to fall," "falling"
Acc	*qīla*	"to fall," "falling"

III-y infinitives sometimes have contraction of *y* and sometimes do not. For example, *šatāyu* or *šatû*, "drinking" (nom).

Free use	*šatāyu* / *šatû*	"to drink"
Nom	*šatāyu* / *šatû*	"to drink," "drinking"
Gen	*šatāyi* / *šatî*	"to drink," "drinking"
Acc	*šatāya* / *šatâ*	"to drink," "drinking"

The **Š-stem infinitive** is *šaqtālu* (e.g., *šabʿāru*, "to illuminate").

Free use	*šabʿāru*	"to illuminate"
Nom	*šabʿāru*	"to illuminate," "illuminating"
Gen	*šabʿāri*	"to illuminate," "illuminating"
Acc	*šabʿāra*	"to illuminate," "illuminating"

The infinitive is a verbal noun and can be translated as such, for example, *laḥāmu*, "eating." As a verbal noun, the infinitive can appear (in the genitive) with *bi* or *lê*, whose meanings give the overall phrase temporal or goal semantics. For example, *bi laḥāmina*, "in our eating" or "when we ate"; *lê šatî*, "for drinking" or "in order to drink."

The infinitive can also serve as a complement to a finite verb, with or without *lê*, for example, *šaʾila lê šatî*, "he asked [us] to drink." Free infinitives (which take nominative masculine morphology) are also used to intensify a finite verb, for example, ***šatāyu*** *šatîtu*, woodenly translated "drinking I drank," meaning "I surely drank."

Finally, it is possible that free infinitives can be used in place of a finite verb to express contingent actions, with TAM features dependent on the verb on which the infinitive is contingent. An infinitive following an imperative, for example, would have the force of an imperative whose action is contingent on the preceding imperative: *šôṣiʾ* (Š imperative; see §7.4) *ʾakla wa* ***laḥāmu***, "bring out food and eat." Even in such cases, infinitives are not inflected for agreement with the subject.

7.3. Cardinal Numerals

Like numerals in any language, cardinal numerals in Ugaritic are neither nouns nor adjectives but something in between (see below). There are masculine and feminine cardinal numerals for the values 1–10 ("ones digits"); because the numeral for 10 is singular, we include it as a "ones digit."

Tens digits (20, 30, etc.) are indicated by a cardinal numeral in the plural. *Ṯamāniyūma*, for example, is the plural of *ṯamāniyu* ("eight") and means "eighty." Similarly, *ṯalāṯūma* (plural of *ṯalāṯu*, "three") means "thirty," *ʾarbaʿūma* (plural of *ʾarbaʿu*, "four") means "forty," and so on. There are two exceptions to this pattern: first, there is a simple numeral for "ten" (*ʿašru*), so no plural of *ʾaḥḥadu* ("one") is ever used. Second, the word for "twenty" (*ʿašrūma*) is the plural of "ten" (*ʿašru*); the numeral for "two" (*ṯinayā*) is dual and is not used to form "twenty" or any other singular or plural numeral.

The forms and their values are as follows:

Value	Masc	Fem	Value of Plural
1	*ʾaḥḥadu* *ʿaštayu* / *ʿaštû*	*ʾaḥḥattu*	—
2	*ṯinayā* / *ṯinâ* (dual nom)	*ṯinêtā* / *ṯittâ* (dual nom)	—
3	*ṯalāṯu*	*ṯalāṯatu*	30
4	*ʾarbaʿu*	*ʾarbaʿatu*	40
5	*ḫamišu*	*ḫamišatu*	50
6	*ṯiṯṯu*	*ṯiṯṯatu*	60
7	*šabʿu*	*šabʿatu*	70
8	*ṯamāniyu* / *ṯamānû*	*ṯamānîtu*	80

Value	Masc	Fem	Value of Plural
9	*tišʿu*	*tišʿatu*	90
10	*ʿašru*	*ʿašratu*	20

Besides the simple numerals for values 1–10, there are lexemes for the values 100 (*miʾtu*) and 1,000 (*ʾalpu*).

In terms of **syntax**, there is some variation in how numerals behave. *ʾaḥḥadu*, "one," is fully adjectival, following the word it modifies and taking the same gender. The other numerals are closer in syntax to nouns: they precede the noun they quantify, in apposition to the noun; *šabʿa lubūšīma*, for example, is accusative "seven lubushus." The numerals *miʾtu* and *ʾalpu* behave entirely like nouns (e.g., they can be quantified by other numerals).

Like other nominal words, numerals take their case based on their syntactic role in a clause. For example, *ṯiṯṯu malakūma qarabū*, "six kings approached," with nominative for the subject, and *qabaʾtu ṯiṯṯa malakīma*, "I summoned six kings," with accusative for the complement of the verb.

There is another numeral, *ʿaštayu*, which also means "one." As in Hebrew, this numeral usually appears together with *ʿašru* in a complex teen numeral, together meaning "eleven." In one text, however, it appears to be used independently. Based on the Akkadian cognate *ištēn*, the Ugaritic numeral *ʿaštayu* would have behaved more like the numerals for 2–10 than like *ʾaḥḥadu*, preceding the noun it quantifies, in apposition. Though it is written /ʿšty/ once in our extant evidence, typically the *y* has contracted, reflected in the spelling /ʿšt/. It is unknown whether the triphthong *ayu* has reduced (*ʿaštû*) or whether the final vowel dropped and the resulting diphthong *ay* reduced (*ʿaštê*; as with the preposition *lê*, c.f. §4.1).

Unlike other Semitic languages, there is no consistent use of "chiastic concord" (feminine numerals with masculine nouns and vice versa) in Ugaritic; numerals often agree in gender with the nouns they quantify, though not always.

The grammatical number of the noun follows a pattern similar to other Semitic languages: a noun quantified by 1 is singular, a noun quantified by 2 is dual, a noun quantified by 3–10 is plural, and a noun quantified by 11 or more is singular (e.g., *šabʿūma lubūšu*, "seventy lubushu-garments").

Multiplying-numerals are formed by combining a cardinal numeral 3-9 with *miʾtu*, "hundred," or *ʾalpu*, "thousand," using the same syntax as with nouns (i.e., *miʾtu* and *ʾalpu* are quantified by the lower numeral). "Three hundred," for example, is *ṯalāṯu miʾātu* (*KTU* 4.337:28), with apposition and plural *miʾātu*. *Miʾtu* and *ʾalpu* are always feminine and masculine, respectively.

Adding-numerals in all languages are in fact two or more individual number phrases joined by a conjunction; the English "two hundred and five books," for example, is derived from "two hundred books and five books." In Ugaritic, the postposition *kubda* ("plus," "and") is often used to conjoin number phrases, as in *ṯamāniyūma ṯiqlu ṯalāṯu kubda*, "eighty shekels plus three," that is, "eighty-three shekels" (cf. similar phrases in *KTU* 4.337:5 and *KTU* 4.777:2). The underlying phrase is *ṯamāniyūma ṯiqlu ṯalāṯu ṯiqalūma kubda*, "eighty shekels plus three shekels"; the second occurrence of the noun *ṯiqlu* has simply been removed (the linguistic term for this syntax in numerals is "deletion"). Ugaritic also uses "right node raising" in adding numerals.[1] For example, *ṯamāniyūma ṯalāṯu kubda ṯiqlu*, "eighty plus three shekels," comes from the same underlying phrase as above, *ṯamāniyūma ṯiqlu ṯalāṯu ṯiqalūma kubda*. In the underlying phrase, *ṯiqlu* is present within the noun phrases *ṯamāniyūma ṯiqlu* and *ṯalāṯu ṯiqlūma*; in the phrase with right node raising, *ṯiqlu/ūma* has been moved out of both of these phrases to the "right" edge (i.e., the end) of the larger phrase.

Besides *kubda*, the preposition *lê* can be used to construct an adding numeral. For example, *ʾarbaʿūma lê miʾti*, "forty to a hundred [=140]" (*KTU* 4.158:3).

Teen numerals are formed by combining a numeral for 1–9 with the numeral for ten, both in the same gender. For example, *ṯalāṯu ʿašru*, "thirteen" (*KTU* 4.342:2), and *ṯamānîti ʿašrati*, "fifteen (dative)" (*KTU* 4.337:15). Another special numeral, based on the numeral for ten, is used in teen numerals: *ʿašrihu*. For example, *ṯalāṯa ʿašrihu*, "thirteen" (acc) (*KTU* 4.777:5), and *ṯamānîta ʿašrihu*, "fifteen" (acc) (*KTU* 4.777:8). It is unclear where the element *-h* in this numeral stems from and whether or not the final vowel is a case vowel (and thus whether or not the word is declined). The ending *-ihu* may be adverbial (*ṯamānîta ʿašrihu*, "eight with

1. Right node raising is a widespread linguistic phenomenon. Contemporary English, for example, uses right node raising with adding numerals, but also in a variety of other contexts. In the sentence *Sarah completed, but William did not complete, the Ugaritic homework*, the constituent *the Ugaritic homework* is the complement in both verb phrases (*completed* [*the Ugaritic homework*] and *did not complete* [*the Ugaritic homework*]). It has been taken from both verb phrases and raised to the right edge (the end), streamlining the utterance so that the phrase *the Ugaritic homework* is stated only once.

respect to ten [=18]"), or it may reflect a genitive ending and suffixed pronoun on the masculine numeral for ten (*ṯamānîta ʿašrihu*, "eight of its ten [=18]"). Though these analyses may seem strange to native English speakers, teen numerals in many languages are formed through similar means (e.g., English "eleven" and "twelve" are from proto-Germanic *ainalif*, "one left [after ten]," and *twalif*, "two left [after ten]").

Numerals with values 11–19 can also be formed as adding numerals, for example, *ʿašru ṯinâ kubda*, "ten plus two" (KTU 4.270:10).

7.4. Weak Verbs in the Š-Stem

Weak verbs in the Š-stem follow rules articulated previously for weak verbs in §§2.8, 3.5, 4.5, 6.3, and 6.4.

The *n* in **I-n verbs in the Š-stem** assimilates in all conjugations, for example, 3ms QATALA *šaggiša* (<*šangiša*) *muta*, "he caused the man to approach." Paradigm forms with NGŠ, "to cause to approach" in the Š-stem, are as follows:

QATALA	*šaggiša*, "he caused [someone/thing] to approach"
YAQTULU	*yašaggišu*, "he causes [someone/thing] to approach"
Imperative	*šaggiš*, "cause [someone/thing] to approach" (2ms)
Participle	*mušaggišu*, "one who causes to approach" (nom ms)
Infinitive	*šaggāšu*, "to cause to approach" (nom)

In **III-y Š-stem verbs**, the final *y* radical sometimes contracts and sometimes remains, as in the G-stem. For example, *šaʿliya muta* and *šaʿlî muta*, "he caused the man to go up." If contraction has occurred, simply apply the rules for contraction (§2.7) to the Š-stem paradigm forms above to determine the nature of the contraction. Paradigm forms with ʿLY, "to cause to go up" in the Š-stem, are as follows:

QATALA	*šaʿliya* or *šaʿlî*, "he caused [someone/thing] to go up"
YAQTULU	*yašaʿliyu* or *yašaʿlû*, "he causes [someone/thing] to go up"
Imperative	*šaʿli*, "cause [someone/thing] to go up" (2ms)
	šaʿlî (< *šaʿliyī*) "cause [someone/thing] to go up" (2fs)
Participle	*mušaʿliyu* or *mušaʿlû*, "one who causes to go up" (nom ms)
Infinitive	*šaʿlāyu* or *šaʿlû*, "to cause to go up" (nom)

Hollow verbs in the Š-stem take lengthened theme-vowels—*ṯaṯībī rigma*, "send (2fs) word." If the syllable is closed, however, the vowel is short: *ṯaṯib rigma*, "send (2ms) word." Paradigm forms with ṮB, "to return [something]" in the Š-stem, are as follows (note that prefixed *š* of the Š-stem has become *ṯ*; cf. §7.5):

QATALA	*ṯaṯība*, "he returned [someone/thing]"
YAQTULU	*yaṯaṯību*, "he returns [someone/thing]"
Imperative	*ṯaṯib*, "return [someone/thing]" (2ms)
	ṯaṯībī, "return [someone/thing]" (2fs)
Participle	*muṯaṯību*, "one who returns [someone/thing]" (nom ms)
Infinitive	*ṯaṯābu*, "to return [someone/thing]" (nom)

7.5. Š-Stem ṮB, "to return"

One hollow verb that is often used in the Š-stem is notable for its form. ṮB, which means intransitive "to return" in the G-stem, has the sense of transitive "to return" (i.e., "to send back") in the Š-stem. The consonant *š* in the prefix *ša-* harmonizes with the following consonant *ṯ*, resulting in *ṯaṯīb-*. This produces forms like *ṯaṯība* (Š QATALA 3ms), "he returned [something]," and *ʾaṯaṯib* (Š jussive 1cs), "let me return [something]."

7.6. Weak Verbs: I-y/w

The initial radical *y* in I-y/w verbs like YRD, "to descend," was historically *w* (WRD). In the G-stem, word-initial *y* occurs in the QATALA conjugation and contraction of *y* in the YAQTULU conjugation. Initial *w* is retained, however, in the N- and D-stems, and it is reflected in the contraction that takes place in the Š-stem (*aw* > *ô*). The lexical form of a I-y/w verb reflects the radicals of the G-stem; thus you will find the entry YRD, not WRD.

7.6.1. G-Stem I-y/w Verbs

In **QATALA** forms, G-stem I-y/w verbs are regular. For example:

YRD 3ms	*yarada*	"he descended"
YṢʾ 3ms	*yaṣaʾa*	"he went out"

In the **YAQTULU**, **jussive**, and **volitive** conjugations, the *y* of the root is elided without any contraction. For example:

YRD 3ms	*yaridu* (< *yayridu*)	"he descends"
YDʿ 3fs	*tidaʿu* (< *tiydaʿu*)	"she knows"
YṢʾ 3fs	*taṣiʾu* (<*tayṣiʾu*)	"she goes out"

The **imperative**—built off the YAQTULU form—retains only the second and third radicals:

YRD 2mp	*ridū*	"descend"
YDʿ 2ms	*daʿ*	"know"

Using the verb YRD (theme vowel *i*), the full paradigms of the YAQTULU, jussive, volitive, and imperative conjugations of I-y/w verbs are as follows:

YAQTULU		Jussive		Volitive		Imperative	
3ms	*yaridu*	3ms	*yarid*	3ms	*yarida*		
3fs	*taridu*	3fs	*tarid*	3fs	*tarida*		
2ms	*taridu*	2ms	*tarid*	2ms	*tarida*	2ms	*rid*
2fs	*taridīna*	2fs	*taridī*	2fs	*taridī*	2fs	*ridī*
1cs	*ʾaridu*	1cs	*ʾarid*	1cs	*ʾarida*		
3md	*taridā(na)*	3md	*taridā*	3md	*taridā*		
3fd	*taridā(na)*	3fd	*taridā*	3fd	*taridā*		
2cd	*taridā(na)*	2cd	*taridā*	2cd	*taridā*	2cd	*ridā*
1cd	*naridā*	1cd	*naridā*	1cd	*naridā*		
3mp	*taridū(na)*	3mp	*taridū*	3mp	*taridū*		
3fp	*taridna*	3fp	*taridna*	3fp	*taridna*		
2mp	*taridū(na)*	2mp	*taridū*	2mp	*taridū*	2mp	*ridū*
2fp	*taridna*	2fp	*taridna*	2fp	*taridna*	2fp	*ridā*
1cp	*naridū*	*1cp*	*narid*	*1cp*	*narida*		

Verbs with an *a* theme vowel (see *tidaʿu* above) take the vowels *i* and *a* in the YAQTULU, jussive, and volitive conjugations, instead of *a* and *i* in the paradigms above for YRD; the imperative, similarly, has *a* instead of *i*.

The **participle** behaves like a strong verb, retaining *y*:

YRD	*yāridu*	"the one descending"
YṢʾ	*yāṣiʾūma*	"those who go out"

The **infinitive** of I-y/w verbs is often strong, retaining *y*: *yarādu* (YRD), "to descend." However, I-y/w verbs sometimes drop *y* and add feminine morphology, for example, *ridatu*, "to descend."

7.6.2. N- and D-Stems

The N- and D-stems of I-y/w verbs are only extant in the YAQTULU conjugation, where the first radical is preserved as *w*.

In the N-stem, the *n* of the prefix assimilates to *w*. For example, YḤL N-stem 3ms *yiwwaḥilu* (< *yinwaḥilu*), "he is discouraged."

N yaqtulu YḤL

3ms	*yiwwaḥilu*	"he is discouraged"
3fs	*tiwwaḥilu*	"she is discouraged"
2ms	*tiwwaḥilu*	"you are discouraged"
2fs	*tiwwaḥilīna*	"you are discouraged"
1cs	*ʾiwwaḥilu*	"I am discouraged"
3md	*tiwwaḥilā(na)*	"the two of them are discouraged"
3fd	*tiwwaḥilā(na)*	"the two of them are discouraged"
2cd	*tiwwaḥilā(na)*	"the two of you are discouraged"
1cd	*niwwaḥilā*	"the two of us are discouraged"
3mp	*tiwwaḥilū(na)*	"they are discouraged"
3fp	*tiwwaḥilna*	"they are discouraged"
2mp	*tiwwaḥilū(na)*	"you are discouraged"
2fp	*tiwwaḥilna*	"you are discouraged"
1cp	*niwwaḥilu*	"we are discouraged"

In the D-stem YAQTULU, *w* is also preserved. For example, YTḤ D-stem 3fs *tawattiḥu*, "she hastens."

D yaqtulu YTḤ		
3ms	*yawattiḥu*	"he hastens"
3fs	*tawattiḥu*	"she hastens"
2ms	*tawattiḥu*	"you hasten"
2fs	*tawattiḥīna*	"you hasten"
1cs	*ʾawattiḥu*	"I hasten"
3md	*tawattiḥā(na)*	"the two of them hasten"
3fd	*tawattiḥā(na)*	"the two of them hasten"
2cd	*tawattiḥā(na)*	"the two of you hasten"
1cd	*nawattiḥā*	"the two of us hasten"
3mp	*tawattiḥū(na)*	"they hasten"
3fp	*tawattiḥna*	"they hasten"
2mp	*tawattiḥū(na)*	"you hasten"
2fp	*tawattiḥna*	"you hasten"
1cp	*nawattiḥu*	"we hasten"

7.6.3. Š-Stem

In the Š-stem, all conjugations have the prefix *ša-* followed by the first and second radical as a consonant cluster (e.g., ***šaqt**ila*). I-y/w verbs that are historically I-w have contraction of *aw* to *ô*. Examples, using Š-stem YṢʾ, "to bring out" (i.e., "cause to go out"):

QATALA	*šôṣiʾa* (< *šawṣiʾa*), "he brought out"
YAQTULU	*yašôṣiʾu* (< *yašawṣiʾu*), "he brings out"
Imperative	*šôṣiʾ* (< *šawṣiʾ*), "bring out" (2ms)
Participle	*mušôṣiʾu* (< *mušawṣiʾu*), "one who brings out" (nom ms)
Infinitive	*šôṣāʾu* (< *šawṣāʾu*), "to bring out" (nom)

7.7. Weak Verbs: HLK and HLM

The verbs HLK and HLM are the only I-h II-l verbs extant in Ugaritic.

HLK behaves like a I-y verb in the G-stem YAQTULU (*yaliku*, "he goes"), imperative (*lik*, "go"), and sometimes infinitive (*halāku* or *likatu*, "to go"). In the G-stem QATALA and in all forms of other stems, HLK behaves like a strong verb.

QATALA	*halaka*, "he goes"
YAQTULU	*yaliku* (< *yahliku*), "he goes"
Imperative	*lik*, "go" (2ms)
Participle	*hāliku*, "one who goes"
Infinitive	*halāku* and *likatu*, "to go" (nom)

HLM is weak in the G-stem YAQTULU, where *h* assimilates with *l* (as in I-n verbs): *yallumu* (<*yahlumu*), "he will strike." HLM is not extant in any other stems, though presumably the same assimilation would occur wherever the consonant cluster *hl* occurs. Outside of the YAQTULU conjugation, HLM is strong, including in the imperative (*hulum*, "strike").

QATALA	*halama*, "he struck"
YAQTULU	*yallumu* (< *yahlumu*), "he strikes"
Imperative	*hulum*, "strike" (2ms)
Participle	*hālimu*, "one who strikes" (nom ms)
Infinitive	*halāmu*, "to strike" (nom)

Other I-h verbs (e.g., HBR, HBṬ/Ẓ, HDY) occur in Ugaritic, with no abnormalities around the radical *h* (i.e., they are strong, with the exception of HDY being a III-y verb).

7.8. YAQTULU in Past-Tense Contexts

In contrast to some other Semitic languages, there is no prefix conjugation past tense in Ugaritic (cf. the Hebrew preterite *yiqtol* in *wayyiqtol*; and Akkadian *iprus*). Despite the obscurity of vocalization in Ugaritic, this aspect of the language is fairly well-established. However, YAQTULU forms are often used in narratives whose events occur in the past. This use may result from a desire for imperfect aspect in the past, or it may result from a "narrative present" style. Such YAQTULU forms can be translated by English past tense or present tense.

7.9. Locative Accusatives

Ugaritic verbs of motion take locations as complements. These complements can be prepositional phrases or may be noun phrases (compare English "he went to the store" and "he went home"). When the complement is a noun phrase, it takes accusative case ("locative accusative"), though in the English equivalent the noun phrase is not the object of the verb. For example, *taʿliyu bêta*, "she went up **to** the house"; *yarada ʾarṣa*, "he went down **to** the earth."

7.10. Vocabulary

ʿaparu	noun, masc., "dust"
HLM	verb, "to strike" (G QATALA *halama*, YAQTULU *yallumu*)
katipu	noun, fem., "shoulder"
MK	verb, "to fall, collapse" (G QATALA *māka*, YAQTULU *yamūku*)
ŠPL	verb, "to bend down" (G QATALA *šapala*, YAQTULU *yišpalu*)
tôku	noun, masc., "midst," i.e., place that is within
YḤL	verb, N "to be discouraged" (no G-stem)
YRD	verb, "to descend, go down" (G QATALA *yarada*, YAQTULU *yaridu*)
YṮB	verb, "to sit, to dwell" (G QATALA *yaṯiba*, YAQTULU *yaṯibu*)
BṢR	verb, "to observe" (G QATALA *baṣara*, YAQTULU *yabṣuru*)
darkatu	noun, fem., "dominion, rule"
HLK	verb, "to go" (G QATALA *halaka*, YAQTULU *yaliku*)
kaḥṯu	noun, masc., "chair"
KN	verb, "to be" (G QATALA *kāna*, YAQTULU *yakūnu*); Š "to establish"
lubūšu	noun, masc., "lubushu," a basic type of garment
yasīmu	adjective, "beautiful"

YṢQ	verb, "to pour out" (G QATALA *yaṣaqa*, YAQTULU *yaṣṣuqu*[2])
YTḤ	verb, D "to hasten" (no G-stem)
zabūlu	noun, masc., "prince"
ʾaḥḥadu	numeral, "one"
ʿaštayu	numeral, "one" (typically as part of the teen numeral "eleven")
ṯinayā/ṯinâ	numeral, "two"
ṯalāṯu	numeral, "three"
ʾarbaʿu	numeral, "four"
ḫamišu	numeral, "five"
ṯiṯṯu	numeral, "six"
šabʿu	numeral, "seven"
ṯamānû/iyu	numeral, "eight"
tišʿu	numeral, "nine"
ʿašru	numeral, "ten"
miʾtu	numeral, fem., "hundred" (pl. *miʾātu*)
ʾalpu	numeral, masc., "thousand"
kubda	postposition, "plus" (used in compound number phrases)
ʾana	adverb, "where," "wherever"

7.11. Exercises

A. Translate the following into English.

1. *ʿāliyu yaridu*
2. *qāla ʾilu kama mīti, ʾilu ka yāridīma ʾarṣa* (*KTU* 1.114:21–22)
3. *ṣimdu yallumu katipa zabūli yammi, bêna yadê ṯāpiṭi nahari. ʿazzu yammu, lā yamūku.* (adapted from *KTU* 1.2 iv:16–17)
4. *ṯalāṯu lubūšūma bîdê ʾalaḫini* (personal name) *bi ʿašrati kaspi* (adapted from *KTU* 4.337:11)

2. The reconstructed vocalization of the YAQTULU form is irregular, on the basis of comparative evidence. See Bordreuil and Pardee, *Manual of Ugaritic*, 224.

5. *ʾilu halāmu yallumuka bi tišʿi miʾāti yadi*
6. *laqaḥa huwa šamna bi qarnihu wa yaṣaqa huwa lê raʾši* ("head") *bitti malki ʾamurri* ("Amuru") (*KTU* 2.72:29–32)

B. Vocalize and translate the following Ugaritic.

1. 𐎀𐎘𐎗
   𐎁𐎓𐎍𐎋 𐎟 𐎀𐎗𐎕 𐎟 𐎗𐎄 𐎟 𐎀𐎗𐎕
   𐎗𐎄 𐎟 𐎆𐎌𐎔𐎍 𐎟 𐎓𐎔𐎗 (*KTU* 1.161:20–22)
2. 𐎓𐎐𐎚 𐎅𐎊 𐎟 𐎅𐎎 𐎟 𐎚𐎗𐎄 𐎟 𐎙𐎗
   𐎚𐎌𐎓𐎍𐎅𐎎
3. w dʿ . k yṣảt . ảp (ʾapa, "also"). mlkt (*KTU* 2.88:38)
4. 𐎗𐎂𐎎 𐎘𐎘𐎁 𐎟 𐎍𐎊 (*KTU* 2.71:8)
5. bʿl . yṯb . k ṯbt (ṯubatu, "seat"). ǵr. hd (haddu, "Hadad").
   k mdb (mādābu, "ocean-tide") . b tk. ǵrh (*KTU* 1.101:1–2)

C. Write in vocalized Ugaritic and cuneiform.

1. I know who struck me. I will strike him and make him go out from the palace. He will know that I know, because I will make him know.
2. If you (f. sg) are not my enemy, I will surely go.
3. When you (m. du.) established my throne, they (m. du.) descended, I went up, and I went to my beautiful house.

D. Read the following passage and answer the questions (using full sentences in Ugaritic).

kôṯaru ṣimdêma yanaḥḥitu wa yipʿaru šumatêhumā: "šumuka ʾatta yagrušu. yagruši, guruš yamma! guruš yamma lê kussaʾihu, nahara lê kaḥṯi darkatihu." (*KTU* 1.2 iv:11–13)

1. *ma šumu ṣimdi hannadī?*
2. *ma ragama kôṯaru lê ṣimdi?*
   a. *šakīn kaḥṯa lê yammi*

b. *guruš yamma lê kaḥṯihu*
c. *šumuka ʾatta baʿlu*
d. *rabbatu kussaʾu yammi*

3. *mī ragama kôṯaru lê garāši?*
4. *lê ʾana yagrušuhu* (irreal) *ṣimdu?*

E. Translate the following passage into English.

lê malki baʿliya, rugum: taḥmu ṯipṭibaʿli (personal name) *ʿabdika. lê paʿnê baʿliya, šabʿida* ("seven times") *šabʿida, marḥaqtama, qālātu. ʿabduka bi lawasanda ʾabṣuru ʿimma malki. wa hatti, malku sēyēra* (proper noun) *nāsa, wa ṯammāniya yidbaḥu malġatêma* ("sacrifices"). *wa malku baʿluya yidaʿ*. (*KTU* 2.40:1–19)

Short Story 5
Šaʿrūḫurāṣitu

ʾamatu naʿīmatu wa **qaṭanatu** ʾiṯu bi ʾarṣi ʾugarit, dātu šumuha **šaʿrūḫurāṣitu**. Taliku šaʿrūḫurāṣitu bi qirbi ʿiṣīma bi ǵūri **ṣapuni**. Tiqqaḥu **ṣumlalîma** lê **tani** lê ʿummiha. Wa taliku wa taʿlû wa tiʾatû lê bêti naʿīmi. Ka qarābiha lê bêti hannadī targumu, "Hannaniya, bêtu hannadū naʿīmu. ʾiʿrab bêta hannadā wa ʾidaʿ mā bi qirbi bêti." ʾū tiʿrabu bêta.

Bi yômi hannadī, kīya taliku šaʿrūḫurāṣitu bi qirbi ʿiṣīma wa tiʿrabu bêta, talikū ṯalāṯu **dābūma** bi qirbi ʿiṣīma. ʾiṯu ʾabû wa ʿummu wa binuhumā—ǵazru dū bêti. Wa hannanna, bêtu dū ʿarabat lêhu šaʿrūḫurāṣitu, hannadū ʾiṯu bêtu dābīma! Lā yadaʿat šaʿrūḫurāṣitu. Bi yômi hannadī, kīya tiʿrabu šaʿrūḫurāṣitu bêta dābīma, wa yaridū dābūma ǵūra lê laqāḥi ǵalamīma—**naʿarīma**—wa ʾamatīma qaṭanīma, lê laḥāmihumu ka ʾakli, kama **naʿāri**. (Kama targumū: naʿru lê naʿāri wa ǵalmu lê **gulliya**.)

Bi qarābi šaʿrūḫurāṣiti lê bêti, yabīnu ʾappuha kīya ʾaklu naʿīmu ʾiṯu biya bêti, bi **ṯulḥani**. Hannana, ṯalāṯu gullūma ʾiṯu bi ṯulḥani, wa ʾaklu bihumu ʾiṯu naʿāru. Naʿāra taʾuhubu šaʿrūḫurāṣitu. Tilḥamu kalīla dā bi ṯalāṯi gullīma. Wa hannana taliku šaʿrūḫurāṣitu lê **ʾibūsāni**, wa ṯamma **yênu** maʾadu ʾiṯu. Tištû šaʿrūḫurāṣitu kulla yêni. **ʾapana** taqīlu.[1] Wa tarīmu ʿadê paʿnêha, wa taliku bêna ṯammi wa bêna ṯammi, wa tašaqīlu ṯalāṯa kaḥaṯīma dūti biya ʾibūsāni. Wa kama hannadī taqīlu wa tarīmu wa taqīlu. ʾapana tiškabu wa **tišanu** marḥaqta lê ṯalāṯi **ʿarašīma** dūti lê dābīma.

Taṯūbū ṯalāṯu dābūma wa lā laḥamū—kī ʾênu naʿarūma bi qirbi ʿiṣīma—wa ʾappuhumu **baʿara** kama šapši. Wa hannannana, gullūhumu **mušaqālūmu**, wa ʾakluhumu **laḥūmu**. Kaḥaṯūhumu mušaqālūmu, wa hanna—wa hannannannana!—kalīlu yênihumu **šatūyu**. "Yênuna ʾênu," yiqraʾu dābu qaṭanu bi gî rabbi, "Lā lā lā, ʾênu ʾênu!" Yargumu ʾabûhu, "Mī yištû yênana? Mī **yaʿsiyu** rigma **rašaʿa** hannadā?" Huwa yiwwaḥilu maʾda.

---

1. Kama targumū: wan taqīla tu taqīla ṯari taqīla, taqīlu.

Kīya taliku šaʿrūḫurāṣitu lê ʾibūsāni, taṣiʾū ʾappūma rašaʿūma lê ṯalāṯi dābīma. Tiqqaḥū šaʿrūḫurāṣita wa tilḥamūha kama naʿāri. "Ṭabu," targumu ʾummu. "ʾapana niškab wa nišan."

Vocabulary

qaṭanu—adjective, "small, little" (unattested)
šaʿrūḫurāṣitu—personal name, fem., "Shaʿru-huratsitu" (unattested)
ṣapunu—proper noun, masc., "Zaphon"
ṣumlalû—noun, an unknown aromatic plant
tanu—infinitive of YTN, "to give"
dābu—noun, "bear" (unattested)
naʿru—noun, "lad," "boy"
naʿāru—noun, some type of food (perhaps "flour")
gullu—noun, "bowl"
ṯulḥanu—noun, "table"
ʾibūsānu—noun, "storeroom," "wine-cellar"
yênu—noun, "wine"
ʾapana—particle "then," "next"
YŠN—verb, "to sleep" (G QATALA *yašana*, YAQTULU *yišanu*)
ʿaršu—noun, "bed"
BʿR—verb, "to burn" (intransitive; not attested in the G-stem) (G QATALA *baʿara*, YAQTULU *yabʿiru*)
mušaqālu—Š-passive participle of QL, "overturned"
laḥūmu—G-passive participle of LḤM, "eaten"
šatūyu—G-passive participle of ŠTY, "drunk, imbibed"
ʿSY—verb, "to do" (G QATALA *ʿasaya*, YAQTULU *yaʿsiyu* / *yaʿsû*)
rašaʿu—adjective, "evil"

Lesson 8

8.1. Weak Verbs: YTN and III-n
8.2. Passive Stem Verbs: Gp, Dp, and Šp
8.3. Stems with Affixed *t*: Gt, tD, and Št
8.4. L-Stem Verbs
8.5. R-Stem Verbs
8.6. YAQTULU 3md and 3mp Prefix *y*-
8.7. Suffixed Pronouns and Verb Valency
8.8. Vocabulary
8.9. Exercises

8.1. Weak Verbs: YTN and III-n

The verb YTN, "to give," is unique in its forms. In the G-stem, the verb behaves like a I-y/w verb: QATALA and the participle are strong; *y* elides in YAQTULU, the jussive, the volitive, and the imperative. The G-stem infinitive of YTN can be *tanu* or *tatinu*.

QATALA	*yatana*, "he gave"
YAQTULU	*yatinu* (< *yaytinu*), "he gives"
Imperative	*tin*, "give" (2ms)
Participle	*yātinu*, "one who gives" (nom ms)
Infinitive	*tanu* and *tatinu*, "to give" (nom)

Because YTN is a **III-n root**, it has some slightly unusual forms in the G-stem QATALA: with suffixes beginning with a consonant, there is either assimilation of *n* to the following consonant, or a helping vowel *ā* is inserted.

3ms	*yatana*	"he gave"
3fs	*yatanat*	"she gave"
2ms	*yatanāta* or *yatatta* (< *yatanta*)	"you gave"
2fs	*yatanāti* or *yatatti* (< *yatanti*)	"you gave"
1cs	*yatanātu* or *yatattu* (< *yatantu*)	"I gave"

3md	*yatanā*	"the two of them gave"
3fd	*yatanatā*	"the two of them gave"
2cd	*yatanātumā* or *yatattumā* (< *yatantumā*)	"the two of you gave"
1cd	*yatannāyā*	"the two of us gave"
3mp	*yatanū*	"they gave"
3fp	*yatanā*	"they gave"
2mp	*yatanātumu* or *yatattumu* (< *yatantumu*)	"you gave"
2fp	*yatanātina* or *yatattina* (< *yatantina*)	"you gave"
1cp	*yatannū*	"we gave"

Such assimilation of *n* occurs with all III-n verbs.

In the **Š-stem for YTN**, we take the historical root to be YTN (not WTN), and thus the contracted vowel is *ê* rather than *ô* (as in other I-y/w roots). The pattern of the YAQTULU conjugation, moreover, is irregular, with prefix vowel *i* instead of *a*, perhaps under influence of the contracted vowel *ê*.

QATALA	*šêtina* (< *šaytina*), "he sent"
YAQTULU	*yišêtinu* (< *yašaytinu*), "he sends"
Imperative	*šêtin* (< *šaytin*), "send" (2ms)
Participle	*mušêtinu* (< *mušaytinu*), "one who sends" (nom ms)
Infinitive	*šêtānu* (< *šaytānu*), "to send" (nom)

Note that the assimilation of *n* occurs in the Š-stem as well; for example, *šêtinātu* (< *šaytinātu*) or *šêtittu* (< *šaytintu*), "I sent" (Š-stem QATALA 1cs).

The verb YTN requires a first complement in the accusative (the thing that is given) and a second complement in a prepositional phrase (the person to whom something is given). For example, *yatana ʾakla lê ʿabdiya*, "he gave my servant food."

8.2. Passive Stem Verbs: Gp, Dp, and Šp

There are multiple cases where context suggests a passive meaning for what is typically an active verb form. Because other Semitic languages use changes in vowel quality (*Ablaut*) to indicate passives, it seems likely that the same or similar forms are occurring in Ugaritic. The consonantal text shows no difference between these forms, which differ only in their vocalization.

Although it is difficult to know for certain, it is likely that G, D, and Š-stems had such passive forms, which we call the Gp-stem, Dp-stem, and Šp-stem. These stems are characterized by the occurrence of the vowel *u* between the first and the second radical of the QATALA form (e.g., *quraʾa*, "he was called") and in the prefix of the YAQTULU form (e.g., *yuraʾu*, "he is called").

The passive stems occur with finite verbs and participles but not with imperatives.

The QATALA, YAQTULU, and participle paradigms of QRʾ, "to call," in the **Gp-stem**, are as follows:

Gp QATALA

3ms	*quraʾa*	"he was called"
3fs	*quraʾat*	"she was called"
2ms	*quraʾta*	"you were called"
2fs	*quraʾti*	"you were called"
1cs	*quraʾtu*	"I was called"
3md	*quraʾā*	"the two of them were called"
3fd	*quraʾatā*	"the two of them were called"
2cd	*quraʾtumā*	"the two of you were called"
1cd	*quraʾnāyā*	"the two of us were called"
3mp	*quraʾū*	"they were called"
3fp	*quraʾā*	"they were called"
2mp	*quraʾtumu*	"you were called"
2fp	*quraʾtina*	"you were called"
1cp	*quraʾnū*	"we were called"

Gp YAQTULU

3ms	*yuqraʾu*	"he is called"
3fs	*tuqraʾu*	"she is called"
2ms	*tuqraʾu*	"you are called"
2fs	*tuqraʾīna*	"you are called"
1cs	*ʾuqraʾu*	"I am called"

3md	*tuqra'ā(na)*	"the two of them are called"
3fd	*tuqra'ā(na)*	"the two of them are called"
2cd	*tuqra'ā(na)*	"the two of you are called"
1cd	*nuqra'ā*	"the two of us are called"
3mp	*tuqra'ū(na)*	"they are called"
3fp	*tuqra'na*	"they are called"
2mp	*tuqra'ū(na)*	"you are called"
2fp	*tuqra'na*	"you are called"
1cp	*nuqra'u*	"we are called"

Gp participle

ms	*qarū'u*	"called one"
fs	*qarū'atu*	"called one"
mp	*qarū'ūma*	"called ones"
fp	*qarū'ātu*	"called ones"

The **Dp-stem** probably used the pattern *quttila* in the QATALA conjugation, *yuqattalu* in the YAQTULU conjugation, and *muqattalu* for the participle. The QATALA, YAQTULU, and participle paradigms for Bʿ R are as follows:

Dp QATALA

3ms	*buʿʿira*	"he was burned"
3fs	*buʿʿirat*	"she was burned"
2ms	*buʿʿirta*	"you were burned"
2fs	*buʿʿirti*	"you were burned"
1cs	*buʿʿirtu*	"I was burned"
3md	*buʿʿirā*	"the two of them were burned"
3fd	*buʿʿiratā*	"the two of them were burned"
2cd	*buʿʿirtumā*	"the two of you were burned"
1cd	*buʿʿirnāyā*	"the two of us were burned"
3mp	*buʿʿirū*	"they were burned"
3fp	*buʿʿirā*	"they were burned"
2mp	*buʿʿirtumu*	"you were burned"
2fp	*buʿʿirtina*	"you were burned"
1cp	*buʿʿirnū*	"we were burned"

Dp YAQTULU

3ms	*yubaʿʿaru*	"he is burned"
3fs	*tubaʿʿaru*	"she is burned"
2ms	*tubaʿʿaru*	"you are burned"
2fs	*tubaʿʿarīna*	"you are burned"
1cs	*ʾubaʿʿaru*	"I am burned"
3md	*tubaʿʿarā(na)*	"the two of them are burned"
3fd	*tubaʿʿarā(na)*	"the two of them are burned"
2cd	*tubaʿʿarā(na)*	"the two of you are burned"
1cd	*nubaʿʿarā*	"the two of us are burned"
3mp	*tubaʿʿarū(na)*	"they are burned"
3fp	*tubaʿʿarna*	"they are burned"
2mp	*tubaʿʿarū(na)*	"you are burned"
2fp	*tubaʿʿarna*	"you are burned"
1cp	*nubaʿʿaru*	"we are burned"

Dp participle

ms	*mubaʿʿaru*	"burned one"
fs	*mubaʿʿaratu*	"burned one"
mp	*mubaʿʿarūma*	"burned ones"
fp	*mubaʿʿarātu*	"burned ones"

The **Šp-stem** can be reconstructed as using the pattern *šuqtala* in the QATALA conjugation, *yušaqtalu* in the YAQTULU conjugation, and *mušaqtalu* for the participle. The QATALA, YAQTULU, and participle paradigms with BʿR are as follows:

Šp QATALA

3ms	*šubʿara*	"he was illuminated"
3fs	*šubʿarat*	"she was illuminated"
2ms	*šubʿarta*	"you were illuminated"
2fs	*šubʿarti*	"you were illuminated"
1cs	*šubʿartu*	"I was illuminated"
3md	*šubʿarā*	"the two of them were illuminated"
3fd	*šubʿaratā*	"the two of them were illuminated"
2cd	*šubʿartumā*	"the two of you were illuminated"

1cd	*šubʿarnāyā*	"the two of us were illuminated"
3mp	*šubʿarū*	"they were illuminated"
3fp	*šubʿarā*	"they were illuminated"
2mp	*šubʿartumu*	"you were illuminated"
2fp	*šubʿartina*	"you were illuminated"
1cp	*šubʿarnū*	"we were illuminated"

Šp YAQTULU

3ms	*yušabʿaru*	"he is illuminated"
3fs	*tušabʿaru*	"she is illuminated"
2ms	*tušabʿaru*	"you are illuminated"
2fs	*tušabʿarīna*	"you are illuminated"
1cs	*ʾušabʿaru*	"I am illuminated"
3md	*tušabʿarā(na)*	"the two of them are illuminated"
3fd	*tušabʿarā(na)*	"the two of them are illuminated"
2cd	*tušabʿarā(na)*	"the two of you are illuminated"
1cd	*nušabʿarā*	"the two of us are illuminated"
3mp	*tušabʿarū(na)*	"they are illuminated"
3fp	*tušabʿarna*	"they are illuminated"
2mp	*tušabʿarū(na)*	"you are illuminated"
2fp	*tušabʿarna*	"you are illuminated"
1cp	*nušabʿaru*	"we are illuminated"

Šp participle

ms	*mušabʿaru*	"illuminated one"
fs	*mušabʿaratu*	"illuminated one"
mp	*mušabʿarūma*	"illuminated ones"
fp	*mušabʿarātu*	"illuminated ones"

Because the written text—consonants without vocalization—shows no difference between active and passive forms, only context can indicate whether the verb is active or passive.

8.3. Stems with Affixed *t*: Gt, tD, and Št

The so-called t-stems denote a variety of meanings, such as reflexivity, reciprocity, and advantage or disadvantage to the agent.

In the **Gt-stem QATALA** conjugation, prosthetic *ʾi-* is used to enable pronunciation of the initial consonant cluster. The theme vowel is *i*. The paradigm of Gt-stem RQṢ, "to dance," is as follows:

Gt QATALA		
3ms	*ʾirtaqiṣa*	"he danced"
3fs	*ʾirtaqiṣat*	"she danced"
2ms	*ʾirtaqišta*	"you danced"
2fs	*ʾirtaqišti*	"you danced"
1cs	*ʾirtaqištu*	"I danced"
3md	*ʾirtaqiṣā*	"the two of them danced"
3fd	*ʾirtaqiṣatā*	"the two of them danced"
2cd	*ʾirtaqištumā*	"the two of you danced"
1cd	*ʾirtaqiṣnāyā*	"the two of us danced"
3mp	*ʾirtaqiṣū*	"they danced"
3fp	*ʾirtaqiṣā*	"they danced"
2mp	*ʾirtaqištumu*	"you danced"
2fp	*ʾirtaqiština*	"you danced"
1cp	*ʾirtaqiṣnū*	"we danced"

In the **Gt-stem YAQTULU** conjugation, the vowel *i* occurs in the prefix and is again the theme vowel. The paradigm of Gt-stem RQṢ, "to dance," is as follows:

Gt YAQTULU		
3ms	*yirtaqiṣu*	"he dances"
3fs	*tirtaqiṣu*	"she dances"
2ms	*tirtaqiṣu*	"you dance"
2fs	*tirtaqiṣīna*	"you dance"
1cs	*ʾirtaqiṣu*	"I dance"
3md	*tirtaqiṣā(na)*	"the two of them dance"
3fd	*tirtaqiṣā(na)*	"the two of them dance"

2cd	*tirtaqiṣā(na)*	"the two of you dance"
1cd	*nirtaqiṣā*	"the two of us dance"
3mp	*tirtaqiṣū(na)*	"they dance"
3fp	*tirtaqiṣna*	"they dance"
2mp	*tirtaqiṣū(na)*	"you dance"
2fp	*tirtaqiṣna*	"you dance"
1cp	*nirtaqiṣu*	"we dance"

With **I-n verbs**, the t-infix stems may result in the consonant cluster *nt*, in which case there is assimilation of *n* to *t*, as in other stems with I-n verbs; for example, *ʾittasû* (< *ʾintasiyu*), "I will try," from NSY.

In the **tD-stem**, the consonant *t* is prefixed, instead of infixed between the first and second radicals. The theme vowel of the QATALA form is *a*. The paradigm of tD-stem QATALA, using the verb KMS, "to collapse" (from the G-stem meaning "to squat"), is as follows:

tD QATALA		
3ms	*takammasa*	"he collapsed"
3fs	*takammasat*	"she collapsed"
2ms	*takammasta*	"you collapsed"
2fs	*takammasti*	"you collapsed"
1cs	*takammastu*	"I collapsed"
3md	*takammasā*	"the two of them collapsed"
3fd	*takammasatā*	"the two of them collapsed"
2cd	*takammastumā*	"the two of you collapsed"
1cd	*takammasnāyā*	"the two of us collapsed"
3mp	*takammasū*	"they collapsed"
3fp	*takammasā*	"they collapsed"
2mp	*takammastumu*	"you collapsed"
2fp	*takammastina*	"you collapsed"
1cp	*takammasnū*	"we collapsed"

The theme vowel of the YAQTULU form is *a*. The paradigm of tD-stem YAQTULU, using the verb KMS, "to collapse," is as follows:

tD YAQTULU

3ms	*yitkammasu*	"he collapses"
3fs	*titkammasu*	"she collapses"
2ms	*titkammasu*	"you collapse"
2fs	*titkammasīna*	"you collapse"
1cs	*ʾitkammasu*	"I collapse"
3md	*titkammasā(na)*	"the two of them collapse"
3fd	*titkammasā(na)*	"the two of them collapse"
2cd	*titkammasā(na)*	"the two of you collapse"
1cd	*nitkammasā*	"the two of us collapse"
3mp	*titkammasū(na)*	"they collapse"
3fp	*titkammasna*	"they collapse"
2mp	*titkammasū(na)*	"you collapse"
2fp	*titkammasna*	"you collapse"
1cp	*nitkammasu*	"we collapse"

If a tD-stem verb has a sibilant as its first radical, then metathesis occurs between the sibilant and prefixed *t*: *yišta*ʾʾ*al* (< *yitša*ʾʾ*al*).

Only a few **Št-stem** forms are attested, with weak verbs. QL (Št-stem "to arrive"), for example, is *ʾištaqīla*, "he arrived," in the Št-stem QATALA, and *yištaqīlu*, "he arrives," in the Št-stem YAQTULU. Another example is the root ḤWY (Št-stem "to bow"), whose form is *ʾištaḥwiya* or *ʾištaḥwî* (*iya* > *î*), "he bowed," in the Št-stem QATALA, and *yištaḥwiyu* or *yištaḥwû* (*iyu* > *û*), "he bows," in the Št-stem YAQTULU. To illustrate the strong verb pattern, the following paradigm use the heuristic root QTL.

Št QATALA

3ms	*ʾištaqtila*
3fs	*ʾištaqtilat*
2ms	*ʾištaqtilta*
2fs	*ʾištaqtilti*
1cs	*ʾištaqtiltu*
3md	*ʾištaqtilā*
3fd	*ʾištaqtilatā*
2cd	*ʾištaqtiltumā*
1cd	*ʾištaqtilnāyā*

3mp	*ʾištaqtilū*
3fp	*ʾištaqtilā*
2mp	*ʾištaqtiltumu*
2fp	*ʾištaqtiltina*
1cp	*ʾištaqtilnū*

Št YAQTULU

3ms	*yištaqtilu*
3fs	*tištaqtilu*
2ms	*tištaqtilu*
2fs	*tištaqtilīna*
1cs	*ʾištaqtilu*
3md	*tištaqtilā(na)*
3fd	*tištaqtilā(na)*
2cd	*tištaqtilā(na)*
1cd	*ništaqtilā*
3mp	*tištaqtilū(na)*
3fp	*tištaqtilna*
2mp	*tištaqtilū(na)*
2fp	*tištaqtilna*
1cp	*ništaqtilu*

8.4. L-Stem Verbs

The L-stem (*lengthened* stem) occurs only with biconsonantal and geminate roots. With biconsonantal roots, it presents a long vowel after the first radical and a reduplicated second/third radical. The meaning is mostly factitive. For instance, the biconsonantal root RM is *rāma* in the G-stem (3ms QATALA) with the meaning of "he was high"; in the L-stem it occurs as *rāmama* (3ms QATALA), "he raised." With geminate roots, the L-stem has an intensive meaning: e.g., 3ms YAQTULU *yaʿāzizu* "he will become more powerful," from ʿZZ.

8.5. R-Stem Verbs

The R-stem reduplicates the first radical of geminate roots. Semantically, it is parallel to the D-stem, often having an intensive or factitive meaning.

The R-stem QATALA follows the pattern *qalqala*. For example, G-stem 3ms QATALA KRR is *karra* ("he turned"), while R-stem 3ms QATALA KRR is *karkara* ("he twisted"). Another example is R-stem 3ms QATALA MRR: *marmara* ("he shook [something]"; G-stem MRR means "to pass through"). The R-stem YAQTULU follows the pattern *yaqalqilu*. For example, R-stem 3ms YAQTULU KRR *yakarkiru* ("he will twist") and MRR *yamarmiru* ("he will shake [something]").

There is also a related stem with reduplication and an infixed *t*—either Rt or tR. The verb YPY, "to be beautiful," appears written as /ttpp/. This form can be analyzed as Rt-stem or tR-stem *titapêpû* (< *tiytapaypiyu* or *titaypaypiyu*). In either case, the meaning is "she makes herself beautiful," with both *p* and *y* reduplicated.

8.6. YAQTULU 3md and 3mp Prefix *y-*

In a handful of cases in poetic texts, the 3md and 3mp YAQTULU forms have a *y-* prefix instead of *t-*. In the G-stem, for example, 3md *yaqtulā(na)* occurs instead of *taqtulā(na)*, and 3mp *yaqtulū(na)* instead of *taqtulū(na)*. Though uncommon, these alternate forms appear a few times in the mythological texts. The variation is possibly for literary purposes.

8.7. Suffixed Pronouns and Verb Valency

When the suffixed pronouns were introduced in lesson 4, we learned that they indicate a complement of the verb when attached to a verb. For example, *yagrušu**nī***, "he drives **me** out." Some verbs require multiple complements. Verbs of speaking, for example, often take a patient (the thing spoken) and a recipient: *ragamtu rigma lêki*, "I spoke a word to you." While the more internal complement (in the case of RGM, the patient) is more likely to be attached directly to the verb, it is also possible for the second complement to be attached to the verb. Continuing with the example phrase *ragamtu rigma lêki*, we could find the second complement as a suffixed pronoun: *šamaʿtu rigma, wa ragamtu**ki** rigma*, "I heard a word, and I spoke the word **to you**." More often, we would find the first complement as a suffixed pronoun: *šamaʿtu rigma, wa ragamtu**hu** lêki*, "I heard a word, and I spoke **it** to you."

8.8. Vocabulary

ʾabnu	noun, fem., "stone"
ʿiṣu	noun, masc., "tree, wood"
didānu	noun, "Didanu" (mythic figure, founder of Ugarit?)
kalbu	noun, masc., "dog"
našru	noun, masc., "raptor"
MRR	verb, "to pass, go through" (G QATALA *marra*, YAQTULU *yamurru*); R "to cause to move back and forth, to shake"
NǴṢ	verb, "to shake [something]" (transitive) (G QATALA *naǵaṣa*, YAQTULU *yaǵǵuṣu*); N "to tremble, go slack"
NSY	verb, "to test [someone]" (transitive) (G QATALA *nasaya/nasâ* YAQTULU *yassiyu/yassû*); Gt "to try, to venture"
QṮṮ	verb, "to drag [something]" (G QATALA *qaṯṯa*, YAQTULU *yaquṯṯu*); R "to drag [something]"
qudšu	noun, masc., "holiness," "holy thing," "holy place"
RQṢ	verb, Gt "to dance" (no G-stem)

ʾuṣbaʿu	noun, fem., "finger" (pl. *ʾuṣbaʿātu*)
DLP	verb, "to weaken, slump, break apart" (G QATALA *dalapa*, YAQTULU *yadlupu*)
naḥlatu	noun, fem., "inheritance"
našu	noun, masc., "man, person," only attested as pl. *našūma*, "humankind"
pinnatu	noun, fem., "joint"
tamūnu	noun, masc., "body," "frame"
YPY	verb, "to be beautiful" (G QATALA *yapiya/yapî*, YAQTULU *yipayu/yipû*); Rt "to beautify oneself"
YTN	verb, "to give" (G QATALA *yatana*, YAQTULU *yatinu*); Š "to send, make delivery" (YAQTULU *yišêtinu*)

BKY	verb, "to mourn, weep" (intransitive), "to mourn [someone], weep for [someone]" (transitive) (G QATALA *bakaya / bakâ*, YAQTULU *yabkiyu / yabkû*)
huwatu	noun, fem., "word"
laḫaštu	noun, fem., "whisper"

QBʾ — verb, "to invoke, summon" (G QATALA *qabaʾa*, YAQTULU *yaqbiʾu*)

ṮNY — verb, "to say, repeat" (G QATALA *ṯaniya*/*ṯanî*, YAQTULU *yaṯniyu*/*yaṯnû*)

KRR — verb, "to turn, return" (G QATALA *karra*, YAQTULU *yakurru*); R "to twist"

la — particle, "certainly"

MLʾ — verb, "to be full" (G QATALA *maliʾa*, YAQTULU *yimlaʾu*)

RḤṢ — verb, "to wash" (G QATALA *raḥaṣa*, YAQTULU *yirḥaṣu*)

8.9. Exercises

A. Translate the following into English.

1. *yatattu šalāma lêki*
2. *tugrašu wa tiʾtabidu*
3. *ʾalpu hannadū ʾênu ṭābu. šêtin ʾalpa wa ʾummahu lê ʿabdiya.*
4. *yuttiḥū lê malkati*
5. *ṯamma ʾittasiyu lê nasāyi yamma* (adapted from *KTU* 1.2 iv:4)
6. *ʾanāku ʾamarmiru ʿiṣa qudši* (*KTU* 1.178:2–3)
7. *yitapêpû bi qudši wa bi huwāti ṭābāti*
8. *ʾarāmimuki wa taʿāzizīna bi kussaʾi hêkali*

B. Vocalize and translate the following into English.

1. 
 (adapted from *KTU* 2.70:20–22)
2. 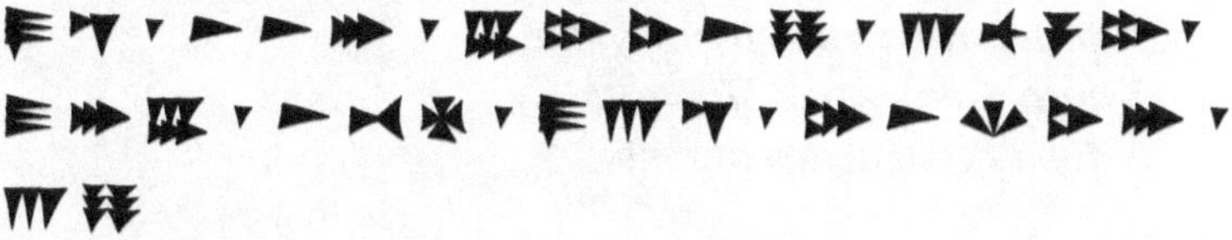
3. b ḥlmh (ḥulumu, "dream") ỉl yrd ...
w yqrb b šảl krt
m ảt krt k ybky … ǵlm ỉl (KTU 1.14 i:35–41)

C. Compose in Ugaritic.

1. The two of them (fem.) gave their lady a strong and beautiful throne.
2. Yariḫu, like a dog, drags (use the R-stem) his goblet (*gūbu*) under the tables. (adapted from *KTU* 1.114:4–6)
3. I myself took their food from the hands of the chief of the shipwreck, returning (use *wa* plus infinitive verb for contingent action) it myself to them. (adapted from *KTU* 2.38:21–24)

D. Translate the following passages into English.

1. *yirtaqiṣu ṣimdu bîdi baʿli, kama našri bi ʾuṣbaʿātihu. yallumu katipa zabūli yammi, bêna yadêma ṯāpiṭi nahari. ʿazzu yammu. lā yamūku. lā tinnaǵiṣna pinnātuhu. lā yadlupu tamūnuhu.* (*KTU* 1.2 iv:15–18)
2. *rigmu ʾiṯu layya wa ʾargumuki, huwatu wa ʾaṯniyuki. rigmu ʿiṣi wa laḫaštu ʾabni; taʾanatu* (fem. noun, "communication, word") *šamîma ʿimma ʾarṣi. ʾabīnu baraqa dā lā tidaʿū šamûma, rigma dā lā tidaʿū našūma, wa lā tabīnu hamullatu* (fem. noun, "horde") *ʾarṣi. ʾatî, wa ʾanāku ʾibǵayuhu, bi tôki ǵūriya, bi qudši, bi ǵūri naḥlatiya, bi naʿīmi.* (adapted from *KTU* 1.3 iii:20–31)

E. Translate the following funerary ritual text into English, and answer the questions that follow. (adapted from *KTU* 1.161)

1 *sipru dabḥi rapaʾīma*
2 *quraʾtumu rapaʾī ʾarṣi*
3 *qubaʾtumu qibūṣi didāni*
4 *quraʾa šamumānu rapaʾu*
5 *quraʾā šiqlašu* (personal name) *wa tiršênu* (personal name)
6 *qaraʾū rapaʾīma qadmiyyīma*
7 *quraʾtumu rapaʾī ʾarṣi*
8 *qubaʾtumu qibūṣi didāni*

1. Write lines 2–3 with consonants only. How would you vocalize the text with active verbs, and how would you translate it?
2. Write line 6 with consonants only. Can you vocalize the text with a passive verb instead (with contextual sensitivity)?

Transitioning to Other Resources

There are a number of good resources for further study of Ugaritic. These include the following:

Bordreuil, Pierre, and Dennis Pardee. *A Manual of Ugaritic*. LSAWS 3. Winona Lake, IN: Eisenbrauns, 2009.

Boyes, Philip. *Script and Society: The Social Context of Writing Practices in Late Bronze Age Ugarit*. Oxford: Oxbow, 2021.

Cunchillos, Jesús-Luis, Juan-Pablo Vita, and José-Ángel Zamora. *A Concordance of Ugaritic Words*. Piscataway, NJ: Gorgias, 2003.

Del Olmo Lete, Gregorio, and Joaquín Sanmartín. *A Dictionary of the Ugaritic Language in the Alphabetic Tradition*. 3rd rev. ed. HdO 112. Leiden: Brill, 2015.[1]

Dietrich, Manfried, et al. *The Cuneiform Alphabetic Texts from Ugarit, Ras Ibn Hani, and Other Places*. 3rd enlarged ed. AOAT 360. Münster: Ugarit-Verlag, 2013.[2]

Huehnergard, John. *An Introduction to Ugaritic*. Peabody, MA: Hendrickson, 2012.

———. *Ugaritic Vocabulary in Syllabic Transcription*. HSS 32. Atlanta: Scholars Press, 1987.

Schniedewind, William M., and Joel H. Hunt. *A Primer on Ugaritic*. Cambridge: Cambridge University Press, 2007.

Sivan, Daniel. *A Grammar of the Ugaritic Language*. Leiden: Brill, 2001.

Smith, Mark S. *The Ugaritic Baal Cycle*. Vol. 1. Leiden: Brill, 1994.

Smith, Mark S., and Wayne T. Pitard. *The Ugaritic Baal Cycle*. Vol. 2. Leiden: Brill, 2009.

Strawn, Brent A., Joel M. LeMon, and Christopher B. Hays. *An Ugaritic Handbook: Vocalization Helps, Paradigms, Word Lists, Sample Texts, and Bibliography*. Winona Lake, IN: Eisenbrauns, forthcoming.

1. This dictionary appears in a few different editions, the most recent of which should be used if possible.

2. This resource appears in a few different editions, the most recent of which should be used if possible.

Tropper, Josef. *Ugaritische Grammatik*. 2nd ed. AOAT 273. Münster: Ugarit-Verlag, 2012.[3]

Tropper, Josef, and Juan-Pablo Vita. *Lehrbuch der ugaritischen Sprache*. Münster: Zaphon, 2020.

Watson, Wilfred, and Nicolas Wyatt. *Handbook of Ugaritic Studies*. Leiden: Brill, 1999.

Yon, Marguerite. *The City of Ugarit at Tell Ras Shamra*. Winona Lake, IN: Eisenbrauns, 2006.

Bordreuil and Pardee's *Manual of Ugaritic* and Huehnergard's *Introduction to Ugaritic* are excellent resources to use upon completion of this grammar. Both contain texts with vocalization and grammatical notes, and both present outlines of Ugaritic grammar that will introduce students to areas of debate in the reconstruction of Ugaritic. *A Manual of Ugaritic* is particularly useful, given the large number of texts it presents and the addition of line-drawings and images. Students should also become familiar with *A Dictionary of the Ugaritic Language in the Alphabetic Tradition* and *The Cuneiform Alphabetic Texts from Ugarit, Ras Ibn Hani and Other Places* (referred to as *CAT*, *KTU*, or *KTU*³), the standard dictionary and text edition, respectively, in the field.

The reconstruction of Ugaritic presented in our grammar aligns in most respects with the reconstruction used in Bordreuil and Pardee's *A Manual of Ugaritic* and Huehnergard's *Introduction to Ugaritic* and with the vocabulary definitions found in those works and in the *Dictionary of the Ugaritic Language*. There are, however, some points of disagreement. The present chapter flags the main disagreements and briefly presents the alternative reconstructions and definitions.

The remarks here are keyed to the lessons in which each topic occurs.

Abjad Order—§1.1

The order of the Ugaritic abjad differs from book to book. Resources such as *An Introduction to Ugaritic* and *Dictionary of the Ugaritic Language* follow the order of the letters in the Latin alphabet, as is done in this grammar. Others, however, follow the typical order of the Phoenician

3. The first edition of this grammar, published in 2000, has been significantly revised in the 2012 edition. See also Dennis Pardee's extensive review of the 2000 edition, *Ugaritische Grammatik*, by Josef Tropper, *AfO* 50 (2003–2004): 1–404.

(and Hebrew and Aramaic) abjad—for example, *A Concordance of Ugaritic Words* and Huehnergard's *Ugaritic Vocabulary in Syllabic Transcription*. In *A Manual of Ugaritic*, Bordreuil and Pardee attempt to reconstruct what the order would have been for ancient users of the Ugaritic abjad—similar to the Phoenician abjad but not entirely. Students should take care when using lexicons and glossaries to know what order is being used. Words starting with *y*, for example, appear near the end of the first system, but closer to the beginning in the second and third; words starting with *š̀* are near the end in the first two systems, but closer to the beginning in *Manual of Ugaritic*.

Vocalization of *lê* —§§1.10, 4.1

The common preposition *lê* (< *lay* < *laya*), "to," is vocalized *le* by Huehnergard.[4] He argues that the form was initially *li* (parallel to *bi*, "with"), and the vowel *i* was shaded to *e* by the preceding "sonorant" *l*. Consequently, the preposition *le* with the 1cs suffixed pronoun *-ya* is vocalized *leya*, not (as here and in *A Manual of Ugaritic*) *layya* (cf. §4.1).

Morphology of QATALA Third Feminine Dual—§2.4

Bordreuil, Pardee, and Huehnergard reconstruct the QATALA 3fd form to end in *tā*, that is, *qatal**tā***. We understand this form to be built off of the 3fs without any vowel reduction: *qatal**atā*** with the dual *ā* appended to the 3fs *at*.

Triphthong Reduction—§2.7

Whereas we view the contraction of *y* and *w* with surrounding vowels to occur inconsistently in our period of Ugaritic, Huehnergard believes there are specific circumstances under which triphthongs do not reduce in III-w/y verbs. His rules for contraction are summarized as follows:[5]

> Where a long vowel is the first vowel of the triphthong (e.g., *ūwa*), there is no contraction.

---

4. Huehnergard, *Introduction to Ugaritic*, 29; Huehnergard, *Ugaritic Vocabulary*, 257–64, esp. 261–62.

5. Huehnergard, *Introduction to Ugaritic*, 28–29.

Where a short vowel is the first vowel of the triphthong (e.g., *uwa*):

	-a	-i	-u
aw-, ay-	*â* (but also archaizing *awa / aya*)	*î* (but also archaizing *awi / ayi*)	*û* (but also archaizing *awu / ayu*)
iy-	no contraction	no contraction	no contraction
uw-	no contraction		*û* or archaizing *uwu*

Theme Vowels of Hollow Verbs—§2.8

In their vocalization of texts, Bordreuil and Pardee vocalize the theme vowel of most hollow verbs as long without contraction (e.g., *ā*, not *â*), in keeping with the analysis of these verbs as biradicals. However, with MT, "to die," they often (though not always) represent contraction of the theme vowel with the radical *y*. For example, 3ms QATALA *mêta*, "he died," whereas we would vocalize *mīta*.[6]

Theme vowel of YAQTULU RM—§2.9

We present the theme vowel of G-stem YAQTULU RM as *ī* (*yarīmu*). In the syllabic evidence, provided in *Dictionary of the Ugaritic Language*, there are some cases with an *ī* theme vowel and some with a *ū* theme vowel.[7] The difference in theme vowel likely indicates a synchronic feature of the verbal system. It is possible that the variation marks a distinction between stative ("be high") and fientive ("become high") or between permanent and temporary state ("he is high," always versus merely at the present moment). It is more likely, however, that the feature distinguishes between an active G-stem (*yarūmu*, "to raise") and a middle G-stem (*yarīmu*, "to be high"). Several Semitic languages show traces of this kind of variation for active and middle voice in the G-stem,[8] and

6. This is perhaps an accidental retention of an earlier analysis published in the French edition, *A Manual of Ugaritic: Manuel d'ougaritique* (Paris: Geuthner, 2004). See similarly below on "Past Tense YAQTUL." We, unfortunately, do not have access to this earlier French edition.

7. Del Olmo Lete and Sanmartín, *Dictionary of the Ugaritic Language*, /r-m/.

8. For example, Hebrew ML', "to fill" or "to be full." See Jan Joosten, "The Func-

there are other potential examples in Ugaritic (e.g., NḤT; see "Stem and Meaning of NḤT" below).

Optional *-na* in Dual and Plural YAQTULU Forms—§3.4

In Huehnergard's *Introduction to Ugaritic*, the final *-na* of the 3md, 3fd, 2cd, 3mp, and 2mp YAQTULU is presented as obligatory, not optional. In Bordreuil and Pardee's *Manual*, the *-na* of the 3mp YAQTULU is likewise presented as obligatory, while *-na* in 3md, 3fd, 2cd, and 2mp YAQTULU is presented as optional. We take *-na* to be optional in all of these cases.

It is possible that, historically, presence versus absence of *-na* in these forms distinguished the YAQTULU conjugation from the jussive (cf. §5.4)—as we find in Phoenician. We take *-na* to be optional in YAQTULU, however, given the use of parallel forms with and without *-na* in poetic texts.[9]

For Huehnergard, presence of final *-na* indicates YAQTULU, while absence of final *-na* indicates jussive or preterite (on which, see below). In our view, use of final *-na* distinguishes YAQTULU from the jussive, but cases without final *-na* may be YAQTULU or jussive.

Quantifiers—§3.7

Our grammar presents one quantifier, *kullu* ("each, every, all"), and the related noun *kalīlu* ("everything, entirety"). There is another quantifier, *kulkulu*, which is not presented in our grammar. *Kulkulu* may have an element of irreality: *Dictionary of the Ugaritic Language* gives the glosses "anything possible" and "anything at all."

In *A Manual of Ugaritic*, Bordreuil and Pardee do not distinguish between quantifier and noun. They label all of these related nominals derived from KLL ("to complete") as nouns, and they define each simply with the gloss "all." In addition to *kullu*, *kulkulu*, and *kalīlu*, Bordreuil and Pardee present a fourth word with feminine morphology: *kullatu*, "all." *Dictionary of the Ugaritic Language*, in contrast, understands this word to indicate specifically an unknown measure of grain. The word can plausibly

tions of the Semitic D Stem: Biblical Hebrew Materials for a Comparative-Historical Approach," *Or* 67 (1998): 209–12.

9. See, for example, *KTU* 1.3 iii:26–28, *lā tidaʿū* (3mp), occurring twice within relative clauses (where we do not expect jussives), parallel to *lā tabīnu* (3fs) in the same passage.

be interpreted as "all" or as "a measure [of grain]" in each case where it occurs, making it difficult to determine which definition is correct.[10]

1cs Suffixed Pronoun *-ī* and Enclitic *-ya*—§§4.1, 5.2

Most grammars understand the 1cs suffixed pronoun on nominative nouns to take the form *-ī* or *-î*, not *-ya*. These include *A Manual of Ugaritic* and Huehnergard's *Introduction*. This is incorrect, in our opinion: although *-uya* (nominative *u* + 1cs *ya*) sometimes reduces to *-î*, there are also many cases where *-uya* remains without any reduction.[11]

Particularly in epistolary texts, nominative nouns often end with *-ya* in contexts where a 1cs suffixed pronoun should be understood. Bordreuil and Pardee consistently analyze such nouns in the following way: *-uya* (nominative case ending *u* + 1cs pronoun *-ya*) has reduced to *-î* (< *-uy* < *-uya*), and subsequently the enclitic particle *-ya* has been added. For example, the word /bʿly/ in *KTU* 2.40 is understood as the subject of the clause, vocalized *baʿlîya*, and translated "my master": *baʿlu* + 1cs *ya* becomes *baʿlî*, to which is appended the enclitic *-ya*, resulting in *baʿlîya*. In this way, they maintain that the 1cs suffixed pronoun is always *-î*.

Indeed, the 1cs suffixed pronoun often contracts to *-î*: we regularly see words like /ủm/, *ʾummî*, "my mother," where the nominative noun is clearly modified by a 1cs pronoun. However, it seems much more likely that /y/ found in other cases is simply the 1cs suffixed pronoun without contraction. Whether or not the spoken language consistently reduced to *-î*, the evidence in written texts is best interpreted as variable. We therefore analyze cases like nom sg /bʿly/ as *baʿluya*, "my master," with *-ya* as the 1cs pronoun and no reduction of the triphthong.

The use of *-ya* with these nominative nouns also goes against the analysis that *-ī* (not contracted *-î*) is the 1cs suffixed pronoun with nomina-

---

10. See also Holger Gzella, "Some Penciled Notes on Ugaritic Lexicography," *BibOr* 64 (2007): 547, who supports the definition "all." Gzella argues that it is simpler to interpret *klt* as a "substantivized feminine form of *kl*" than to posit a new lexical entry; Semitic clearly possesses, however, a related root (KWL) that refers to measuring.

11. Cf. Simon B. Parker, "Studies in the Grammar of Ugaritic Prose Texts" (PhD diss., The Johns Hopkins University, 1967), 11–16. For a recent overview of positions on the 1cs pronoun, see Jason A. Riley, "'Why, O -y?' The 1cs Suffix in Ugaritic and Its Bearing on the Case of the Vocative," *UF* 44 (2013): 261–84.

tives, replacing the case vowel.[12] In this view, too, the frequent appearance of /y/ with nominative nouns suggests that *-ya* was the 1cs suffixed pronoun with nominatives as well.

Relative Words—§5.1

We follow Josef Tropper and Robert Holmstedt in reconstructing an inflected relative marker that coexisted with an uninflected relative particle.[13] Huehnergard takes the same approach. Pardee instead postulates one system that accounts for all relative words in our evidence. For Pardee, there is a masculine singular, feminine singular, and common plural form of the relative, with only the masculine singular inflected for case.[14] The ending *ti* is optional for the plural and feminine singular forms. This approach is reflected in the *Manual of Ugaritic*, for both relatives and demonstratives.

Relative Pronouns in *Manual of Ugaritic*

	masc sg	fem sg	com pl
Nom	*dū*		
Gen/Voc	*dī*	*dā(ti)*	*dū(ti)*
Acc	*dā*		

Demonstrative Pronouns in *Manual of Ugaritic*

	masc sg	fem sg	com pl
Nom	*hannadū*		
Gen/Voc	*hannadī*	*hannadā*(*ti*)	*hannadū*(*ti*)
Acc	*hannadā*		

12. So Huehnergard, *Introduction to Ugaritic*, 33.

13. Tropper, *Ugaritische Grammatik*, 234–38; Robert Holmstedt, "The Relative Clause in Canaanite Epigraphic Texts," *JNSL* 34 (2008): 25–26; Holmstedt, *The Relative Clause in Biblical Hebrew*, LSAWS 10 (Winona Lake, IN: Eisenbrauns, 2016), 267–68.

14. Pardee, review of *Ugaritische Grammatik*, 137–38.

Holmstedt argues persuasively that use of the relative marker in Ugaritic was breaking down by the time of our evidence and that Ugaritic was consequently moving to an uninflected, relative complementizer instead—what we have, for simplicity, called a relative particle. Similar processes can be observed in other Semitic languages.[15]

Stem and Meaning of NḤT—§5.9

We define the verb NḤT as "to prepare [something]" in both the G- and D-stems. This essentially agrees with Bordreuil and Pardee, who gloss the G-stem as "prepare" and treat the D-stem as an "intensive" of the G-stem (335). The *Dictionary of the Ugaritic Language*, however, understands only a D-stem in Ugaritic, with the sense "to reach for."

These definitions all stem from the core idea of "to go down." *Dictionary of the Ugaritic Language* indicates that the D-stem meaning "to reach for" is a development from "to take down,"[16] which itself looks like a causative of "to go down." Our definition (and the *Manual*'s) "to prepare" agrees with the Hebrew cognate NḤT, which means "to go down" in the G-stem and "to press down" in the D-stem. The D-stem meaning is causative of the G-stem, connoting that some tool is caused to go down into something. When D-stem NḤT is said to happen to a bow (e.g., Ps 18) or a furrow (e.g., Ps 65), it connotes that the bow or furrow is *made* or *prepared* by pressing a tool down; thus, the sense "to prepare."

Evidence from *KTU* 1.23 indicates that the Ugaritic verb does not behave exactly like the Hebrew cognate; specifically, the G-stem takes a complement, and therefore it is more or less synonymous with the D-stem, rather than the D-stem being a causative of the G-stem as in Hebrew. The verb first appears in line 37, *ʾilu ḫaṭṭahu* ***naḥata***, "Ilu prepared his staff"; the verb could, of course, be D-stem *niḥḥata*. In three subsequent places (lines 40, 43, 47), however, Ilu is referred to as /nḥtm ḫṭk/, which reasonably should be vocalized as a vocative G-stem participle (with enclitic *-ma*) followed by a complement, *nāḥitima ḫaṭṭaka*, "O you who prepares your staff." The participle has no preformative *m-* indicative of a D-stem participle, yet it clearly takes a complement. Probably what has occurred here is that the original G-stem middle

15. Holmstedt, "Relative Clause," 28–30; Holmstedt, *Relative Clause*, 268.
16. Del Olmo Lete and Sanmartín, *Dictionary of the Ugaritic Language*, /n-ḥ-t/.

sense "to go down" fell out of use,[17] leaving the G-stem active sense "to bring down" alongside the D-stem "to cause to go down," both of which developed in parallel to the meaning "to prepare" (via a route similar to D-stem NḤT in Hebrew).

In our analysis, then, both the G-stem and D-stem of this verb occur, and both stems take a complement. The sense "to prepare" fits cognate evidence within Northwest Semitic and works better contextually than *Dictionary of the Ugaritic Language*'s definition "to reach for" in the places where it occurs (in both the G- and D-stems).

Location of I-y/w Verbs in Lexicons—§7.6

We note that I-y/w verbs are listed in lexicons and glossaries according to the radicals of the G-stem, where the first radical is *y*. In *Dictionary of the Ugaritic Language*, however, several verbs are listed under *w*, for example, YSR ("to teach") is given as "/w-s-r/". In *Dictionary of the Ugaritic Language*, students should first look for such roots under *y* but consult the *w* section if the verb cannot be found.

Contraction of *y* in I-y YAQTULU Forms—§7.6.1

Like Huehnergard and Bordreuil and Pardee, we understand the *y* of I-*y* verbs to elide, without contraction, in YAQTULU forms. The principle evidence for this view is the spelling of certain 1cs YAQTULU verbs with /å/, e.g., /ård/, indicating the vocalization *ʾaridu* (< *ʾayridu*), "I descend." If contraction had occurred, we would expect /ỉ/ to be used: /ỉrd/, *ʾêridu* (*ay* > *ê*).

In some of the texts presented in *A Manual of Ugaritic*, however, we find vocalizations that seem to assume contraction of *y*, though Bordreuil and Pardee's grammatical outline states otherwise. For example, *yîšanu* (YŠN), "he falls asleep," with *iy* contracted to *î* (**yiyšanu*).[18]

It is certainly possible that the use of the three *alef* signs is not entirely consistent across the corpus, in which case the evidence of /ård/ and a few other 1cs YAQTULU forms may be misleading. If *y* contracted in I-y YAQTULU verbs, the forms would be as follows (compare the forms given in §7.6.1):

---

17. We consider the G-stem to have had both an active and middle sense at an earlier period; cf. "Theme vowel of YAQTULU RM," above.

18. Bordreuil and Pardee, *Manual of Ugaritic*, 171.

YRD YAQTULU 3ms	*yêridu* (< *yayridu*), "he descends"
YRD jussive 3ms	*yêrid* (< *yayrid*), "may he descend"
YRD volitive 3ms	*yêrida* (< *yayrida*), "let him descend"
YDʿ YAQTULU 3fs	*tîdaʿu* (< *tiydaʿu*), "she knows"
YṢʾ YAQTULU 3fs	*têṣiʾu* (<*tayṣiʾu*), "she goes out"

Past Tense YAQTUL—§7.8

For a long time scholars held that Ugarit used a short YAQTUL form, identical to the jussive, as a preterite (past tense) verb. Evidence in other Semitic languages suggests as much.[19] In the last twenty years, however, the existence of such a form in Ugaritic has been questioned.

The argument against a preterite YAQTUL is presented most compellingly by Edward Greenstein in a 2006 study.[20] Another interpretation of the evidence is presented, in response to Greenstein, by Jo Ann Hackett.[21] The crucial evidence on this issue comes from III-ʾ verbs, which in theory should reflect whether a long YAQTULU or short YAQTUL has been used—the former spelled with /ủ/ as the final character, the latter with /ỉ/.[22] Grenstein argues that there are no cases where such verbs are written with /ỉ/ in a past tense context. Hackett argues that there are, in fact, cases of past tense III-ʾ verbs written with /ỉ/. In our opinion, though there are a few cases that can be interpreted in different ways, the high number of III-ʾ

---

19. In Hebrew, for example, most scholars believe an old preterite *yiqtol* is preserved in the narrative *wayyiqtol* form.

20. Edward Greenstein, "Forms and Functions of the Finite Verb in Ugaritic Narrative Verse," in *Biblical Hebrew in Its Northwest Semitic Setting: Typological and Historical Perspectives*, ed. Steven E. Fassberg and Avi Hurvitz (Winona Lake, IN: Eisenbrauns, 2006), 75–102.

21. Jo Ann Hackett, "*Yaqtul* and a Ugaritic Incantation," in *Language and Nature: Papers Presented to John Huehnergard on the Occasion of His Sixtieth Birthday*, ed. Rebecca Hasselbach and Na'ama Pat-El, SAOC 67 (Chicago: Oriental Institute, 2012), 111–17.

22. There is other evidence, but its reliability is uncertain: some take the presence or absence of *-na* at the end of some forms to indicate YAQTULU versus jussive/YAQTUL (see above on "Optional *-na* in Dual and Plural YAQTULU Forms"). Moreover, the presence or absence of *y* in III-*y* verbs also provides evidence that can be interpreted in various ways (cf. the jussive, where *y* of III-y verbs drops; the YAQTUL form would be identical).

verbs used in past tense contexts and written with /ủ/ (not /ỉ/)[23] suggests that there was no past tense YAQTUL form.

Huehnergard believes that there is a short preterite YAQTUL.[24] The grammatical outline in *A Manual of Ugaritic*, on the other hand, agrees more or less with Greenstein's position.[25] The vocalizations for some of the mythological texts, however, reflect the understanding that a short YAQTUL preterite was used for past tense in poetry. In *KTU* 1.3, for example, they vocalize /tǵṣ/ *taǵǵuṣ* (not *taǵǵuṣu*) but translate with a present-tense English verb and parse the form as "imperfective [= YAQTULU]" in a note.[26] We assume that such vocalizations have been accidentally retained from the earlier French edition of *A Manual of Ugaritic*.[27] In such a large undertaking—the translation and updating of a grammatical outline and editions of texts—it is, of course, unsurprising that some of these vocalizations from the first edition have been accidentally retained, despite the clear effort to reflect their new understanding everywhere in the book.[28] Students should be aware of this phenomenon in the vocalizations of *A Manual of Ugaritic*.

Root and Stem of YTḤ/WḤY, "to hasten"—§7.10

The verb presented as YTḤ in *A Manual of Ugaritic* is instead understood as WḤY in *Dictionary of the Ugaritic Language*. The word in question appears in only one form, /twtḥ/, in a phrase repeated in several places the Baal Cycle (e.g., *KTU* 1.3 iii:20): /ʿmy **twtḥ** ỉšdk/, "let your legs hasten to me." Though the root is clearly I-y/w and the form is a third person dual YAQTULU (or jussive or volitive), the third and fourth letters (/tḥ/) can be accounted for using different roots and stems.

---

23. See Greenstein, "Forms and Functions," 90–91 for a summary.

24. Huehnergard, *Introduction to Ugaritic*, 56–57.

25. Bordreuil and Pardee, *Manual of Ugaritic*, 45–46, 49. Specifically, they believe the YAQTUL/jussive form was not the only form used for past tense in poetry, but rather it was used "in free variation with [YAQTULU] forms" (46). Significantly, they indicate in the outline (46) that they treat prefix conjugation verbs in poetry as YAQTULU forms, and within their presentation of texts they follow this statement fairly consistently (see the translation and parsing of /tǵṣ/ in the example cited here).

26. Bordreuil and Pardee, *Manual of Ugaritic*, 165, 167–68.

27. Bordreuil and Pardee, *Manuel d'ougaritique*.

28. Cf. Bordreuil and Pardee, *Manual of Ugaritic*, ix.

Bordreuil and Pardee understand a D-stem from YTḤ; the original first radical *w* is preserved in the D-stem, while the third and fourth letters are simply the other letters of the root: *tawattiḥā*, "may the two of them hasten." *Dictionary of the Ugaritic Language*, however, argues that YTḤ (WTḤ) "[probably] does not exist in [Semitic] with this meaning."[29] They instead posit the root WḤY, known from Arabic and other Semitic languages with the meaning "to hasten." The form /twtḥ/, in that case, is a Gt-stem, which we would vocalize *tiwtaḥî* (< *tiwtaḥiyā*). We are not aware of any other I-y/w verbs that preserve *w* in the Gt-stem, though there are not many Gt-stem verbs attested in general in our evidence.

Š-Stem YTN—§8.1

Bordreuil and Pardee treat Š-stem YAQTULU YTN as if it is formed from the biradical root TN.[30]

QATALA 3ms	*šatina*, "he sent"
YAQTULU 3ms	*yišatinu*, "he sends"

This is also their analysis of G-stem YAQTULU YTN, where we have evidence in the form of the 1cs written with /å/ (*ʾatinu*, not *ʾêtinu* with contraction from *ʾaytinu*). We understand the G-stem to behave like other I-*y* verbs, thus the form *ʾatinu* reflects elision of *y* without contraction (cf. §7.6.1 and "Contraction of *y* in I-*y* YAQTULU Forms" above). Whereas most I-*y* verbs in the Š-stem reflect contraction of *w* (historically, these roots begin with *w*; cf. §7.6.3), with Huehnergard we understand YTN to be a I-*y* (not I-w) verb;[31] for example, QATALA *šêtina* (< *šaytina*), "he sent."[32]

Meaning of G-Stem NSY—§8.8

We have defined the verb NSY as "to test" in the G-stem and "to try" in the Gt-stem. *A Manual of Ugaritic*, however, defines the G-stem as "to banish"

29. Del Olmo Lete and Sanmartín, *Dictionary of the Ugaritic Language*, /w-ḥ-y/.

30. Bordreuil and Pardee, *Manual of Ugaritic*, 54–55. Note that they do not treat TN as a hollow verb with long theme vowels.

31. Huehnergard, *Introduction to Ugaritic*, 68.

32. The evidence is difficult; like Ugaritic, Phoenician has YTN for the verb "to give," but most other Semitic languages reflect the root NTN/NDN.

and gives no separate gloss for the Gt-stem.[33] The lack of a separate definition for the Gt-stem is not uncommon compared to elsewhere in the *Manual*'s glossary: Bordreuil and Pardee sometimes provide separate glosses for derived stems and sometimes do not. The Gt-stem occurrence of NSY in *KTU* 1.2 iv:4 is translated "to lay waste" by Bordreuil and Pardee.[34]

A Dictionary of the Ugaritic Language is closer to our definition: according to them, the Gt-stem means "to try, venture." They also offer an uncertain definition of "to venture" for one occurrence that may be G- or N-stem in their estimation.[35]

Our definition follows the sense of the root attested in Hebrew and Aramaic—"to test" (i.e., to test someone) in the G-stem and "to try" (i.e., to try to do something) in the Gt-stem. Though the Ugaritic evidence is sparse and found in broken contexts, this analysis provides a reasonable interpretation of passages where the verb occurs and has the benefit of aligning with uses of the same root in the other branches of Northwest Semitic.

YDʿ in the QATALA Conjugation

In *A Manual of Ugaritic*, Bordreuil and Pardee treat the verb YDʿ as though the guttural ʿ (*ayin*) requires the helping vowel *ā* before a consonant. Such cases arise particularly in the QATALA conjugation where the suffix begins with *t* or *n*.

2ms	*yadaʿāta*, "you know" (compare our vocalization *yadaʿta*)
2fs	*yadaʿāti*, "you know" (compare *yadaʿti*)
1cs	*yadaʿātu*, "I know" (compare *yadaʿtu*)
3fd	*yadaʿātā*,[36] "the two of them know" (compare *yadaʿatā*)
2cd	*yadaʿātumā*, "the two of you know" (compare *yadaʿtumā*)
1cd	*yadaʿānāyā*, "the two of us know" (compare *yadaʿnāyā*)

33. Bordreuil and Pardee, *Manual of Ugaritic*, 335.
34. Bordreuil and Pardee, *Manual of Ugaritic*, 159.
35. Del Olmo Lete and Sanmartín, *Dictionary of the Ugaritic Language*, /n-s(-y)/.
36. Based on their 3fd form *qataltā*; cf. "Morphology of QATALA Third Feminine Dual" above.

2mp	*yadaʿātumu*, "you know" (compare *yadaʿtumu*)
2fp	*yadaʿātina*, "you know" (compare *yadaʿtina*)
1cp	*yadaʿānū*, "we know" (compare *yadaʿnū*)

Bordreuil and Pardee do not, however, treat any of the other III-guttural verbs in this way,[37] and all of our other evidence suggests that ʿ is strong and completely regular. Students who have learned forms like *yadaʿti*, without a helping vowel, should keep in mind Bordreuil and Pardee's practice of inserting *ā*, since YDʿ occurs frequently in *A Manual of Ugaritic*'s texts.

37. With the root ŠMʿ, for example, they never use a helping vowel for these forms.

Ugaritic to English Glossary

ʾabnu	noun, fem., "stone" (§8)
ʾabû	noun, masc., "father" (§2)
ʾadānu	noun, masc., "lord" (§6)
ʾadattu	noun, fem., "lady" (pl. *ʾadānātu*) (§6)
ʾaduru	adjective, "powerful," "magnificent," "worthy" (§4)
ʾaḥḥadu	numeral, "one" (§7)
ʾaḫâtu	noun, fem., "sister" (pl. *ʾaḫḫâtu*) (§2)
ʾaḫû	noun, masc., "brother" (pl. *ʾaḫḫûma*) (§2)
ʾaklu	noun, masc., "food" (§2)
ʾal	particle, "not," negation with irrealis verbs (§6)
ʾalpu	numeral, masc., "thousand" (§7)
ʾalpu	noun, masc., "bovid," "ox" (§2)
ʾamatu	noun, fem., "servant," "maidservant" (§1)
ʾana	adverb, "where," "wherever" (§7)
ʾanāku, ʾanā	pronoun, "I" (§3)
ʾappu	noun, masc., "nose" (dual "nostrils"), "anger" (§4)
ʾarbaʿu	numeral, "four" (§7)
ʾarṣu	noun, fem., "earth, land" (§6)
ʾatta	pronoun, "you" (masc. sg.) (§3)
ʾatti	pronoun, "you" (fem. sg.) (§3)
ʾattumā	pronoun, "(the two of) you" (dual) (§3)
ʾattumu	pronoun, "you," "y'all" (plural) (§3)
ʾaṯra	preposition, "after, behind" (§3)
ʾaṯṯatu	noun, fem., "woman" (§4)
ʾBD	verb, D "to destroy," Gt "to perish" (no G-stem) (§4)
ʾêbu	noun, masc., "enemy" (§3)
ʾêka, ʾêkaya	interrogative particle, "how?" (§4)
ʾênu, ʾênuna	indeclinable negated copula, "there is not" (§2)
ʾHB	verb, "to love" (G QATALA *ʾahiba*, YAQTULU *yaʾhubu* or *yaʾuhubu*); D "to love strongly" (§4)

ʾḪD	verb, "to seize, take, hold" (G QATALA *ʾaḫada*, YAQTULU *yaʾḫudu* or *yaʾuḫudu*) (§4)
ʾilu	noun, masc., "god"; personal name "Ilu," "El" (§1)
ʾimma, himma	particle, "if"; conjunction "or" (§4)
ʾišdu	noun, fem., "leg" (§4)
ʾiṯu	indeclinable copula, "to be" (§1)
ʾô	conjunction, "or" (§5)
ʾTY	verb, "to come" (G QATALA *ʾatawa* / *ʾatâ*, YAQTULU *yiʾtayu* / *yiʾatayu* / *yiʾtû* / *yiʾatû*) (§6)
ʾū	conjunction, "and" (§5)
ʾudnu	noun, fem., "ear" (§4)
ʾummu	noun, fem., "mother" (pl. *ʾummahātu*) (§2)
ʾuṣbaʿu	noun, fem., "finger" (pl. *ʾuṣbaʿātu*) (§8)
ʿabdu	noun, masc., "servant" (§1)
ʿadê	preposition, "up to" (§3)
ʿālamu	noun, masc., "long duration of time" (§3)
ʿaparu	noun, masc., "dust" (§7)
ʿašru	numeral, "ten" (§7)
ʿaštayu	numeral, "one" (typically as part of the teen numeral "eleven") (§7)
ʿazzu	adjective, "strong" (§2)
ʿimma, ʿimmānu	preposition, "with," "to" (§1)
ʿiṣu	noun, masc., "tree, wood" (§8)
ʿLY	verb, "to go up" (G QATALA *ʿalaya* / *ʿalâ*, YAQTULU *yaʿliyu* / *yaʿlû*), Št "to present an offering" (§6)
ʿNY	verb, "to answer" (G QATALA *ʿanaya* / *ʿanâ*, YAQTULU *yaʿniyu* / *yaʿnû*) (§6)
ʿRB	verb, "to enter" (G QATALA *ʿaraba*, YAQTULU *yiʿrabu*) (§1)
ʿuṣṣūru	noun, fem., "bird" (§3)
ʿuzzu	noun, masc., "strength" (§2)
BʿR	verb, D "to burn [something]," Š "to illuminate" (no G-stem) (§4)
baʿlu	noun, masc., "master," "lord"; personal name "Baʿlu," "Baal" (§1)
baraqu	noun, masc., "lightning" (§5)
bêna	preposition, "between" (§2)
bêtu	noun, masc., "house," "household" (pl. *bahatūma*) (§1)

BǴY	verb, "to explain" (G QATALA *baǵaya* / *baǵâ*, YAQTULU *yibǵayu* / *yibǵû*) (§6)
bi, biya	preposition, "in," "on," "to," "by (= agent or instrument)," "from," "for (= exchange)" (cf. §5.7) (§1)
bîdi, bîdê	complex preposition, "in the hand(s) of," "in the authority of" (§2)
binu	noun, masc., "son" (pl. *banūma*) (§2)
bittu	noun, fem., "daughter" (pl. *banātu*) (§2)
BKY	verb, "to mourn, weep" (intransitive), "to mourn [someone], weep for [someone]" (transitive) (G QATALA *bakaya* / *bakâ*, YAQTULU *yabkiyu* / *yabkû*) (§8)
BN	verb, "to understand" (G QATALA *bāna*, YAQTULU *yabīnu*) (§5)
BRK	verb, D "to bless" (no G-stem) (§4)
dabḥu	noun, masc., "sacrifice" (§3)
darkatu	noun, fem., "dominion, rule" (§7)
DBḤ	verb, "to sacrifice, slaughter" (G QATALA *dabaḥa*, YAQTULU *yidbaḥu*) (§3)
didānu	noun, "Didanu" (mythic figure, founder of Ugarit?) (§8)
DLP	verb, "to weaken, slump, break apart" (G QATALA *dalapa*, YAQTULU *yadlupu*) (§8)
du	relative particle, "that, who, which" (§5)
dū	relative marker, "that, who, which" (§5)
GRŠ	verb, "to drive away" (G QATALA *garaša*, YAQTULU *yagrušu*) (§3)
gû	noun, masc., "voice" (§4)
ǵalmu	noun, masc., "boy" (§5)
ǵazru	noun, masc., "young man," "hero" (§3)
ǵūru	noun, masc., "mountain" (§5)
hanna	interjection, "look, behold"; adverb, "here" (also *hannana*, *hannaniya*, *halli*, *hatti*, *halliha*, *hallima*, *hallina*, *halliniya*) (§5)
hannadū	demonstrative pronoun, "this" (§5)
hêkalu	noun, masc., "palace" (§6)
hiya	pronoun, "she" (oblique *hiyati*) (§3)
HLK	verb, "to go" (G QATALA *halaka*, YAQTULU *yaliku*) (§7)

HLM	verb, "to strike" (G QATALA *halama*, YAQTULU *yallumu*) (§7)
humā	pronoun, "they," "the two of them" (dual) (oblique *humāti*) (§3)
humū	pronoun, "they" (plural) (oblique *humūti*) (§3)
huwa	pronoun, "he" (oblique *huwati*) (§3)
huwatu	noun, fem., "word" (§8)
ḥadaṯu	adjective, "new" (§3)
ḫaṭṭu	noun, masc., "staff," "rod" (§1)
ḫamišu	numeral, "five" (§7)
ka, kama	preposition, "like, as" (§4)
kaḥṯu	noun, masc., "chair" (§7)
kalbu	noun, masc., "dog" (§8)
kalīlu	noun, masc., only sg., "all, entirety, everything" (§3)
kāma, kamāma	adverb, "thus" (§5)
kaspu	noun, masc., "silver" (§4)
katipu	noun, fem., "shoulder" (§7)
kī, kīya, kīma	conjunction, circumstantial "when," "if," "because"; complementizer "that"; emphatic "indeed" (§5)
kirta	personal name, masc., "Kirta" (indeclinable) (§3)
KN	verb, "to be" (G QATALA *kāna*, YAQTULU *yakūnu*); Š "to establish" (§7)
KRR	verb, "to turn, return" (G QATALA *karra*, YAQTULU *yakurru*); R "to twist" (§8)
kubda	postposition, "plus" (used in compound number phrases) (§7)
kullu	quantifier, masc., only sg., "each, every, all" (§3)
kussa'u	noun, fem., "chair," "throne" (§5)
la	particle, "certainly" (§8)
lā	particle, "not," negation (§1)
laḫaštu	noun, fem., "whisper" (§8)
lawasanda	proper noun, place, "Lawasanda" (indeclinable) (§5)
lê, lêya	preposition, "to," "for," "from," "before" (§1)
lê panî	complex preposition, "before" (§2)
LḤM	verb, "to eat" (G QATALA *laḥama*, YAQTULU *yilḥamu*) (§2)
LQḤ	verb, "to take" (G QATALA *laqaḥa*, YAQTULU *yiqqaḥu*) (§4)
lubūšu	noun, masc., "lubushu," a basic type of garment (§7)

ma	pronoun, "what?" (only extant in *lê ma*, "why?") (§6)
maʾadu	adjective, "much" (§3)
maʾda	adverb, "very" (acc. of noun maʾdu, "muchness") (§3)
malkatu	noun, fem., "queen" (§1)
malku	noun, masc., "king" (§1)
manna	pronoun, "whatever" (also *mannaka*, *mannama*) (§6)
marḥaqtu	noun, fem., "distant place"; often adverbial "[from] far away" (§5)
marziḥu	noun, masc., "drinking club" (§6)
MḪṢ	verb, "to strike, smite" (G QATALA *maḫaṣa*, YAQTULU *yimḫaṣu*) (§3)
mī	pronoun, "who?" (§6)
miʾtu	numeral, fem., "hundred" (pl. *miʾātu*) (§7)
MK	verb, "to fall, collapse" (G QATALA *māka*, YAQTULU *yamūku*) (§7)
MLʾ	verb, "to be full" (G QATALA *maliʾa*, YAQTULU *yimlaʾu*) (§8)
MRR	verb, "to pass, go through" (G QATALA *marra*, YAQTULU *yamurru*); R "to shake [something]" (transitive), "to cause to move back and forth" (§8)
MT	verb, "to die" (G QATALA *mīta*, YAQTULU *yamūtu*) (§2)
mutu	noun, masc., "man" (§4)
naʿīmu	adjective, "pleasant," "gracious" (§4)
naharu	noun, masc., "river" (§2)
naḥlatu	noun, fem., "inheritance" (§8)
našru	noun, masc., "raptor" (§8)
našu	noun, masc., "man, person," only attested as pl. *našūma*, "humankind" (§8)
NDR	verb, "to make a vow" (G QATALA *nadara*, YAQTULU *yadduru*) (§4)
NGŠ	verb, "to approach" (G QATALA *nagaša*, YAQTULU *yiggašu*) (§4)
NǴR	verb, "to guard" (G QATALA *naǵara*, YAQTULU *yaǵǵuru*) (§4)
NǴṢ	verb, "to shake [something]" (transitive) (G QATALA *naǵaṣa*, YAQTULU *yaǵǵuṣu*) ; N "to tremble, go slack" (§8)
NḤT	verb, "to prepare [something]" (G QATALA *naḥata*, YAQTULU *yiḥḥatu*), D "to prepare [something]" (§5)

NPL	verb, "to fall" (G QATALA *napala*, YAQTULU *yappulu*) (§4)
NR	verb, "to shine" (G QATALA *nāra*, YAQTULU *yanūru*) (§2)
NS	verb, "to flee" (G QATALA *nāsa*, YAQTULU *yanūsu*) (§6)
NSʿ	verb, "to pay" (G QATALA *nasaʿa*, YAQTULU *yissaʿu*) (§5)
NSY	verb, "to test [someone]" (transitive) (G QATALA *nasaya* / *nasâ* YAQTULU *yassiyu* / *yassû*); Gt "to try, to venture" (§8)
PʿR	verb, "to proclaim" (G QATALA *paʿara*, YAQTULU *yipʿaru*) (§5)
paʿnu	noun, fem., "foot" (dl. *paʿnāma*) (§4)
panûma	noun, masc., only pl., "face" (§2)
pinnatu	noun, fem., "joint" (§8)
pû	noun, masc., "mouth" (§4)
qadmiyyu	adjective, "ancient" (§3)
qarnu	noun, fem., "horn" (§4)
QBʾ	verb, "to invoke, summon" (G QATALA *qabaʾa*, YAQTULU *yaqbiʾu*) (§8)
qibūṣu	noun, masc., "assembly," "clan" (§3)
qirbu	noun, masc., "middle," "midst" (§6)
QL	verb, "to fall" (G QATALA *qāla*, YAQTULU *yaqīlu*) (§2)
QNY	verb, "to acquire" (G QATALA *qanaya* / *qanâ*, YAQTULU *yaqniyu* / *yaqnû*) (§6)
QRʾ	verb, "to call" (G QATALA *qaraʾa*, YAQTULU *yiqraʾu*) (§1)
QRB	verb, "to approach" (G QATALA *qaraba*, YAQTULU *yiqrabu*) (§1)
QṮṮ	verb, "to drag [something]" (G QATALA *qaṯṯa*, YAQTULU *yaquṯṯu*); R "to drag [something]" (§8)
qudšu	noun, masc., "holiness," "holy thing," "holy place" (§8)
rabbu	adjective, "great" (§4)
rapaʾu	noun, masc., "ancestral being," "shade" (§2)
RBB	verb, "to be great, become great" (G QATALA *rabba*, YAQTULU *yarubbu*) (§5)
RGM	verb, "to say" (G QATALA *ragama*, YAQTULU *yargumu*) (§1)

RḤṢ	verb, "to wash" (G QATALA *raḥaṣa*, YAQTULU *yirḥaṣu*) (§8)
rigmu	noun, masc., "word," "thing," "matter" (§1)
RM	verb, "to be/become high" (G QATALA *rāma*, YAQTULU *yarīmu*) (§2)
RQṢ	verb, Gt "to dance" (no G-stem) (§8)
sipru	noun, masc., "document," "account" (§6)
ṣimdu	noun, masc., "mace" (§5)
Š'L	verb, "to request" (G QATALA *šaʾila*, YAQTULU *yišʾalu*) (§3)
šabʿu	numeral, "seven" (§7)
šalāmu	noun, masc., "peace," "well-being" (§1)
šamnu	noun, masc., "oil" (§4)
šamûma	noun, masc., only pl., "heavens" (§6)
šamumānu	personal name, masc., diptotic, "Shamumanu" (§5)
šapšu	noun, fem., "sun" (§1)
ŠKB	verb, "to lie down" (G QATALA *šakaba*, YAQTULU *yiškabu*) (§3)
ŠLM	verb, "to be well" (G QATALA *šalima*, YAQTULU *yišlamu*) (§1)
ŠMʿ	verb, "to hear" (G QATALA *šamaʿa*, YAQTULU *yišmaʿu*) (§3)
ŠPL	verb, "to bend down" (G QATALA *šapala*, YAQTULU *yišpalu*) (§7)
ŠQY	verb, D "to give drink" (no G-stem) (§6)
ŠT	verb, "to put, place" (G QATALA *šāta*, YAQTULU *yašītu*) (§3)
ŠTY	verb, "to drink" (G QATALA *šatiya* / *šatî* , YAQTULU *yištayu* / *yištû*) (§6)
šumu	noun, masc., "name" (dual *šumatā*, pl. *šumātu*) (§5)
taḥmu	noun, masc., "message," "word" (§2)
taḥta	preposition, "under" (§3)
tamūnu	noun, masc., "body," "frame" (§8)
tamūtatu	noun, fem., "shipwreck" (§6)
tišʿu	numeral, "nine" (§7)
tôku	noun, masc., "midst," i.e., place that is within (§7)
TRḪ	verb, "to marry" (G QATALA *taraḫa*, YAQTULU *yitraḫu*) (§4)
ṭābu	adjective, "good" (§2)

ṯalāṯu	numeral, "three" (§7)
ṯamānû/iyu	numeral, "eight" (§7)
ṯamma	adverb, "there" (also *ṯammāna*, *ṯammāniya*, *ṯammati*) (§5)
ṮB	verb, "to return" (G QATALA *ṯāba*, YAQTULU *yaṯūbu*) (§3)
ṯinayā/ṯinâ	numeral, "two" (§7)
ṯiqlu	noun, masc., "shekel" (§4)
ṯiṯṯu	numeral, "six" (§7)
ṮNY	verb, "to say, repeat" (G QATALA *ṯaniya* / *ṯanî*, YAQTULU *yaṯniyu* / *yaṯnû*) (§8)
ṮPṬ	verb, "to rule, judge" (G QATALA *ṯapaṭa*, YAQTULU *yaṯputu*) (§3)
ṯulḥanu	noun, masc., "table" (pl. *ṯulḥanātu*) (§6)
wa	coordinating particle and phrase-edge marker (cf. §4.7), "and" (§1)
yadu	noun, masc. or fem., "hand" (dual *yadāma*; pl. *yadātu*); preposition, "together with" (§2)
yammu	noun, masc., "sea"; personal name "Yam" (§5)
yasīmu	adjective, "beautiful" (§7)
YDʿ	verb, "to know" (G QATALA *yadaʿa*, YAQTULU *yidaʿu*) (§1)
YḪL	verb, N "to be discouraged" (no G-stem) (§7)
yômu	noun, masc., "day" (§2)
YPY	verb, "to be beautiful" (G QATALA *yapiya* / *yapî*, YAQTULU *yipayu* / *yipû*); Rt "to beautify oneself" (§8)
YRD	verb, "to descend, go down" (G QATALA *yarada*, YAQTULU *yaridu*) (§7)
YṢʾ	verb, "to go out" (G QATALA *yaṣaʾa*, YAQTULU *yaṣiʾu*) (§2)
YṢQ	verb, "to pour out" (G QATALA *yaṣaqa*, YAQTULU *yaṣṣuqu*) (§7)
YTḤ	verb, D "to hasten" (no G-stem) (§7)
YTN	verb, "to give" (G QATALA *yatana*, YAQTULU *yatinu*); Š "to send, make delivery" (YAQTULU *yišêtinu*) (§8)
YṮB	verb, "to sit, to dwell" (G QATALA *yaṯiba*, YAQTULU *yaṯibu*) (§7)
zabūlu	noun, masc., "prince" (§7)

English to Ugaritic Glossary

account	*sipru*, noun, masc. (§6)
acquire	QNY, verb (G QATALA *qanaya* / *qanâ*, YAQTULU *yaqniyu* / *yaqnû*) (§6)
after	*ʾaṯra*, preposition (§3)
all	*kalīlu*, noun, masc., only sg. (§3); *kullu*, quantifier, masc., only sg. (§3)
ancestral being	*rapaʾu*, noun, masc. (§2)
ancient	*qadmiyyu*, adjective (§3)
and	*ʾū*, conjunction (§5); *wa*, coordinating particle and phrase-edge marker (cf. §4.7) (§1)
anger	*ʾappu*, noun, masc. (§4)
answer	ʿNY, verb (G QATALA *ʿanaya* / *ʿanâ*, YAQTULU *yaʿniyu* / *yaʿnû*) (§6)
approach	NGŠ, verb (G QATALA *nagaša*, YAQTULU *yiggašu*) (§4); QRB, verb (G QATALA *qaraba*, YAQTULU *yiqrabu*) (§1)
as	*ka*, *kama*, preposition (§4)
assembly	*qibūṣu*, noun, masc. (§3)
Baʿlu	*baʿlu*, personal name (§1)
Baal	*baʿlu*, personal name (§1)
be	KN, verb (G QATALA *kāna*, YAQTULU *yakūnu*); *ʾiṯu*, indeclinable copula (§1)
be high	RM, verb (G QATALA *rāma*, YAQTULU *yarīmu*) (§2)
be beautiful	YPY, verb (G QATALA *yapiya* / *yapî*, YAQTULU *yipayu* / *yipû*) (§8)
be discouraged	YḤL, verb, N (no G-stem) (§7)
be full	MLʾ, verb (G QATALA *maliʾa*, YAQTULU *yimlaʾu*) (§8)
be great	RBB, verb (G QATALA *rabba*, YAQTULU *yarubbu*) (§5)

be well	ŠLM, verb (G QATALA *šalima*, YAQTULU *yišlamu*) (§1)
beautiful	*yasīmu*, adjective (§7)
beautify oneself	YPY, verb, Rt (see "be beautiful") (§8)
because	*kī*, *kīya*, *kīma*, conjunction, circumstantial (§5)
become great	RBB, verb (G QATALA *rabba*, YAQTULU *yarubbu*) (§5)
become high	RM, verb (G QATALA *rāma*, YAQTULU *yarīmu*) (§2)
before	*lê*, *lêya*, preposition (§1); *lê panî*, complex preposition (§2)
behind	*ʾaṯra*, preposition (§3)
behold	*hanna*, interjection (also *hannana*, *hannaniya*, *halli*, *hatti*, *halliha*, *hallima*, *hallina*, *halliniya*) (§5)
bend down	ŠPL, verb (G QATALA *šapala*, YAQTULU *yišpalu*) (§7)
between	*bêna*, preposition (§2)
bird	*ʿuṣṣūru*, noun, fem. (§3)
bless	BRK, verb, D (no G-stem) (§4)
body	*tamūnu*, noun, masc. (§8)
bovid	*ʾalpu*, noun, masc. (§2)
boy	*ǵalmu*, noun, masc. (§5)
break apart	DLP, verb (G QATALA *dalapa*, YAQTULU *yadlupu*) (§8)
brother	*ʾaḫû*, noun, masc. (pl. *ʾaḫḫûma*) (§2)
burn [something]	BʿR, verb, D (no G-stem) (§4)
by	*bi*, *biya*, preposition (= agent or instrument) (cf. §5.7) (§1)
call	QRʾ, verb (G QATALA *qaraʾa*, YAQTULU *yiqraʾu*) (§1)
certainly	*la*, particle (§8)
chair	*kaḥṯu*, noun, masc. (§7); *kussaʾu*, noun, fem. (§5)
clan	*qibūṣu*, noun, masc. (§3)
collapse	MK, verb (G QATALA *māka*, YAQTULU *yamūku*) (§7)
come	ʾTY, verb (G QATALA *ʾatawa* / *ʾatâ*, YAQTULU *yiʾtayu* / *yiʾatayu* / *yiʾtû* / *yiʾatû*) (§6)
dance	RQṢ, verb, Gt (no G-stem) (§8)
daughter	*bittu*, noun, fem. (pl. *banātu*) (§2)
day	*yômu*, noun, masc. (§2)
descend	YRD, verb (G QATALA *yarada*, YAQTULU *yaridu*) (§7)

destroy	ʾBD, verb, D (no G-stem) (§4)
Didanu	*didānu*, noun (mythic figure, founder of Ugarit?) (§8)
die	MT, verb (G QATALA *mīta*, YAQTULU *yamūtu*) (§2)
distant place	*marḥaqtu*, noun, fem. (§5)
document	*sipru*, noun, masc. (§6)
dog	*kalbu*, noun, masc. (§8)
dominion	*darkatu*, noun, fem. (§7)
drag [something]	QṮṮ, verb (G QATALA *qaṯṯa*, YAQTULU *yaquṯṯu*); QṮṮ, verb, R (§8)
drink	ŠTY, verb (G QATALA *šatiya / šatî*, YAQTULU *yištayu / yištû*) (§6)
drinking club	*marziḥu*, noun, masc. (§6)
drive away	GRŠ, verb (G QATALA *garaša*, YAQTULU *yagrušu*) (§3)
dust	*ʿaparu*, noun, masc. (§7)
dwell	YṮB, verb (G QATALA *yaṯiba*, YAQTULU *yaṯibu*) (§7)
each	*kullu*, quantifier, masc., only sg. (§3)
ear	*ʾudnu*, noun, fem. (§4)
earth	*ʾarṣu*, noun, fem. (§6)
eat	LḤM, verb (G QATALA *laḥama*, YAQTULU *yilḥamu*) (§2)
eight	*ṯamānû/iyu*, numeral (§7)
El	*ʾilu*, personal name (§1)
enemy	*ʾêbu*, noun, masc. (§3)
enter	ʿRB, verb (G QATALA *ʿaraba*, YAQTULU *yiʿrabu*) (§1)
entirety	*kalīlu*, noun, masc., only sg. (§3)
establish	KN, verb, Š (see "be") (§7)
every	*kullu*, quantifier, masc., only sg. (§3)
everything	*kalīlu*, noun, masc., only sg. (§3)
explain	BǴY, verb (G QATALA *baǵaya / baǵâ*, YAQTULU *yibǵayu / yibǵû*) (§6)
face	*panûma*, pl. noun, masc. (always plural) (§2)
fall	MK, verb (G QATALA *māka*, YAQTULU *yamūku*) (§7); NPL, verb (G QATALA *napala*, YAQTULU *yappulu*) (§4); QL, verb (G QATALA *qāla*, YAQTULU *yaqīlu*) (§2)
[from] far away	*marḥaqtu*, adverb (§5)
father	*ʾabû*, noun, masc. (§2)

finger	*ʾuṣbaʿu*, noun, fem. (pl. *ʾuṣbaʿātu*) (§8)
five	*ḫamišu*, numeral (§7)
flee	NS, verb (G QATALA *nāsa*, YAQTULU *yanūsu*) (§6)
food	*ʾaklu*, noun, masc. (§2)
foot	*paʿnu*, noun, fem. (dl. *paʿnāma*) (§4)
four	*ʾarbaʿu*, numeral (§7)
for	*bi*, *biya*, preposition (=exchange) (cf. §5.7) (§1); *lê*, *lêya*, preposition (§1)
frame	*tamūnu*, noun, masc. (§8)
from	*bi*, *biya*, preposition (cf. §5.7) (§1); *lê*, *lêya*, preposition (§1)
give	YTN, verb (G QATALA *yatana*, YAQTULU *yatinu*)
give drink	ŠQY, verb, D (no G-stem) (§6)
go	HLK, verb (G QATALA *halaka*, YAQTULU *yaliku*) (§7)
go down	YRD, verb (G QATALA *yarada*, YAQTULU *yaridu*) (§7)
go out	YṢʾ, verb (G QATALA *yaṣaʾa*, YAQTULU *yaṣiʾu*) (§2)
go slack	NǴṢ, verb, N (see "shake [something]") (§8)
go through	MRR, verb (G QATALA *marra*, YAQTULU *yamurru*) (§8)
go up	ʿLY, verb (G QATALA *ʿalaya* / *ʿalâ*, YAQTULU *yaʿliyu* / *yaʿlû*)
god	*ʾilu*, noun, masc. (§1)
good	*ṭābu*, adjective (§2)
gracious	*naʿīmu*, adjective (§4)
great	*rabbu*, adjective (§4)
guard	NǴR, verb (G QATALA *naǵara*, YAQTULU *yaǵǵuru*) (§4)
hand	*yadu*, noun, masc. or fem. (dual *yadāma*; pl. *yadātu*) (§2)
hasten	YTḤ, verb, D (no G-stem) (§7)
he	*huwa*, pronoun (oblique *huwati*) (§3)
hear	ŠMʿ, verb (G QATALA *šamaʿa*, YAQTULU *yišmaʿu*) (§3)
heavens	*šamûma*, noun, masc., only pl. (§6)
here	*hanna*, adverb (also *hannana*, *hannaniya*, *halli*, *hatti*, *halliha*, *hallima*, *hallina*, *halliniya*) (§5)
hero	*ǵazru*, noun, masc. (§3)

hold	ʾḪD, verb (G QATALA *ʾaḫada*, YAQTULU *yaʾḫudu* or *yaʾuḫudu*) (§4)
holiness	*qudšu*, noun, masc. (§8)
holy place	*qudšu*, noun, masc. (§8)
holy thing	*qudšu*, noun, masc. (§8)
horn	*qarnu*, noun, fem. (§4)
house	*bêtu*, noun, masc. (pl. *bahatūma*) (§1)
household	*bêtu*, noun, masc. (pl. *bahatūma*) (§1)
how?	*ʾêka*, *ʾêkaya*, interrogative particle (§4)
humankind	*našūma*, noun, masc., pl. (§8)
hundred	*miʾtu*, numeral, fem. (pl. *miʾātu*) (§7)
I	*ʾanāku*, *ʾanā*, pronoun (§3)
if	*ʾimma*, *himma*, particle (§4); *kī*, *kīya*, *kīma*, conjunction, circumstantial (§5)
illuminate	BʿR, verb, Š (no G-stem) (§4)
Ilu	*ʾilu*, personal name (§1)
in	*bi*, *biya*, preposition (cf. §5.7) (§1)
in the authority of	*bîdi*, *bîdê*, complex preposition (§2)
in the hand(s) of	*bîdi*, *bîdê*, complex preposition (§2)
indeed	*kī*, *kīya*, *kīma*, conjunction, emphatic (§5)
inheritance	*naḥlatu*, noun, fem. (§8)
invoke	QBʾ, verb (G QATALA *qabaʾa*, YAQTULU *yaqbiʾu*) (§8)
joint	*pinnatu*, noun, fem. (§8)
judge	ṮPṬ, verb (G QATALA *ṯapaṭa*, YAQTULU *yaṯpuṭu*) (§3)
king	*mallku*, noun, masc. (§1)
Kirta	personal name, masc. (indeclinable) (§3)
know	YDʿ, verb (G QATALA *yadaʿa*, YAQTULU *yidaʿu*) (§1)
lady	*ʾadattu*, noun, fem. (pl. *ʾadānātu*) (§6)
land	*ʾarṣu*, noun, fem. (§6)
Lawasanda	*lawasanda*, proper noun, place (indeclinable) (§5)
leg	*ʾišdu*, noun, fem. (§4)
lie down	ŠKB, verb (G QATALA *šakaba*, YAQTULU *yiškabu*) (§3)
lightning	*baraqu*, noun, masc. (§5)
like	*ka*, *kama*, preposition (§4)
long duration of time	*ʿālamu*, noun, masc. (§3)
look	*hanna*, interjection (also *hannana*, *hannaniya*, *halli*, *hatti*, *halliha*, *hallima*, *hallina*, *halliniya*) (§5)

lord	*ʾadānu*, noun, masc. (§6); *baʿlu*, noun, masc. (§1)
love	ʾHB, verb (G QATALA *ʾahiba*, YAQTULU *yaʾhubu* or *yaʾuhubu*)
love strongly	ʾHB, verb, D (see "love") (§4)
lubushu	*lubūšu*, noun, masc., a basic type of garment (§7)
mace	*ṣimdu*, noun, masc. (§5)
magnificent	*ʾaduru*, adjective (§4)
maidservant	*ʾamatu*, noun, fem. (§1)
make a vow	NDR, verb (G QATALA *nadara*, YAQTULU *yadduru*) (§4)
make delivery	YTN, verb, Š (YAQTULU *yišêtinu*) (see "give") (§8)
man	*mutu*, noun, masc. (§4); *našu*, noun, masc., only attested as pl. (see "humankind") (§8)
marry	TRḪ, verb (G QATALA *taraḫa*, YAQTULU *yitraḫu*) (§4)
master	*baʿlu*, noun, masc. (§1)
matter	*rigmu*, noun, masc. (§1)
message	*taḥmu*, noun, masc. (§2)
middle	*qirbu*, noun, masc. (§6)
midst	*qirbu*, noun, masc. (§6); *tôku*, noun, masc., i.e., place that is within (§7)
mother	*ʾummu*, noun, fem. (pl. *ʾummahātu*) (§2)
mountain	*ǵūru*, noun, masc. (§5)
mourn	BKY, verb (G QATALA *bakaya* / *bakâ*, YAQTULU *yabkiyu* / *yabkû*) (§8)
mouth	*pû*, noun, masc. (§4)
much	*maʾadu*, adjective (§3)
name	*šumu*, noun, masc. (dual *šumatā*, pl. *šumātu*) (§5)
new	*ḥadaṯu*, adjective (§3)
nine	*tišʿu*, numeral (§7)
nose	*ʾappu*, noun, masc. (dual "nostrils") (§4)
not	*ʾal*, particle, negation with irrealis verbs (§6); *lā*, particle, negation (§1)
oil	*šamnu*, noun, masc. (§4)
on	*bi*, *biya*, preposition (cf. §5.7) (§1)
one	*ʾaḥḥadu*, numeral (§7); *ʿaštayu*, numeral (typically as part of the teen numeral "eleven") (§7)
or	*ʾimma*, *himma*, conjunction (§4); *ʾô*, conjunction (§5)

ox	*ʾalpu*, noun, masc. (§2)
palace	*hêkalu*, noun, masc. (§6)
pass	MRR, verb (G QATALA *marra*, YAQTULU *yamurru*) (§8)
pay	NSʿ, verb (G QATALA *nasaʿa*, YAQTULU *yissaʿu*) (§5)
peace	*šalāmu*, noun, masc. (§1)
perish	ʾBD, verb, Gt (no G-stem) (§4)
person	*našu*, noun, masc., only attested as pl. (see "humankind") (§8)
place	ŠT, verb (G QATALA *šāta*, YAQTULU *yašītu*) (§3)
pleasant	*naʿīmu*, adjective (§4)
plus	*kubda*, postposition (used in compound number phrases) (§7)
pour out	YṢQ, verb (G QATALA *yaṣaqa*, YAQTULU *yaṣṣuqu*) (§7)
powerful	*ʾaduru*, adjective (§4)
prepare [something]	NḤT, verb (G QATALA *naḥata*, YAQTULU *yiḥḥatu*); NḤT, verb, D (§5)
present offering	ʿLY, verb, Št (see "go up") (§6)
prince	*zabūlu*, noun, masc. (§7)
proclaim	PʿR, verb (G QATALA *paʿara*, YAQTULU *yipʿaru*) (§5)
put	ŠT, verb (G QATALA *šāta*, YAQTULU *yašītu*) (§3)
queen	*malkatu*, noun, fem. (§1)
raptor	*našru*, noun, masc. (§8)
repeat	ṮNY, verb (G QATALA *ṯaniya* / *ṯanî*, YAQTULU *yaṯniyu* / *yaṯnû*) (§8)
request	ŠʾL, verb (G QATALA *šaʾila*, YAQTULU *yišʾalu*) (§3)
return	KRR, verb (G QATALA *karra*, YAQTULU *yakurru*) (§8); ṮB, verb (G QATALA *ṯāba*, YAQTULU *yaṯūbu*) (§3)
river	*naharu*, noun, masc. (§2)
rod	*ḫaṭṭu*, noun, masc. (§1)
rule	*darkatu*, noun, fem. (§7); ṮPṬ, verb (G QATALA *ṯapaṭa*, YAQTULU *yaṯpuṭu*) (§3)
sacrifice	*dabḥu*, noun, masc. (§3); DBḤ, verb (G QATALA *dabaḥa*, YAQTULU *yidbaḥu*) (§3)
say	RGM, verb (G QATALA *ragama*, YAQTULU *yargumu*) (§1); ṮNY, verb (G QATALA *ṯaniya* / *ṯanî*, YAQTULU *yaṯniyu* / *yaṯnû*) (§8)

sea	*yammu*, noun, masc. (§5)
seize	ʾḪD, verb (G QATALA *ʾaḫada*, YAQTULU *yaʾḫudu* or *yaʾuḫudu*) (§4)
send	YTN, verb, Š (YAQTULU *yišêtinu*) (see "give") (§8)
servant	*ʿabdu*, noun, masc. (§1); *ʾamatu*, noun, fem. (§1)
seven	*šabʿu*, numeral (§7)
shade	*rapaʾu*, noun, masc. (§2)
shake [something]	MRR, verb, R (see "pass" or "go through") (§8); NǴṢ, verb (G QATALA *naǵaṣa*, YAQTULU *yaǵǵuṣu*) (§8)
Shamumanu	*šamumānu*, personal name, masc., diptotic (§5)
she	*hiya*, pronoun (oblique *hiyati*) (§3)
shekel	*ṯiqlu*, noun, masc. (§4)
shine	NR, verb (G QATALA *nāra*, YAQTULU *yanūru*) (§2)
shipwreck	*tamūtatu*, noun, fem. (§6)
shoulder	*katipo*, noun, fem. (§7)
silver	*kaspu*, noun, masc. (§4)
sister	*ʾaḫâtu*, noun, fem. (pl. *ʾaḫḫâtu*) (§2)
sit	YṮB, verb (G QATALA *yaṯiba*, YAQTULU *yaṯibu*) (§7)
six	*ṯiṯṯu*, numeral (§7)
slaughter	DBḤ, verb (G QATALA *dabaḥa*, YAQTULU *yidbaḥu*) (§3)
slump	DLP, verb (G QATALA *dalapa*, YAQTULU *yadlupu*) (§8)
smite	MḪṢ, verb (G QATALA *maḫaṣa*, YAQTULU *yimḫaṣu*) (§3)
son	*binu*, noun, masc. (pl. *banūma*) (§2)
staff	*ḫaṭṭu*, noun, masc. (§1)
stone	*ʾabnu*, noun, fem. (§8)
strength	*ʿuzzu*, noun, masc. (§2)
strike	HLM, verb (G QATALA *halama*, YAQTULU *yallumu*) (§7); MḪṢ, verb (G QATALA *maḫaṣa*, YAQTULU *yimḫaṣu*) (§3)
strong	*ʿazzu*, adjective (§2)
summon	QBʾ, verb (G QATALA *qabaʾa*, YAQTULU *yaqbiʾu*) (§8)
sun	*šapšu*, noun, fem. (§1)
table	*ṯulḥanu*, noun, masc. (pl. *ṯulḥanātu*) (§6)

take	ʾḪD, verb (G QATALA *ʾaḫada*, YAQTULU *yaʾḫudu* or *yaʾuḫudu*) (§4); LQḤ, verb (G QATALA *laqaḥa*, YAQTULU *yiqqaḥu*) (§4)
ten	*ʿašru*, numeral (§7)
test [someone]	NSY, verb (G QATALA *nasaya* / *nasâ* YAQTULU *yas-siyu* / *yassû*) (§8)
try	NSY, verb, Gt (see "test [someone]") (§8)
that	*du*, relative particle (§5); *dū*, relative marker (§5); *kī*, *kīya*, *kīma*, conjunction, complementizer (§5)
there	*ṯamma*, adverb (also *ṯammāna*, *ṯammāniya*, *ṯammati*) (§5)
there is not	*ʾênu*, *ʾênuna*, indeclinable negated copula (§2)
they	*humā*, pronoun (oblique *humāti*) (§3); *humū*, pronoun (plural) (oblique *humūti*) (§3)
thing	*rigmu*, noun, masc. (§1)
this	*hannadū*, demonstrative pronoun (§5)
thousand	*ʾalpu*, numeral, masc. (§7)
three	*ṯalāṯu*, numeral (§7)
throne	*kussaʾu*, noun, fem. (§5)
thus	*kāma*, *kamāma*, adverb (§5)
to	*bi*, *biya*, preposition (cf. §5.7) (§1); *ʿimma*, *ʿimmānu*, preposition (§1); *lê*, *lêya*, preposition (§1)
together with	*yadu*, preposition (§2)
tree	*ʿiṣu*, noun, masc. (§8)
tremble	NǴṢ, verb, N (see "shake [something]") (§8)
turn	KRR, verb (G QATALA *karra*, YAQTULU *yakurru*)
twist	KRR, verb, R (see "turn" or "return") (§8)
two	*ṯinayā*/*ṯinâ*, numeral (§7)
two of them	*humā*, pronoun (dual) (oblique *humāti*) (§3)
(two of) you	*ʾattumā*, pronoun (dual) (§3)
under	*taḥta*, preposition (§3)
understand	BN, verb (G QATALA *bāna*, YAQTULU *yabīnu*) (§5)
up to	*ʿadê*, preposition (§3)
venture	NSY, verb, Gt (see "test [someone]" (§8)
very	*maʾda*, adverb (acc. of noun *maʾdu*, "muchness") (§3)
voice	*gû*, noun, masc. (§4)
wash	RḤṢ, verb (G QATALA *raḥaṣa*, YAQTULU *yirḥaṣu*) (§8)

weaken	DLP, verb (G QATALA *dalapa*, YAQTULU *yadlupu*) (§8)
weep	BKY, verb (G QATALA *bakaya* / *bakâ*, YAQTULU *yabkiyu* / *yabkû*) (§8)
well-being	*šalāmu*, noun, masc. (§1)
what?	*ma*, pronoun (only extant in *lê ma*, "why?") (§6)
whatever	*manna*, pronoun (also *mannaka*, *mannama*) (§6)
when	*kī*, *kīya*, *kīma*, conjunction, circumstantial (§5)
where	*ʾana*, adverb (§7)
wherever	*ʾana*, adverb (§7)
which	*du*, relative particle (§5); *dū*, relative marker (§5)
whisper	*laḫaštu*, noun, fem. (§8)
who	*du*, relative particle (§5); *dū*, relative marker (§5); *mī*, pronoun (§6)
why?	*lê ma* (see "what?") (§6)
with	*ʿimma*, *ʿimmānu*, preposition (§1)
woman	*ʾaṯṯatu*, noun, fem. (§4)
wood	*ʿiṣu*, noun, masc. (§8)
word	*huwatu*, noun, fem. (§8); *rigmu*, noun, masc. (§1); *taḥmu*, noun, masc. (§2)
worthy	*ʾaduru*, adjective (§4)
y'all	*ʾattumu*, pronoun (plural) (§3)
Yam	*yammu*, personal name (§5)
you	*ʾatta*, pronoun (masc. sg.) (§3); *ʾatti*, pronoun (fem. sg.) (§3); *ʾattumu*, pronoun (plural) (§3)
young man	*ǵazru*, noun, masc. (§3)

Paradigms

Nominals

Case Endings

<table>
<tr><th></th><th></th><th colspan="2">Masculine</th><th colspan="2">Feminine</th></tr>
<tr><th></th><th></th><th>free form</th><th>bound form</th><th>free form</th><th>bound form</th></tr>
<tr><td rowspan="3">Sg</td><td>Nom</td><td colspan="2">–u</td><td colspan="2">–atu</td></tr>
<tr><td>Gen/Voc</td><td colspan="2">–i</td><td colspan="2">–ati</td></tr>
<tr><td>Acc</td><td colspan="2">–a</td><td colspan="2">–ata</td></tr>
<tr><td rowspan="2">Dual</td><td>Nom</td><td>–āma</td><td>–ā</td><td>–atāma</td><td>–atā</td></tr>
<tr><td>Acc/Gen/Voc (Obl)</td><td>–êma</td><td>–ê</td><td>–atêma</td><td>–atê</td></tr>
<tr><td rowspan="2">Pl</td><td>Nom</td><td>–ūma</td><td>–ū</td><td colspan="2">–ātu</td></tr>
<tr><td>Acc/Gen/Voc (Obl)</td><td>–īma</td><td>–ī</td><td colspan="2">–āti</td></tr>
</table>

Nouns: *malku*, “king,” and *malkatu*, “queen”

<table>
<tr><th></th><th></th><th colspan="2">Masculine</th><th colspan="2">Feminine</th></tr>
<tr><th></th><th></th><th>free form</th><th>bound form</th><th>free form</th><th>bound form</th></tr>
<tr><td rowspan="3">Sg</td><td>Nom</td><td colspan="2">malku</td><td colspan="2">malkatu</td></tr>
<tr><td>Gen/Voc</td><td colspan="2">malki</td><td colspan="2">malkati</td></tr>
<tr><td>Acc</td><td colspan="2">malka</td><td colspan="2">malkata</td></tr>
<tr><td rowspan="2">Dual</td><td>Nom</td><td>malkāma</td><td>malkā</td><td>malkatāma</td><td>malkatā</td></tr>
<tr><td>Acc/Gen/Voc (Obl)</td><td>malkêma</td><td>malkê</td><td>malkatêma</td><td>malkatê</td></tr>
<tr><td rowspan="2">Pl</td><td>Nom</td><td>malakūma</td><td>malakū</td><td colspan="2">malakātu</td></tr>
<tr><td>Acc/Gen/Voc (Obl)</td><td>malakīma</td><td>malakī</td><td colspan="2">malakāti</td></tr>
</table>

Adjectives: *ṭābu*, "good"

		Masculine		Feminine	
		free form	bound form	free form	bound form
Sg	Nom	*ṭābu*		*ṭābatu*	
	Gen/Voc	*ṭābi*		*ṭābati*	
	Acc	*ṭāba*		*ṭābata*	
Dual	Nom	*ṭābāma*	*ṭābā*	*ṭābatāma*	*ṭābatā*
	Acc/Gen/Voc (Obl)	*ṭābêma*	*ṭābê*	*ṭābatêma*	*ṭābatê*
Pl	Nom	*ṭābūma*	*ṭābū*	*ṭābātu*	
	Acc/Gen/Voc (Obl)	*ṭābīma*	*ṭābī*	*ṭābāti*	

Relative Markers

	Masc Sg	Fem Sg	Com Pl
Nom	*dū*	*dātu*	*dūtu*
Gen/Voc	*dī*	*dāti*	*dūti*
Acc	*dā*	*dāta*	

Demonstrative Pronouns

	Masc Sg	Fem Sg	Com Pl
Nom	*hannadū*	*hannadātu*	*hannadūtu*
Gen/Voc	*hannadī*	*hannadāti*	*hannadūti*
Acc	*hannadā*	*hannadāta*	

Pronouns

Nominative Independent Pronouns

1cs	*ʾanāku* / *ʾanā*	"I"
2ms	*ʾatta*	"you"
2fs	*ʾatti*	"you"
2cd	*ʾattumā*	"(the two of) you"

2cp	*ʾattumu*	"you," "y'all"
3ms	*huwa*	"he"
3fs	*hiya*	"she"
3cd	*humā*	"they," "the two of them"
3cp	*humū*	"they"

Oblique Independent Pronouns

3ms	*huwati*	"him"
3fs	*hiyati*	"her"
3cd	*humāti*	"them," "the two of them"
3cp	*humūti*	"them"

Suffixed Pronouns with Nouns

1cs	*-ya* (nom *-ya* or *-ī*)	1cd	*-nāyā*	1cp	*-na*
2ms	*-ka*	2cd	*-kumā*	2mp	*-kumu*
2fs	*-ki*			2fp	*-kuna*
3ms	*-hu*	3cd	*-humā*	3mp	*-humu*
3fs	*-ha*			3fp	*-huna*

Suffixed Pronouns with Prepositions

1cs	*-ya*	1cd	*-nāyā*	1cp	*-na*
2ms	*-ka*	2cd	*-kumā*	2mp	*-kumu*
2fs	*-ki*			2fp	*-kuna*
3ms	*-hu*	3cd	*-humā*	3mp	*-humu*
3fs	*-ha*			3fp	*-huna*

Suffixed Pronouns with Verbs

1cs	*-nī*	1cd	*-nāyā*	1cp	*-na*
2ms	*-ka*	2cd	*-kumā*	2mp	*-kumu*
2fs	*-ki*			2fp	*-kuna*

3ms	*-hu*	3cd	*-humā*	3mp	*-humu*
	-annu				
	-annannu				
3fs	*-ha*			3fp	*-huna*

Cardinal Numerals

Value	Masculine	Feminine	Value of Plural
1	*ʾaḥḥadu* *ʿaštayu* / *ʿaštû*	*ʾaḥḥattu*	—
2	*ṯinayā* / *ṯinâ* (dual nom)	*ṯinêtā* / *ṯittâ* (dual nom)	—
3	*ṯalāṯu*	*ṯalāṯatu*	30
4	*ʾarbaʿu*	*ʾarbaʿatu*	40
5	*ḫamišu*	*ḫamišatu*	50
6	*ṯiṯṯu*	*ṯiṯṯatu*	60
7	*šabʿu*	*šabʿatu*	70
8	*ṯamāniyu* / *ṯamānû*	*ṯamānîtu*	80
9	*tišʿu*	*tišʿatu*	90
10	*ʿašru*	*ʿašratu*	20

Verb Endings

	QATALA	YAQTULU		Imperative
	suffix	prefix	suffix	suffix
3ms	*–a*	*y–*	*–u*	
3fs	*–at*	*t–*	*–u*	
2ms	*–ta*	*t–*	*–u*	
2fs	*–ti*	*t–*	*–īna*	*–ī*
1cs	*–tu*	*ʾ–*	*–u*	

3md	*–ā*	*t–*	*–ā(na)*	
3fd	*–atā*	*t–*	*–ā(na)*	
2cd	*–tumā*	*t–*	*–ā(na)*	*–ā*
1cs	*–nāyā*	*n–*	*–ā*	
3mp	*–ū*	*t–*	*–ū(na)*	
3fp	*–ā*	*t–*	*–na*	
2mp	*–tumu*	*t–*	*–ū(na)*	*–ū*
2fp	*–tina*	*t–*	*–na*	*–ā*
1cp	*–nū*	*n–*	*–u*	

Verb Patterns

	QATALA	YAQTULU	Jussive	Imperative	Participle	Infinitive
G-stem	*qatala*	*yaqtulu*	*yaqtul*	*qutul*	*qātilu*	*qatālu*
	qatula	*yaqtilu*	*yaqtil*	*qitil*		
	qatila	*yiqtalu*	*yiqtal*	*qatal*		
Gt-stem	*ʾiqtatila*	*yiqtatilu*	*yiqtatil*			
Gp-stem	*qutala*	*yuqtala*	*yuqtal*		*qatūlu*	
N-stem	*naqtala*	*yiqqatilu*	*yiqqatil*	*ʾiqqatil*		
D-stem	*qittala*	*yaqattilu*	*yaqattil*	*qattil*	*muqattilu*	
tD-stem	*taqattala*	*yitqattalu*	*yitqattal*			
Dp-stem	*quttila*	*yuqattilu*	*yuqattil*		*muqattalu*	
Š-stem	*šaqtila*	*yašaqtilu*	*yašaqtil*	*šaqtil*	*mušaqtilu*	
Št-stem	*ʾištaqtila*	*yištaqtilu*	*yištaqtil*			
Šp-stem	*šuqtala*	*yušaqtalu*	*yušaqtal*		*mušaqtalu*	
L-stem	*qālala*	*yaqālilu*	*yaqālil*			
R-stem	*qalqala*	*yaqalqilu*	*yaqalqil*			
Rt-stem	*ʾiqtaltala*	*yiqtataltilu*	*yiqtataltil*			
tR-stem	*taqalqala*	*yitaqtaltilu*	*yitaqtaltil*			

G-Stem QATALA Verbs

RGM, "to say": *a* theme vowel

3ms	*ragama*	"he said"
3fs	*ragamat*	"she said"
2ms	*ragamta*	"you said"
2fs	*ragamti*	"you said"
1cs	*ragamtu*	"I said"
3md	*ragamā*	"the two of them said"
3fd	*ragamatā*	"the two of them said"
2cd	*ragamtumā*	"the two of you said"
1cd	*ragamnāyā*	"the two of us said"
3mp	*ragamū*	"they said"
3fp	*ragamā*	"they said"
2mp	*ragamtumu*	"you said"
2fp	*ragamtina*	"you said"
1cp	*ragamnū*	"we said"

ŠLM, "to be well": *i* theme vowel

3ms	*šalima*	"he is well"
3fs	*šalimat*	"she is well"
2ms	*šalimta*	"you are well"
2fs	*šalimti*	"you are well"
1cs	*šalimtu*	"I am well"
3md	*šalimā*	"the two of them are well"
3fd	*šalimatā*	"the two of them are well"
2cd	*šalimtumā*	"the two of you are well"
1cd	*šalimnāyā*	"the two of us are well"
3mp	*šalimū*	"they are well"
3fp	*šalimā*	"they are well"
2mp	*šalimtumu*	"you are well"
2fp	*šalimtina*	"you are well"
1cp	*šalimnū*	"we are well"

G-Stem YAQTULU Verbs

ŠLM, "to be well": *a* theme vowel

3ms	*yišlamu*	"he is well"
3fs	*tišlamu*	"she is well"
2ms	*tišlamu*	"you are well"
2fs	*tišlamīna*	"you are well"
1cs	*ʾišlamu*	"I am well"
3md	*tišlamā*(*na*)	"the two of them are well"
3fd	*tišlamā*(*na*)	"the two of them are well"
2cd	*tišlamā*(*na*)	"the two of you are well"
1cd	*nišlamā*	"the two of us are well"
3mp	*tišlamū*(*na*)	"they are well"
3fp	*tišlamna*	"they are well"
2mp	*tišlamū*(*na*)	"you are well"
2fp	*tišlamna*	"you are well"
1cp	*nišlamu*	"we are well"

QBʾ, "to invoke": *i* theme vowel

3ms	*yaqbiʾu*	"he invokes"
3fs	*taqbiʾu*	"she invokes"
2ms	*taqbiʾu*	"you invoke"
2fs	*taqbiʾīna*	"you invoke"
1cs	*ʾaqbiʾu*	"I invoke"
3md	*taqbiʾā*(*na*)	"the two of them invoke"
3fd	*taqbiʾā*(*na*)	"the two of them invoke"
2cd	*taqbiʾā*(*na*)	"the two of you invoke"
1cd	*naqbiʾā*	"the two of us invoke"
3mp	*taqbiʾū*(*na*)	"they invoke"
3fp	*taqbiʾna*	"they invoke"
2mp	*taqbiʾū*(*na*)	"you invoke"
2fp	*taqbiʾna*	"you invoke"
1cp	*naqbiʾu*	"we invoke"

RGM, “to say”: *u* theme vowel

3ms	*yargumu*	“he says”
3fs	*targumu*	“she says”
2ms	*targumu*	“you say”
2fs	*targumīna*	“you say”
1cs	*ʾargumu*	“I say”
3md	*targumā(na)*	“the two of them say”
3fd	*targumā(na)*	“the two of them say”
2cd	*targumā(na)*	“the two of you say”
1cd	*nargumā*	“the two of us say”
3mp	*targumū(na)*	“they say”
3fp	*targumna*	“they say”
2mp	*targumū(na)*	“you say”
2fp	*targumna*	“you say”
1cp	*nargumu*	“we say”

G-Stem Jussive Verbs

ŠLM, “to be well”: *a* theme vowel

3ms	*yišlam*	“may he be well”
3fs	*tišlam*	“may she be well”
2ms	*tišlam*	“may you be well”
2fs	*tišlamī*	“may you be well”
1cs	*ʾišlam*	“may I be well”
3md	*tišlamā*	“may the two of them be well”
3fd	*tišlamā*	“may the two of them be well”
2cd	*tišlamā*	“may the two of you be well”
1cd	*nišlamā*	“may the two of us be well”
3mp	*tišlamū*	“may they be well”
3fp	*tišlamna*	“may they be well”
2mp	*tišlamū*	“may you be well”
2fp	*tišlamna*	“may you be well”
1cp	*nišlam*	“may we be well”

QBʾ, "to invoke": *i* theme vowel

3ms	*yaqbiʾ*	"may he invoke"
3fs	*taqbiʾ*	"may she invoke"
2ms	*taqbiʾ*	"may you invoke"
2fs	*taqbiʾī*	"may you invoke"
1cs	*ʾaqbiʾ*	"may I invoke"
3md	*taqbiʾā*	"may the two of them invoke"
3fd	*taqbiʾā*	"may the two of them invoke"
2cd	*taqbiʾā*	"may the two of you invoke"
1cd	*naqbiʾā*	"may the two of us invoke"
3mp	*taqbiʾū*	"may they invoke"
3fp	*taqbiʾna*	"may they invoke"
2mp	*taqbiʾū*	"may you invoke"
2fp	*taqbiʾna*	"may you invoke"
1cp	*naqbiʾ*	"may we invoke"

RGM, "to say": *u* theme vowel

3ms	*yargum*	"may he say"
3fs	*targum*	"may she say"
2ms	*targum*	"may you say"
2fs	*targumī*	"may you say"
1cs	*ʾargum*	"may I say"
3md	*targumā*	"may the two of them say"
3fd	*targumā*	"may the two of them say"
2cd	*targumā*	"may the two of you say"
1cd	*nargumā*	"may the two of us say"
3mp	*targumū*	"may they say"
3fp	*targumna*	"may they say"
2mp	*targumū*	"may you say"
2fp	*targumna*	"may you say"
1cp	*nargum*	"may we say"

G-Stem Volitive Verbs

ŠLM, "to be well": *a* theme vowel

3ms	*yišlama*	"let him be well"
3fs	*tišlama*	"let her be well"
2ms	*tišlama*	"may you be well"
2fs	*tišlamī*	"may you be well"
1cs	*ʾišlama*	"let me be well"
3md	*tišlamā*	"let the two of them be well"
3fd	*tišlamā*	"let the two of them be well"
2cd	*tišlamā*	"let the two of you be well"
1cd	*nišlamā*	"let the two of us be well"
3mp	*tišlamū*	"let them be well"
3fp	*tišlamna*	"let them be well"
2mp	*tišlamū*	"may you be well"
2fp	*tišlamna*	"may you be well"
1cp	*nišlama*	"let us be well"

QBʾ, "to invoke": *i* theme vowel

3ms	*yaqbiʾa*	"let him invoke"
3fs	*taqbiʾa*	"let her invoke"
2ms	*taqbiʾa*	"may you invoke"
2fs	*taqbiʾī*	"may you invoke"
1cs	*ʾaqbiʾa*	"let me invoke"
3md	*taqbiʾā*	"let the two of them invoke"
3fd	*taqbiʾā*	"let the two of them invoke"
2cd	*taqbiʾā*	"let the two of you invoke"
1cd	*naqbiʾā*	"let the two of us invoke"
3mp	*taqbiʾū*	"let them invoke"
3fp	*taqbiʾna*	"let them invoke"
2mp	*taqbiʾū*	"may you invoke"
2fp	*taqbiʾna*	"may you invoke"
1cp	*naqbiʾa*	"let us invoke"

RGM, "to say": *u* theme vowel

3ms	*yarguma*	"let him say"
3fs	*targuma*	"let her say"
2ms	*targuma*	"may you say"
2fs	*targumī*	"may you say"
1cs	*ʾarguma*	"let me say"
3md	*targumā*	"let the two of them say"
3fd	*targumā*	"let the two of them say"
2cd	*targumā*	"let the two of you say"
1cd	*nargumā*	"let the two of us say"
3mp	*targumū*	"let them say"
3fp	*targumna*	"let them say"
2mp	*targumū*	"may you say"
2fp	*targumna*	"may you say"
1cp	*narguma*	"let us say"

G-Stem Imperative Verbs

ŠLM, "to be well": *a* theme vowel

2ms	*šalam*	"be well"
2fs	*šalamī*	"be well"
2cd	*šalamā*	"be well"
2mp	*šalamū*	"be well"
2fp	*šalamā*	"be well"

QBʾ, "to invoke": *i* theme vowel

2ms	*qibiʾ*	"invoke"
2fs	*qibiʾī*	"invoke"
2cd	*qibiʾā*	"invoke"
2mp	*qibiʾū*	"invoke"
2fp	*qibiʾā*	"invoke"

RGM, "to say": *u* theme vowel

2ms	*rugum*	"say"
2fs	*rugumī*	"say"
2cd	*rugumā*	"say"
2mp	*rugumū*	"say"

2fp	*rugumā*	"say"

G-Stem Participles

RGM, "to say"

		Masculine	Feminine
Sg	Nom	*rāgimu*	*rāgimatu*
	Gen/Voc	*rāgimi*	*rāgimati*
	Acc	*rāgima*	*rāgimata*
Dual	Nom	*rāgimāma*	*rāgimatāma*
		bound: *rāgimā*	bound: *rāgimatā*
	Acc/Gen/Voc (Obl)	*rāgimêma*	*rāgimatêma*
		bound: *rāgimê*	bound: *rāgimatê*
Pl	Nom	*rāgimūma*	*rāgimātu*
		bound: *rāgimū*	
	Acc/Gen/Voc (Obl)	*rāgimīma*	*rāgimāti*
		bound: *rāgimī*	

G-Stem Infinitive Verbs

RGM, "to say"

Free use	*ragāmu*	"to say"
Nom	*ragāmu*	"to say," "saying"
Gen	*ragāmi*	"to say," "saying"
Acc	*ragāma*	"to say," "saying"

Gp-Stem Verbs

Gp QATALA QRʾ, "to be called"

3ms	*quraʾa*	"he was called"
3fs	*quraʾat*	"she was called"
2ms	*quraʾta*	"you were called"
2fs	*quraʾti*	"you were called"
1cs	*quraʾtu*	"I was called"

3md	*quraʾā*	"the two of them were called"
3fd	*quraʾatā*	"the two of them were called"
2cd	*quraʾtumā*	"the two of you were called"
1cd	*quraʾnāyā*	"the two of us were called"
3mp	*quraʾū*	"they were called"
3fp	*quraʾā*	"they were called"
2mp	*quraʾtumu*	"you were called"
2fp	*quraʾtina*	"you were called"
1cp	*quraʾnū*	"we were called"

Gp YAQTULU QRʾ, "to be called"

3ms	*yuqraʾu*	"he is called"
3fs	*tuqraʾu*	"she is called"
2ms	*tuqraʾu*	"you are called"
2fs	*tuqraʾīna*	"you are called"
1cs	*ʾuqraʾu*	"I am called"
3md	*tuqraʾā(na)*	"the two of them are called"
3fd	*tuqraʾā(na)*	"the two of them are called"
2cd	*tuqraʾā(na)*	"the two of you are called"
1cd	*nuqraʾā*	"the two of us are called"
3mp	*tuqraʾū(na)*	"they are called"
3fp	*tuqraʾna*	"they are called"
2mp	*tuqraʾū(na)*	"you are called"
2fp	*tuqraʾna*	"you are called"
1cp	*nuqraʾu*	"we are called"

Gp participle QRʾ, "to be called"

ms	*qarūʾu*	"called one"
fs	*qarūʾatu*	"called one"
mp	*qarūʾūma*	"called ones"
fp	*qarūʾātu*	"called ones"

Gt-Stem Verbs

Gt QATALA RQṢ, "to dance"

3ms	*ʾirtaqiṣa*	"he danced"

3fs *ʾirtaqiṣat* "she danced"
2ms *ʾirtaqišta* "you danced"
2fs *ʾirtaqišti* "you danced"
1cs *ʾirtaqištu* "I danced"

3md *ʾirtaqiṣā* "the two of them danced"
3fd *ʾirtaqiṣatā* "the two of them danced"
2cd *ʾirtaqištumā* "the two of you danced"
1cd *ʾirtaqiṣnāyā* "the two of us danced"

3mp *ʾirtaqiṣū* "they danced"
3fp *ʾirtaqiṣā* "they danced"
2mp *ʾirtaqištumu* "you danced"
2fp *ʾirtaqiština* "you danced"
1cp *ʾirtaqiṣnū* "we danced"

Gt YAQTULU RQṢ, "to dance"

3ms *yirtaqiṣu* "he dances"
3fs *tirtaqiṣu* "she dances"
2ms *tirtaqiṣu* "you dance"
2fs *tirtaqiṣīna* "you dance"
1cs *ʾirtaqiṣu* "I dance"

3md *tirtaqiṣā(na)* "the two of them dance"
3fd *tirtaqiṣā(na)* "the two of them dance"
2cd *tirtaqiṣā(na)* "the two of you dance"
1cd *nirtaqiṣā* "the two of us dance"

3mp *tirtaqiṣū(na)* "they dance"
3fp *tirtaqiṣna* "they dance"
2mp *tirtaqiṣū(na)* "you dance"
2fp *tirtaqiṣna* "you dance"
1cp *nirtaqiṣu* "we dance"

N-Stem Verbs

N QATALA MḪṢ, "to be struck"

3ms *namḫaṣa* "he was struck"
3fs *namḫaṣat* "she was struck"

2ms	*namḫašta*	"you were struck"
2fs	*namḫašti*	"you were struck"
1cs	*namḫaštu*	"I was struck"
3md	*namḫaṣā*	"the two of them were struck"
3fd	*namḫaṣatā*	"the two of them were struck"
2cd	*namḫaštumā*	"the two of you were struck"
1cd	*namḫaṣnāyā*	"the two of us were struck"
3mp	*namḫaṣū*	"they were struck"
3fp	*namḫaṣā*	"they were struck"
2mp	*namḫaštumu*	"you were struck"
2fp	*namḫaština*	"you were struck"
1cp	*namḫaṣnū*	"we were struck"

N YAQTULU MḪṢ, "to be struck"

3ms	*yimmaḫiṣu*	"he is struck"
3fs	*timmaḫiṣu*	"she is struck"
2ms	*timmaḫiṣu*	"you are struck"
2fs	*timmaḫiṣīna*	"you are struck"
1cs	*ʾimmaḫiṣu*	"I am struck"
3md	*timmaḫiṣā(na)*	"the two of them are struck"
3fd	*timmaḫiṣā(na)*	"the two of them are struck"
2cd	*timmaḫiṣā(na)*	"the two of you are struck"
1cd	*nimmaḫiṣā*	"the two of us are struck"
3mp	*timmaḫiṣū(na)*	"they are struck"
3fp	*timmaḫiṣna*	"they are struck"
2mp	*timmaḫiṣū(na)*	"you are struck"
2fp	*timmaḫiṣna*	"you are struck"
1cp	*nimmaḫiṣu*	"we are struck"

N Jussive DBḤ, "to be sacrificed"

3ms	*yiddabiḥ*	"may he be sacrificed"
3fs	*tiddabiḥ*	"may she be sacrificed"
2ms	*tiddabiḥ*	"may you be sacrificed"
2fs	*tiddabiḥī*	"may you be sacrificed"
1cs	*ʾiddabiḥ*	"may I be sacrificed"

3md	*tiddabiḥā*	"may the two of them be sacrificed"
3fd	*tiddabiḥā*	"may the two of them be sacrificed"
2cd	*tiddabiḥā*	"may the two of you be sacrificed"
1cd	*niddabiḥā*	"may the two of us be sacrificed"
3mp	*tiddabiḥū*	"may they be sacrificed"
3fp	*tiddabiḥna*	"may they be sacrificed"
2mp	*tiddabiḥū*	"may you be sacrificed"
2fp	*tiddabiḥna*	"may you be sacrificed"
1cp	*niddabiḥ*	"may we be sacrificed"

N Volitive DBḤ, "to be sacrificed"

3ms	*yiddabiḥa*	"let him be sacrificed"
3fs	*tiddabiḥa*	"let her be sacrificed"
2ms	*tiddabiḥa*	"may you be sacrificed"
2fs	*tiddabiḥī*	"may you be sacrificed"
1cs	*ʾiddabiḥa*	"let me be sacrificed"
3md	*tiddabiḥā*	"let the two of them be sacrificed"
3fd	*tiddabiḥā*	"let the two of them be sacrificed"
2cd	*tiddabiḥā*	"let the two of you be sacrificed"
1cd	*niddabiḥā*	"let the two of us be sacrificed"
3mp	*tiddabiḥū*	"let them be sacrificed"
3fp	*tiddabiḥna*	"let them be sacrificed"
2mp	*tiddabiḥū*	"may you be sacrificed"
2fp	*tiddabiḥna*	"may you be sacrificed"
1cp	*niddabiḥa*	"let us be sacrificed"

N Imperative DBḤ, "to be sacrificed"

2ms	*ʾiddabiḥ*	"be sacrificed"
2fs	*ʾiddabiḥī*	"be sacrificed"
2cd	*ʾiddabiḥā*	"be sacrificed"
2mp	*ʾiddabiḥū*	"be sacrificed"
2fp	*ʾiddabiḥā*	"be sacrificed"

D-Stem Verbs

D QATALA ŠLM, "to make well"

3ms	*šillama*	"he made __ well"
3fs	*šillamat*	"she made __ well"
2ms	*šillamta*	"you made __ well"
2fs	*šillamti*	"you made __ well"
1cs	*šillamtu*	"I made __ well"
3md	*šillamā*	"the two of them made __ well"
3fd	*šillamatā*	"the two of them made __ well"
2cd	*šillamtumā*	"the two of you made __ well"
1cd	*šillamnāyā*	"the two of us made __ well"
3mp	*šillamū*	"they made __ well"
3fp	*šillamā*	"they made __ well"
2mp	*šillamtumu*	"you made __ well"
2fp	*šillamtina*	"you made __ well"
1cp	*šillamnū*	"we made __ well"

D YAQTULU ŠLM, "to make well"

3ms	*yašallimu*	"he makes __ well"
3fs	*tašallimu*	"she makes __ well"
2ms	*tašallimu*	"you make __ well"
2fs	*tašallimīna*	"you make __ well"
1cs	*ʾašallimu*	"I make __ well"
3md	*tašallimā(na)*	"the two of them make __ well"
3fd	*tašallimā(na)*	"the two of them make __ well"
2cd	*tašallimā(na)*	"the two of you make __ well"
1cd	*našallimā*	"the two of us make __ well"
3mp	*tašallimū(na)*	"they make __ well"
3fp	*tašallimna*	"they make __ well"
2mp	*tašallimū(na)*	"you make __ well"
2fp	*tašallimna*	"you make __ well"
1cp	*našallimu*	"we make __ well"

D Jussive ŠLM, "to make well"

3ms	*yašallim*	"may he make __ well"
3fs	*tašallim*	"may she make __ well"
2ms	*tašallim*	"may you make __ well"
2fs	*tašallimī*	"may you make __ well"
1cs	*ʾašallim*	"may I make __ well"
3md	*tašallimā*	"may the two of them make __ well"
3fd	*tašallimā*	"may the two of them make __ well"
2cd	*tašallimā*	"may the two of you make __ well"
1cd	*našallimā*	"may the two of us make __ well"
3mp	*tašallimū*	"may they make __ well"
3fp	*tašallimna*	"may they make __ well"
2mp	*tašallimū*	"may you make __ well"
2fp	*tašallimna*	"may you make __ well"
1cp	*našallim*	"may we make __ well"

D Volitive ŠLM, "to make well"

3ms	*yašallima*	"let him make __ well"
3fs	*tašallima*	"let her make __ well"
2ms	*tašallima*	"may you make __ well"
2fs	*tašallimī*	"may you make __ well"
1cs	*ʾašallima*	"let me make __ well"
3md	*tašallimā*	"let the two of them make __ well"
3fd	*tašallimā*	"let the two of them make __ well"
2cd	*tašallimā*	"let the two of you make __ well"
1cd	*našallimā*	"let the two of us make __ well"
3mp	*tašallimū*	"let them make __ well"
3fp	*tašallimna*	"let them make __ well"
2mp	*tašallimū*	"may you make __ well"
2fp	*tašallimna*	"may you make __ well"
1cp	*našallima*	"let us make __ well"

D Imperative ŠLM, "to make well"

2ms	*šallim*	"make __ well"
2fs	*šallimī*	"make __ well"

2cd	*šallimā*	"make __ well"
2mp	*šallimū*	"make __ well"
2fp	*šallimā*	"make __ well"

D Participle Bʿ R, "to burn [something]"

		Masculine	Feminine
Sg	Nom	*mubaʿʿiru*	*mubaʿʿiratu*
	Gen/Voc	*mubaʿʿiri*	*mubaʿʿirati*
	Acc	*mubaʿʿira*	*mubaʿʿirata*
Dual	Nom	*mubaʿʿirāma* bound: *mubaʿʿirā*	*mubaʿʿiratāma* bound: *mubaʿʿiratā*
	Acc/Gen/Voc (Obl)	*mubaʿʿirêma* bound: *mubaʿʿirê*	*mubaʿʿiratêma* bound: *mubaʿʿiratê*
Pl	Nom	*mubaʿʿirūma* bound: *mubaʿʿirū*	*mubaʿʿirātu*
	Acc/Gen/Voc (Obl)	*mubaʿʿirīma* bound: *mubaʿʿirī*	*mubaʿʿirāti*

Dp-Stem Verbs

Dp QATALA Bʿ R, "to be burned"

3ms	*buʿʿira*	"he was burned"
3fs	*buʿʿirat*	"she was burned"
2ms	*buʿʿirta*	"you were burned"
2fs	*buʿʿirti*	"you were burned"
1cs	*buʿʿirtu*	"I was burned"
3md	*buʿʿirā*	"the two of them were burned"
3fd	*buʿʿiratā*	"the two of them were burned"
2cd	*buʿʿirtumā*	"the two of you were burned"
1cd	*buʿʿirnāyā*	"the two of us were burned"
3mp	*buʿʿirū*	"they were burned"
3fp	*buʿʿirā*	"they were burned"

2mp	*buʿʿirtumu*	"you were burned"
2fp	*buʿʿirtina*	"you were burned"
1cp	*buʿʿirnū*	"we were burned"

Dp YAQTULU BʿR, "to be burned"

3ms	*yubaʿʿaru*	"he is burned"
3fs	*tubaʿʿaru*	"she is burned"
2ms	*tubaʿʿaru*	"you are burned"
2fs	*tubaʿʿarīna*	"you are burned"
1cs	*ʾubaʿʿaru*	"I am burned"
3md	*tubaʿʿarā(na)*	"the two of them are burned"
3fd	*tubaʿʿarā(na)*	"the two of them are burned"
2cd	*tubaʿʿarā(na)*	"the two of you are burned"
1cd	*nubaʿʿarā*	"the two of us are burned"
3mp	*tubaʿʿarū(na)*	"they are burned"
3fp	*tubaʿʿarna*	"they are burned"
2mp	*tubaʿʿarū(na)*	"you are burned"
2fp	*tubaʿʿarna*	"you are burned"
1cp	*nubaʿʿaru*	"we are burned"

Dp participle BʿR, "to be burned"

ms	*mubaʿʿaru*	"burned one"
fs	*mubaʿʿaratu*	"burned one"
mp	*mubaʿʿarūma*	"burned ones"
fp	*mubaʿʿarātu*	"burned ones"

tD-Stem Verbs

tD QATALA KMS, "to collapse"

3ms	*takammasa*	"he collapsed"
3fs	*takammasat*	"she collapsed"
2ms	*takammasta*	"you collapsed"
2fs	*takammasti*	"you collapsed"
1cs	*takammastu*	"I collapsed"
3md	*takammasā*	"the two of them collapsed"
3fd	*takammasatā*	"the two of them collapsed"

2cd	*takammastumā*	"the two of you collapsed"
1cd	*takammasnāyā*	"the two of us collapsed"
3mp	*takammasū*	"they collapsed"
3fp	*takammasā*	"they collapsed"
2mp	*takammastumu*	"you collapsed"
2fp	*takammastina*	"you collapsed"
1cp	*takammasnū*	"we collapsed"

tD YAQTULU KMS, "to collapse"

3ms	*yitkammasu*	"he collapses"
3fs	*titkammasu*	"she collapses"
2ms	*titkammasu*	"you collapse"
2fs	*titkammasīna*	"you collapse"
1cs	*ʾitkammasu*	"I collapse"
3md	*titkammasā(na)*	"the two of them collapse"
3fd	*titkammasā(na)*	"the two of them collapse"
2cd	*titkammasā(na)*	"the two of you collapse"
1cd	*nitkammasā*	"the two of us collapse"
3mp	*titkammasū(na)*	"they collapse"
3fp	*titkammasna*	"they collapse"
2mp	*titkammasū(na)*	"you collapse"
2fp	*titkammasna*	"you collapse"
1cp	*nitkammasu*	"we collapse"

Š-Stem Verbs

Š QATALA BʿR, "to illuminate"

3ms	*šabʿira*	"he illuminated"
3fs	*šabʿirat*	"she illuminated"
2ms	*šabʿirta*	"you illuminated"
2fs	*šabʿirti*	"you illuminated"
1cs	*šabʿirtu*	"I illuminated"
3md	*šabʿirā*	"the two of them illuminated"
3fd	*šabʿiratā*	"the two of them illuminated"
2cd	*šabʿirtumā*	"the two of you illuminated"

1cd	*šabʿirnāyā*	"the two of us illuminated"
3mp	*šabʿirū*	"they illuminated"
3fp	*šabʿirā*	"they illuminated"
2mp	*šabʿirtumu*	"you illuminated"
2fp	*šabʿirtina*	"you illuminated"
1cp	*šabʿirnū*	"we illuminated"

Š YAQTULU BʿR, "to illuminate"

3ms	*yašabʿiru*	"he illuminates"
3fs	*tašabʿiru*	"she illuminates"
2ms	*tašabʿiru*	"you illuminate"
2fs	*tašabʿirīna*	"you illuminate"
1cs	*ʾašabʿiru*	"I illuminate"
3md	*tašabʿirā(na)*	"the two of them illuminate"
3fd	*tašabʿirā(na)*	"the two of them illuminate"
2cd	*tašabʿirā(na)*	"the two of you illuminate"
1cd	*našabʿirā*	"the two of us illuminate"
3mp	*tašabʿirū(na)*	"they illuminate"
3fp	*tašabʿirna*	"they illuminate"
2mp	*tašabʿirū(na)*	"you illuminate"
2fp	*tašabʿirna*	"you illuminate"
1cp	*našabʿiru*	"we illuminate"

Š Jussive BʿR, "to illuminate"

3ms	*yašabʿir*	"may he illuminate"
3fs	*tašabʿir*	"may she illuminate"
2ms	*tašabʿir*	"may you illuminate"
2fs	*tašabʿirī*	"may you illuminate"
1cs	*ʾašabʿir*	"may I illuminate"
3md	*tašabʿirā*	"may the two of them illuminate"
3fd	*tašabʿirā*	"may the two of them illuminate"
2cd	*tašabʿirā*	"may the two of you illuminate"
1cd	*našabʿirā*	"may the two of us illuminate"
3mp	*tašabʿirū*	"may they illuminate"

3fp	*tašabʿirna*	"may they illuminate"
2mp	*tašabʿirū*	"may you illuminate"
2fp	*tašabʿirna*	"may you illuminate"
1cp	*našabʿir*	"may we illuminate"

Š Volitive BʿR, "to illuminate"

3ms	*yašabʿira*	"let him illuminate"
3fs	*tašabʿira*	"let her illuminate"
2ms	*tašabʿira*	"may you illuminate"
2fs	*tašabʿirī*	"may you illuminate"
1cs	*ʾašabʿira*	"let me illuminate"
3md	*tašabʿirā*	"let the two of them illuminate"
3fd	*tašabʿirā*	"let the two of them illuminate"
2cd	*tašabʿirā*	"let the two of you illuminate"
1cd	*našabʿirā*	"let the two of us illuminate"
3mp	*tašabʿirū*	"let them illuminate"
3fp	*tašabʿirna*	"let them illuminate"
2mp	*tašabʿirū*	"may you illuminate"
2fp	*tašabʿirna*	"may you illuminate"
1cp	*našabʿira*	"let us illuminate"

Š Imperative BʿR, "to illuminate"

2ms	*šabʿir*	"illuminate"
2fs	*šabʿirī*	"illuminate"
2cd	*šabʿirā*	"illuminate"
2mp	*šabʿirū*	"illuminate"
2fp	*šabʿirā*	"illuminate"

Š Participle BʿR, "to illuminate"

		Masc	Fem
Sg	Nom	*mušabʿiru*	*mušabʿiratu*
	Gen/Voc	*mušabʿiri*	*mušabʿirati*
	Acc	*mušabʿira*	*mušabʿirata*

Dual	Nom	*mušabʿirāma* bound: *mušabʿirā*	*mušabʿiratāma* bound: *mušabʿiratā*
	Acc/Gen/Voc (Obl)	*mušabʿirêma* bound: *mušabʿirê*	*mušabʿiratêma* bound: *mušabʿiratê*
Pl	Nom	*mušabʿirūma* bound: *mušabʿirū*	*mušabʿirātu*
	Acc/Gen/Voc (Obl)	*mušabʿirīma* bound: *mušabʿirī*	*mušabʿirāti*

Š Infinitive BʿR, "to illuminate"

Free use	*šabʿāru*	"to illuminate"
Nom	*šabʿāru*	"to illuminate," "illuminating"
Gen	*šabʿāri*	"to illuminate," "illuminating"
Acc	*šabʿāra*	"to illuminate," "illuminating"

Šp-Stem Verbs

Šp QATALA BʿR, "to be illuminated"

3ms	*šubʿara*	"he was illuminated"
3fs	*šubʿarat*	"she was illuminated"
2ms	*šubʿarta*	"you were illuminated"
2fs	*šubʿarti*	"you were illuminated"
1cs	*šubʿartu*	"I was illuminated"
3md	*šubʿarā*	"the two of them were illuminated"
3fd	*šubʿaratā*	"the two of them were illuminated"
2cd	*šubʿartumā*	"the two of you were illuminated"
1cd	*šubʿarnāyā*	"the two of us were illuminated"
3mp	*šubʿarū*	"they were illuminated"
3fp	*šubʿarā*	"they were illuminated"
2mp	*šubʿartumu*	"you were illuminated"
2fp	*šubʿartina*	"you were illuminated"
1cp	*šubʿarnū*	"we were illuminated"

Šp YAQTULU Bʿ R, "to be illuminated"

3ms	*yušabʿaru*	"he is illuminated"
3fs	*tušabʿaru*	"she is illuminated"
2ms	*tušabʿaru*	"you are illuminated"
2fs	*tušabʿarīna*	"you are illuminated"
1cs	*ʾušabʿaru*	"I am illuminated"
3md	*tušabʿarā(na)*	"the two of them are illuminated"
3fd	*tušabʿarā(na)*	"the two of them are illuminated"
2cd	*tušabʿarā(na)*	"the two of you are illuminated"
1cd	*nušabʿarā*	"the two of us are illuminated"
3mp	*tušabʿarū(na)*	"they are illuminated"
3fp	*tušabʿarna*	"they are illuminated"
2mp	*tušabʿarū(na)*	"you are illuminated"
2fp	*tušabʿarna*	"you are illuminated"
1cp	*nušabʿaru*	"we are illuminated"

Šp participle Bʿ R, "to be illuminated"

ms	*mušabʿaru*	"illuminated one"
fs	*mušabʿaratu*	"illuminated one"
mp	*mušabʿarūma*	"illuminated ones"
fp	*mušabʿarātu*	"illuminated ones"

Št-Stem Verbs

Št QATALA

3ms	*ʾištaqtila*
3fs	*ʾištaqtilat*
2ms	*ʾištaqtilta*
2fs	*ʾištaqtilti*
1cs	*ʾištaqtiltu*
3md	*ʾištaqtilā*
3fd	*ʾištaqtilatā*
2cd	*ʾištaqtiltumā*
1cd	*ʾištaqtilnāyā*
3mp	*ʾištaqtilū*

3fp	*ʾištaqtilā*
2mp	*ʾištaqtiltumu*
2fp	*ʾištaqtiltina*
1cp	*ʾištaqtilnū*

Št YAQTULU

3ms	*yištaqtilu*
3fs	*tištaqtilu*
2ms	*tištaqtilu*
2fs	*tištaqtilīna*
1cs	*ʾištaqtilu*
3md	*tištaqtilā(na)*
3fd	*tištaqtilā(na)*
2cd	*tištaqtilā(na)*
1cd	*ništaqtilā*
3mp	*tištaqtilū(na)*
3fp	*tištaqtilna*
2mp	*tištaqtilū(na)*
2fp	*tištaqtilna*
1cp	*ništaqtilu*

I-n Verbs in the G-Stem

G QATALA

See paradigm for the strong verb.

G YAQTULU NDR, "to make a vow"

3ms	*yadduru*	"he vows"
3fs	*tadduru*	"she vows"
2ms	*tadduru*	"you vow"
2fs	*taddurīna*	"you vow"
1cs	*ʾadduru*	"I vow"
3md	*taddurā(na)*	"the two of them vow"
3fd	*taddurā(na)*	"the two of them vow"
2cd	*taddurā(na)*	"the two of you vow"
1cd	*naddurā*	"the two of us vow"

3mp	*taddurū(na)*	"they vow"
3fp	*taddurna*	"they vow"
2mp	*taddurū(na)*	"you vow"
2fp	*taddurna*	"you vow"
1cp	*nadduru*	"we vow"

G Jussive NDR, "to make a vow"

3ms	*yaddur*	"let him vow"
3fs	*taddur*	"let her vow"
2ms	*taddur*	"may you vow"
2fs	*taddurī*	"may you vow"
1cs	*ʾaddur*	"let me vow"
3md	*taddurā*	"let the two of them vow"
3fd	*taddurā*	"let the two of them vow"
2cd	*taddurā*	"let the two of you vow"
1cd	*naddurā*	"let the two of us vow"
3mp	*taddurū*	"let them vow"
3fp	*taddurna*	"let them vow"
2mp	*taddurū*	"may you vow"
2fp	*taddurna*	"may you vow"
1cp	*naddur*	"let us vow"

G Volitive NDR, "to make a vow"

3ms	*yaddura*	"let him vow"
3fs	*taddura*	"let her vow"
2ms	*taddura*	"may you vow"
2fs	*taddurī*	"may you vow"
1cs	*ʾaddura*	"let me vow"
3md	*taddurā*	"let the two of them vow"
3fd	*taddurā*	"let the two of them vow"
2cd	*taddurā*	"let the two of you vow"
1cd	*naddurā*	"let the two of us vow"
3mp	*taddurū*	"let them vow"
3fp	*taddurna*	"let them vow"
2mp	*taddurū*	"may you vow"

2fp	*taddurna*	"may you vow"
1cp	*naddura*	"let us vow"

G Imperative NDR, "to make a vow"

2ms	*dur*	"vow"
2fs	*durī*	"vow"
2cd	*durā*	"vow"
2mp	*durū*	"vow"
2fp	*durā*	"vow"

I-n Participle

See paradigm for the strong verb.

I-n Infinitive

See paradigm for the strong verb.

I-n Verbs in the N-Stem

N QATALA NDR, "to be vowed"

3ms	*naddara*	"he was vowed"
3fs	*naddarat*	"she was vowed"
2ms	*naddarta*	"you were vowed"
2fs	*naddarti*	"you were vowed"
1cs	*naddartu*	"I was vowed"
3md	*naddarā*	"the two of them were vowed"
3fd	*naddaratā*	"the two of them were vowed"
2cd	*naddartumā*	"the two of you were vowed"
1cd	*naddarnāyā*	"the two of us were vowed"
3mp	*naddarū*	"they were vowed"
3fp	*naddarā*	"they were vowed"
2mp	*naddartumu*	"you were vowed"
2fp	*naddartina*	"you were vowed"
1cp	*naddarnū*	"we were vowed"

N YAQTULU

See paradigm for the strong verb.

I-n Verbs in the D-Stem

See paradigms for the strong verb.

I-n Verbs in the Š-Stem

NGŠ, "to cause to approach"

QATALA	*šaggiša*, "he caused [someone/thing] to approach"
YAQTULU	*yašaggišu*, "he causes [someone/thing] to approach"
Imperative	*šaggiš*, "cause [someone/thing] to approach" (2ms)
Participle	*mušaggišu*, "one who causes to approach" (nom ms)
Infinitive	*šaggāšu*, "to cause to approach" (nom)

LQḤ, "to take," in the G-Stem

G QATALA

See paradigm for the strong verb.

G YAQTULU

3ms	*yiqqaḥu*	"he takes"
3fs	*tiqqaḥu*	"she takes"
2ms	*tiqqaḥu*	"you take"
2fs	*tiqqaḥīna*	"you take"
1cs	*ʾiqqaḥu*	"I take"
3md	*tiqqaḥā(na)*	"the two of them take"
3fd	*tiqqaḥā(na)*	"the two of them take"
2cd	*tiqqaḥā(na)*	"the two of you take"
1cd	*niqqaḥā*	"the two of us take"
3mp	*tiqqaḥū(na)*	"they take"
3fp	*tiqqaḥna*	"they take"
2mp	*tiqqaḥū(na)*	"you take"
2fp	*tiqqaḥna*	"you take"
1cp	*niqqaḥu*	"we take"

G Jussive

3ms	*yiqqaḥ*	"let him take"
3fs	*tiqqaḥ*	"let her take"

2ms	*tiqqaḥ*	"may you take"
2fs	*tiqqaḥī*	"may you take"
1cs	*ʾiqqaḥ*	"let me take"
3md	*tiqqaḥā*	"let the two of them take"
3fd	*tiqqaḥā*	"let the two of them take"
2cd	*tiqqaḥā*	"let the two of you take"
1cd	*niqqaḥā*	"let the two of us take"
3mp	*tiqqaḥū*	"let them take"
3fp	*tiqqaḥna*	"let them take"
2mp	*tiqqaḥū*	"may you take"
2fp	*tiqqaḥna*	"may you take"
1cp	*niqqaḥ*	"let us take"

G Volitive

3ms	*yiqqaḥa*	"let him take"
3fs	*tiqqaḥa*	"let her take"
2ms	*tiqqaḥa*	"may you take"
2fs	*tiqqaḥī*	"may you take"
1cs	*ʾiqqaḥa*	"let me take"
3md	*tiqqaḥā*	"let the two of them take"
3fd	*tiqqaḥā*	"let the two of them take"
2cd	*tiqqaḥā*	"let the two of you take"
1cd	*niqqaḥā*	"let the two of us take"
3mp	*tiqqaḥū*	"let them take"
3fp	*tiqqaḥna*	"let them take"
2mp	*tiqqaḥū*	"may you take"
2fp	*tiqqaḥna*	"may you take"
1cp	*niqqaḥa*	"let us take"

G Imperative

2ms	*qaḥ*	"take"
2fs	*qaḥī*	"take"
2cd	*qaḥā*	"take"
2mp	*qaḥū*	"take"
2fp	*qaḥā*	"take"

HLM, "to strike," in the G-Stem YAQTULU

3ms	*yallumu*	"he strikes"
3fs	*tallumu*	"she strikes"
2ms	*tallumu*	"you strike"
2fs	*tallumīna*	"you strike"
1cs	*ʾallumu*	"I strike"
3md	*tallumā*(*na*)	"the two of them strike"
3fd	*tallumā*(*na*)	"the two of them strike"
2cd	*tallumā*(*na*)	"the two of you strike"
1cd	*nallumā*	"the two of us strike"
3mp	*tallumū*(*na*)	"they strike"
3fp	*tallumna*	"they strike"
2mp	*tallumū*(*na*)	"you strike"
2fp	*tallumna*	"you strike"
1cp	*nallumu*	"we strike"

I-ʾ Verbs in the G-Stem

G QATALA

See paradigm for the strong verb.

G YAQTULU ʾḪD, "to seize"

3ms	*yaʾḫudu* / *yaʾuḫudu*	"he seizes"
3fs	*taʾḫudu* / *taʾuḫudu*	"she seizes"
2ms	*taʾḫudu* / *taʾuḫudu*	"you seize"
2fs	*taʾḫudīna* / *taʾuḫudīna*	"you seize"
1cs	*ʾaḫudu*	"I seize"
3md	*taʾḫudā*(*nai* / *taʾuḫudā*(*na*)	"the two of them seize"
3fd	*taʾḫudā*(*na*) / *taʾuḫudā*(*na*)	"the two of them seize"
2cd	*taʾḫudā*(*na*) / *taʾuḫudā*(*na*)	"the two of you seize"
1cd	*naʾḫudā* / *naʾuḫudā*	"the two of us seize"
3mp	*taʾḫudū*(*na*) / *taʾuḫudū*(*na*)	"they seize"
3fp	*taʾḫudna* / *taʾuḫudna*	"they seize"
2mp	*taʾḫudū*(*na*) / *taʾuḫudū*(*na*)	"you seize"
2fp	*taʾḫudna* / *taʾuḫudna*	"you seize"

1cp	*naʾḫudu / naʾuḫudu*	"we seize"

G Jussive ʾḪD, "to seize"

3ms	*yaʾḫud / yaʾuḫud*	"let him seize"
3fs	*taʾḫud / taʾuḫud*	"let her seize"
2ms	*taʾḫud / taʾuḫud*	"may you seize"
2fs	*taʾḫudī / taʾuḫudī*	"may you seize"
1cs	*ʾaḫud*	"let me seize"
3md	*taʾḫudā / taʾuḫudā*	"let the two of them seize"
3fd	*taʾḫudā / taʾuḫudā*	"let the two of them seize"
2cd	*taʾḫudā / taʾuḫudā*	"let the two of you seize"
1cd	*naʾḫudā / naʾuḫudā*	"let the two of us seize"
3mp	*taʾḫudū / taʾuḫudū*	"let them seize"
3fp	*taʾḫudna / taʾuḫudna*	"let them seize"
2mp	*taʾḫudū / taʾuḫudū*	"may you seize"
2fp	*taʾḫudna / taʾuḫudna*	"may you seize"
1cp	*naʾḫud*	"let us seize"

G Volitive ʾḪD, "to seize"

3ms	*yaʾḫuda / yaʾuḫuda*	"let him seize"
3fs	*taʾḫuda / taʾuḫuda*	"let her seize"
2ms	*taʾḫuda / taʾuḫuda*	"may you seize"
2fs	*taʾḫudī / taʾuḫudī*	"may you seize"
1cs	*ʾaḫuda*	"let me seize"
3md	*taʾḫudā / taʾuḫudā*	"let the two of them seize"
3fd	*taʾḫudā / taʾuḫudā*	"let the two of them seize"
2cd	*taʾḫudā / taʾuḫudā*	"let the two of you seize"
1cd	*naʾḫudā / naʾuḫudā*	"let the two of us seize"
3mp	*taʾḫudū / taʾuḫudū*	"let them seize"
3fp	*taʾḫudna / taʾuḫudna*	"let them seize"
2mp	*taʾḫudū / taʾuḫudū*	"may you seize"
2fp	*taʾḫudna / taʾuḫudna*	"may you seize"
1cp	*naʾḫuda*	"let us seize"

G Imperative ʾḪD, "to seize"

2ms	*ʾuḫud*	"seize"
2fs	*ʾuḫudī*	"seize"
2cd	*ʾuḫudā*	"seize"
2mp	*ʾuḫudū*	"seize"
2fp	*ʾuḫudā*	"seize"

I-ʾ Verbs in the N-Stem

N QATALA ʾḪD, "to be seized"

3ms	*naʾḫada / naʾaḫada*	"he was seized"
3fs	*naʾḫadat / naʾaḫadat*	"she was seized"
2ms	*naʾḫadta / naʾaḫadta*	"you were seized"
2fs	*naʾḫadti / naʾaḫadti*	"you were seized"
1cs	*naʾḫadtu / naʾaḫadtu*	"I was seized"
3md	*naʾḫadā / naʾaḫadā*	"the two of them were seized"
3fd	*naʾḫadatā / naʾaḫadatā*	"the two of them were seized"
2cd	*naʾḫadtumā / naʾaḫadtumā*	"the two of you were seized"
1cd	*naʾḫadnāyā / naʾaḫadnāyā*	"the two of us were seized"
3mp	*naʾḫadū / naʾaḫadū*	"they were seized"
3fp	*naʾḫadā / naʾaḫadā*	"they were seized"
2mp	*naʾḫadtumu / naʾaḫadtumu*	"you were seized"
2fp	*naʾḫadtina / naʾaḫadtina*	"you were seized"
1cp	*naʾḫadnū / naʾaḫadnū*	"we were seized"

N YAQTULU

See paradigm for the strong verb.

I-y Verbs in the G-Stem

G QATALA

See paradigm for the strong verb.

G YAQTULU YDʿ, "to know": *a* theme vowel

3ms	*yidaʿu*	"he knows"
3fs	*tidaʿu*	"she knows"
2ms	*tidaʿu*	"you know"

2fs	*tidaʿīna*	"you know"
1cs	*ʾidaʿu*	"I know"
3md	*tidaʿā(na)*	"the two of them know"
3fd	*tidaʿā(na)*	"the two of them know"
2cd	*tidaʿā(na)*	"the two of you know"
1cd	*nidaʿā*	"the two of us know"
3mp	*tidaʿū(na)*	"they know"
3fp	*tidaʿna*	"they know"
2mp	*tidaʿū(na)*	"you know"
2fp	*tidaʿna*	"you know"
1cp	*nidaʿu*	"we know"

G YAQTULU YRD, "to descend": *i* theme vowel

3ms	*yaridu*	"he descends"
3fs	*taridu*	"she descends"
2ms	*taridu*	"you descend"
2fs	*taridīna*	"you descend"
1cs	*ʾaridu*	"I descend"
3md	*taridā(na)*	"the two of them descend"
3fd	*taridā(na)*	"the two of them descend"
2cd	*taridā(na)*	"the two of you descend"
1cd	*naridā*	"the two of us descend"
3mp	*taridū(na)*	"they descend"
3fp	*taridna*	"they descend"
2mp	*taridū(na)*	"you descend"
2fp	*taridna*	"you descend"
1cp	*naridu*	"we descend"

G Jussive YDʿ, "to know": *a* theme vowel

3ms	*yidaʿ*	"may he know"
3fs	*tidaʿ*	"may she know"
2ms	*tidaʿ*	"may you know"
2fs	*tidaʿī*	"may you know"
1cs	*ʾidaʿ*	"may I know"

3md	*tidaʿā*	"may the two of them know"
3fd	*tidaʿā*	"may the two of them know"
2cd	*tidaʿā*	"may the two of you know"
1cd	*nidaʿā*	"may the two of us know"
3mp	*tidaʿū*	"may they know"
3fp	*tidaʿna*	"may they know"
2mp	*tidaʿū*	"may you know"
2fp	*tidaʿna*	"may you know"
1cp	*nidaʿ*	"may we know"

G Jussive YRD, "to descend": *i* theme vowel

3ms	*yarid*	"may he descend"
3fs	*tarid*	"may she descend"
2ms	*tarid*	"may you descend"
2fs	*taridī*	"may you descend"
1cs	*ʾarid*	"may I descend"
3md	*taridā*	"may the two of them descend"
3fd	*taridā*	"may the two of them descend"
2cd	*taridā*	"may the two of you descend"
1cd	*naridā*	"may the two of us descend"
3mp	*taridū*	"may they descend"
3fp	*taridna*	"may they descend"
2mp	*taridū*	"may you descend"
2fp	*taridna*	"may you descend"
1cp	*narid*	"may we descend"

G Volitive YDʿ, "to know": *a* theme vowel

3ms	*yidaʿa*	"let him know"
3fs	*tidaʿa*	"let her know"
2ms	*tidaʿa*	"may you know"
2fs	*tidaʿī*	"may you know"
1cs	*ʾidaʿa*	"let me know"
3md	*tidaʿā*	"let the two of them know"
3fd	*tidaʿā*	"let the two of them know"
2cd	*tidaʿā*	"let the two of you know"

1cd	*nidaʿā*	"let the two of us know"
3mp	*tidaʿū*	"let them know"
3fp	*tidaʿna*	"let them know"
2mp	*tidaʿū*	"may you know"
2fp	*tidaʿna*	"may you know"
1cp	*nidaʿa*	"let us know"

G Volitive YRD, "to descend": *i* theme vowel

3ms	*yarida*	"let him descend"
3fs	*tarida*	"let her descend"
2ms	*tarida*	"may you descend"
2fs	*taridī*	"may you descend"
1cs	*ʾarida*	"let me descend"
3md	*taridā*	"let the two of them descend"
3fd	*taridā*	"let the two of them descend"
2cd	*taridā*	"let the two of you descend"
1cd	*naridā*	"let the two of us descend"
3mp	*taridū*	"let them descend"
3fp	*taridna*	"let them descend"
2mp	*taridū*	"may you descend"
2fp	*taridna*	"may you descend"
1cp	*narida*	"let us descend"

G Imperative YDʿ, "to know": *a* theme vowel

2ms	*daʿ*	"know"
2fs	*daʿī*	"know"
2cd	*daʿā*	"know"
2mp	*daʿū*	"know"
2fp	*daʿā*	"know"

G Imperative YRD, "to descend": *i* theme vowel

2ms	*rid*	"descend"
2fs	*ridī*	"descend"
2cd	*ridā*	"descend"
2mp	*ridū*	"descend"
2fp	*ridā*	"descend"

G Participle

See paradigm for the strong verb.

G Infinitive YRD, "to descend"

Free use	*yarādu* or *ridatu*	"to descend"
Nom	*yarādu* or *ridatu*	"to descend," "descending"
Gen	*yarādi* or *ridati*	"to descend," "descending"
Acc	*yarāda* or *ridata*	"to descend," "descending"

HLK, "to go," in the G-Stem

G QATALA

See paradigm for the strong verb.

G YAQTULU

3ms	*yaliku*	"he goes"
3fs	*taliku*	"she goes"
2ms	*taliku*	"you go"
2fs	*talikīna*	"you go"
1cs	*ʾaliku*	"I go"
3md	*talikā(na)*	"the two of them go"
3fd	*talikā(na)*	"the two of them go"
2cd	*talikā(na)*	"the two of you go"
1cd	*nalikā*	"the two of us go"
3mp	*talikū(na)*	"they go"
3fp	*talikna*	"they go"
2mp	*talikū(na)*	"you go"
2fp	*talikna*	"you go"
1cp	*naliku*	"we go"

G Jussive

3ms	*yalik*	"may he go"
3fs	*talik*	"may she go"
2ms	*talik*	"may you go"
2fs	*talikī*	"may you go"
1cs	*ʾalik*	"may I go"

3md	*talikā*	"may the two of them go"
3fd	*talikā*	"may the two of them go"
2cd	*talikā*	"may the two of you go"
1cd	*nalikā*	"may the two of us go"
3mp	*talikū*	"may they go"
3fp	*talikna*	"may they go"
2mp	*talikū*	"may you go"
2fp	*talikna*	"may you go"
1cp	*nalik*	"may we go"

G Volitive

3ms	*yalika*	"let him go"
3fs	*talika*	"let her go"
2ms	*talika*	"may you go"
2fs	*talikī*	"may you go"
1cs	*ʾalika*	"let me go"
3md	*talikā*	"let the two of them go"
3fd	*talikā*	"let the two of them go"
2cd	*talikā*	"let the two of you go"
1cd	*nalikā*	"let the two of us go"
3mp	*talikū*	"let them go"
3fp	*talikna*	"let them go"
2mp	*talikū*	"may you go"
2fp	*talikna*	"may you go"
1cp	*nalika*	"let us go"

G Imperative

2ms	*lik*	"go"
2fs	*likī*	"go"
2cd	*likā*	"go"
2mp	*likū*	"go"
2fp	*likā*	"go"

G Participle

See paradigm for the strong verb.

G Infinitive

Free use	*halāku* or *likatu*	"to go"
Nom	*halāku* or *likatu*	"to go," "going"
Gen	*halāki* or *likati*	"to go," "going"
Acc	*halāka* or *likata*	"to go," "going"

I-y Verbs in the N-Stem

N YAQTULU YḤL, "to be discouraged"

3ms	*yiwwaḥilu*	"he is discouraged"
3fs	*tiwwaḥilu*	"she is discouraged"
2ms	*tiwwaḥilu*	"you are discouraged"
2fs	*tiwwaḥilīna*	"you are discouraged"
1cs	*ʾiwwaḥilu*	"I am discouraged"
3md	*tiwwaḥilā(na)*	"the two of them are discouraged"
3fd	*tiwwaḥilā(na)*	"the two of them are discouraged"
2cd	*tiwwaḥilā(na)*	"the two of you are discouraged"
1cd	*niwwaḥilā*	"the two of us are discouraged"
3mp	*tiwwaḥilū(na)*	"they are discouraged"
3fp	*tiwwaḥilna*	"they are discouraged"
2mp	*tiwwaḥilū(na)*	"you are discouraged"
2fp	*tiwwaḥilna*	"you are discouraged"
1cp	*niwwaḥilu*	"we are discouraged"

I-y Verbs in the D-Stem

D YAQTULU YTḤ, "to hasten"

3ms	*yawattiḥu*	"he hastens"
3fs	*tawattiḥu*	"she hastens"
2ms	*tawattiḥu*	"you hasten"
2fs	*tawattiḥīna*	"you hasten"
1cs	*ʾawattiḥu*	"I hasten"
3md	*tawattiḥā(na)*	"the two of them hasten"
3fd	*tawattiḥā(na)*	"the two of them hasten"
2cd	*tawattiḥā(na)*	"the two of you hasten"
1cd	*nawattiḥā*	"the two of us hasten"

3mp	*tawattiḥū(na)*	"they hasten"
3fp	*tawattiḥna*	"they hasten"
2mp	*tawattiḥū(na)*	"you hasten"
2fp	*tawattiḥna*	"you hasten"
1cp	*nawattiḥu*	"we hasten"

I-y Verbs in the Š-Stem

YṢʾ, "to bring out"

QATALA	*šôṣiʾa* (< *šawṣiʾa*), "he brought out"
YAQTULU	*yašôṣiʾu* (< *yašawṣiʾu*), "he brings out"
Imperative	*šôṣiʾ* (< *šawṣiʾ*), "bring out" (2ms)
Participle	*mušôṣiʾu* (< *mušawṣiʾu*), "one who brings out" (nom ms)
Infinitive	*šôṣāʾu* (< *šawṣāʾu*), "to bring out" (nom)

YTN, "to give," in the G- and Š-Stems

G QATALA

3ms	*yatana*	"he gave"
3fs	*yatanat*	"she gave"
2ms	*yatanāta* or *yatatta* (< *yatanta*)	"you gave"
2fs	*yatanāti* or *yatatti* (< *yatanti*)	"you gave"
1cs	*yatanātu* or *yatattu* (< *yatantu*)	"I gave"
3md	*yatanā*	"the two of them gave"
3fd	*yatanatā*	"the two of them gave"
2cd	*yatanātumā* or *yatattumā* (< *yatantumā*)	"the two of you gave"
1cd	*yatannāyā*	"the two of us gave"
3mp	*yatanū*	"they gave"
3fp	*yatanā*	"they gave"
2mp	*yatanātumu* or *yatattumu* (< *yatantumu*)	"you gave"
2fp	*yatanātina* or *yatattina* (< *yatantina*)	"you gave"
1cp	*yatannū*	"we gave"

G YAQTULU

3ms	*yatinu*	"he gives"
3fs	*tatinu*	"she gives"
2ms	*tatinu*	"you give"
2fs	*tatinīna*	"you give"
1cs	*ʾatinu*	"I give"
3md	*tatinā(na)*	"the two of them give"
3fd	*tatinā(na)*	"the two of them give"
2cd	*tatinā(na)*	"the two of you give"
1cd	*natinā*	"the two of us give"
3mp	*tatinū(na)*	"they give"
3fp	*tatinna*	"they give"
2mp	*tatinū(na)*	"you give"
2fp	*tatinna*	"you give"
1cp	*natinu*	"we give"

G Jussive

3ms	*yatin*	"may he give"
3fs	*tatin*	"may she give"
2ms	*tatin*	"may you give"
2fs	*tatinī*	"may you give"
1cs	*ʾatin*	"may I give"
3md	*tatinā*	"may the two of them give"
3fd	*tatinā*	"may the two of them give"
2cd	*tatinā*	"may the two of you give"
1cd	*natinā*	"may the two of us give"
3mp	*tatinū*	"may they give"
3fp	*tatinna*	"may they give"
2mp	*tatinū*	"may you give"
2fp	*tatinna*	"may you give"
1cp	*natin*	"may we give"

G Volitive

3ms	*yatina*	"let him give"
3fs	*tatina*	"let her give"

2ms	*tatina*	"may you give"
2fs	*tatinī*	"may you give"
1cs	*ʾatina*	"let me give"
3md	*tatinā*	"let the two of them give"
3fd	*tatinā*	"let the two of them give"
2cd	*tatinā*	"let the two of you give"
1cd	*natinā*	"let the two of us give"
3mp	*tatinū*	"let them give"
3fp	*tatinna*	"let them give"
2mp	*tatinū*	"may you give"
2fp	*tatinna*	"may you give"
1cp	*natina*	"let us give"

G Imperative

2ms	*tin*	"give"
2fs	*tinī*	"give"
2cd	*tinā*	"give"
2mp	*tinū*	"give"
2fp	*tinā*	"give"

G Participle

See paradigm for the strong verb.

G Infinitive

Free use	*tanu* or *tatinu*	"to give"
Nom	*tanu* or *tatinu*	"to give," "giving"
Gen	*tani* or *tatini*	"to give," "giving"
Acc	*tana* or *tatina*	"to give," "giving"

Š-Stem

QATALA	*šêtina* (< *šaytina*), "he sent"
YAQTULU	*yišêtinu* (< *yašaytinu*), "he sends"
Imperative	*šêtin* (< *šaytin*), "send" (2ms)
Participle	*mušêtinu* (< *mušaytinu*), "one who sends" (nom ms)
Infinitive	*šêtānu* (< *šaytānu*), "to send" (nom)

Hollow Verbs in the G-Stem

G QATALA QL, "to fall"

3ms	*qāla*	"he fell"
3fs	*qālat*	"she fell"
2ms	*qālāta*	"you fell"
2fs	*qālāti*	"you fell"
1cs	*qālātu*	"I fell"
3md	*qālā*	"the two of them fell"
3fd	*qālatā*	"the two of them fell"
2cd	*qālātumā*	"the two of you fell"
1cd	*qālānāyā*	"the two of us fell"
3mp	*qālū*	"they fell"
3fp	*qālā*	"they fell"
2mp	*qālātumu*	"you fell"
2fp	*qālātina*	"you fell"
1cp	*qālānū*	"we fell"

G YAQTULU QL, "to fall"

3ms	*yaqīlu*	"he falls"
3fs	*taqīlu*	"she falls"
2ms	*taqīlu*	"you fall"
2fs	*taqīlīna*	"you fall"
1cs	*ʾaqīlu*	"I fall"
3md	*taqīlā(na)*	"the two of them fall"
3fd	*taqīlā(na)*	"the two of them fall"
2cd	*taqīlā(na)*	"the two of you fall"
1cd	*naqīlā*	"the two of us fall"
3mp	*taqīlū(na)*	"they fall"
3fp	*taqilna*	"they fall"
2mp	*taqīlū(na)*	"you fall"
2fp	*taqilna*	"you fall"
1cp	*naqīlu*	"we fall"

G Jussive QL, “to fall”

3ms	*yaqil*	“let him fall”
3fs	*taqil*	“let her fall”
2ms	*taqil*	“may you fall”
2fs	*taqīlī*	“may you fall”
1cs	*ʾaqil*	“let me fall”
3md	*taqīlā*	“let the two of them fall”
3fd	*taqīlā*	“let the two of them fall”
2cd	*taqīlā*	“let the two of you fall”
1cd	*naqīlā*	“let the two of us fall”
3mp	*taqīlū*	“let them fall”
3fp	*taqilna*	“let them fall”
2mp	*taqīlū*	“may you fall”
2fp	*taqilna*	“may you fall”
1cp	*naqil*	“let us fall”

G Volitive QL, “to fall”

3ms	*yaqīla*	“let him fall”
3fs	*taqīla*	“let her fall”
2ms	*taqīla*	“may you fall”
2fs	*taqīlī*	“may you fall”
1cs	*ʾaqīla*	“let me fall”
3md	*taqīlā*	“let the two of them fall”
3fd	*taqīlā*	“let the two of them fall”
2cd	*taqīlā*	“let the two of you fall”
1cd	*naqīlā*	“let the two of us fall”
3mp	*taqīlū*	“let them fall”
3fp	*taqilna*	“let them fall”
2mp	*taqīlū*	“may you fall”
2fp	*taqilna*	“may you fall”
1cp	*naqīla*	“let us fall”

G Imperative QL, “to fall”

2ms	*qil*	“fall”
2fs	*qīlī*	“fall”

2cd	*qīlā*	"fall"
2mp	*qīlū*	"fall"
2fp	*qīlā*	"fall"

G Participle QL, "to fall," and MT, "to die"

		Masculine		Feminine	
Sg	Nom	*qālu*	*mītu*	*qālatu*	*mītatu*
	Gen/Voc	*qāli*	*mīti*	*qālati*	*mītati*
	Acc	*qāla*	*mīta*	*qālata*	*mītata*
Dual	Nom	*qālāma* bound: *qālā*	*mītāma* bound: *mītā*	*qālatāma* bound: *qālatā*	*mītatāma* bound: *mītatā*
	Acc/Gen/Voc (Obl)	*qālêma* bound: *qālê*	*mītêma* bound: *mītê*	*qālatêma* bound: *qālatê*	*mītatêma* bound: *mītatê*
Pl	Nom	*qālūma* bound: *qālū*	*mītūma* bound: *mītū*	*qālātu*	*mītātu*
	Acc/Gen/Voc (Obl)	*qālīma* bound: *qālī*	*mītīma* bound: *mītī*	*qālāti*	*mītāti*

G Infinitive QL, "to fall"

Free use	*qīlu*	"to fall"
Nom	*qīlu*	"to fall," "falling"
Gen	*qīli*	"to fall," "falling"
Acc	*qīla*	"to fall," "falling"

Hollow Verbs in the N-Stem

N QATALA ŠT, "to be placed"

3ms	*našāta*	"he was placed"
3fs	*našātat*	"she was placed"
2ms	*našatta*	"you were placed"
2fs	*našatti*	"you were placed"

1cs	*našattu*	"I was placed"
3md	*našātā*	"the two of them were placed"
3fd	*našātatā*	"the two of them were placed"
2cd	*našāttumā*	"the two of you were placed"
1cd	*našatnāyā*	"the two of us were placed"
3mp	*našātū*	"they were placed"
3fp	*našātā*	"they were placed"
2mp	*našattumu*	"you were placed"
2fp	*našattina*	"you were placed"
1cp	*našatnū*	"we were placed"

N YAQTULU ŠT, "to be placed"

3ms	*yiššītu*	"he is placed"
3fs	*tiššītu*	"she is placed"
2ms	*tiššītu*	"you are placed"
2fs	*tiššītīna*	"you are placed"
1cs	*ʾiššītu*	"I am placed"
3md	*tiššītā*(*na*)	"the two of them are placed"
3fd	*tiššītā*(*na*)	"the two of them are placed"
2cd	*tiššītā*(*na*)	"the two of you are placed"
1cd	*niššītā*	"the two of us are placed"
3mp	*tiššītū*(*na*)	"they are placed"
3fp	*tiššitna*	"they are placed"
2mp	*tiššītū*(*na*)	"you are placed"
2fp	*tiššitna*	"you are placed"
1cp	*niššītu*	"we are placed"

Hollow Verbs in the Š-Stem

ṮB, "to return [something]"

QATALA	*taṯība*, "he returned [someone/thing]"
YAQTULU	*yaṯaṯību*, "he returned [someone/thing]"
Imperative	*taṯib*, "return [someone/thing]" (2ms)
	taṯībī, "return [someone/thing]" (2fs)
Participle	*muṯaṯību*, "one who returns [someone/thing]" (nom ms)

Infinitive	*ṯaṯābu*, "to return [someone/thing]" (nom)	

Geminate Verbs in the G-Stem

G QATALA RBB, "to be great, become great"

3ms	*rabba*	"he is great"
3fs	*rabbat*	"she is great"
2ms	*rabbāta*	"you are great"
2fs	*rabbāti*	"you are great"
1cs	*rabbātu*	"I am great"
3md	*rabbā*	"the two of them are great"
3fd	*rabbatā*	"the two of them are great"
2cd	*rabbātumā*	"the two of you are great"
1cd	*rabbānāyā*	"the two of us are great"
3mp	*rabbū*	"they are great"
3fp	*rabbā*	"they are great"
2mp	*rabbātumu*	"you are great"
2fp	*rabbātina*	"you are great"
1cp	*rabbānū*	"we are great"

G YAQTULU RBB, "to be great, become great"

3ms	*yarubbu*	"he will become great"
3fs	*tarubbu*	"she will become great"
2ms	*tarubbu*	"you will become great"
2fs	*tarubbīna*	"you will become great"
1cs	*ʾarubbu*	"I will become great"
3md	*tarubbā(na)*	"the two of them will become great"
3fd	*tarubbā(na)*	"the two of them will become great"
2cd	*tarubbā(na)*	"the two of you will become great"
1cd	*narubbā*	"the two of us will become great"
3mp	*tarubbū(na)*	"they will become great"
3fp	*tarubna*	"they will become great"
2mp	*tarubbū(na)*	"you will become great"
2fp	*tarubna*	"you will become great"
1cp	*narubbu*	"we will become great"

G Jussive RBB, "to be great, become great"

3ms	*yarub* (< *yarubb*)	"may he become great"
3fs	*tarub* (< *tarubb*)	"may she become great"
2ms	*tarub* (< *tarubb*)	"may you become great"
2fs	*tarubbī*	"may you become great"
1cs	*ʾarub* (< *ʾarubb*)	"may I become great"
3md	*tarubbā*	"may the two of them become great"
3fd	*tarubbā*	"may the two of them become great"
2cd	*tarubbā*	"may the two of you become great"
1cd	*narubbā*	"may the two of us become great"
3mp	*tarubbū*	"may they become great"
3fp	*tarubna* (< *tarubbna*)	"may they become great"
2mp	*tarubbū*	"may you become great"
2fp	*tarubna*	"may you become great"
1cp	*narub* (< *narubb*)	"may we become great"

G Volitive RBB, "to be great, become great"

3ms	*yarubba*	"let him become great"
3fs	*tarubba*	"let her become great"
2ms	*tarubba*	"may you become great"
2fs	*tarubbī*	"may you become great"
1cs	*ʾarubba*	"let me become great"
3md	*tarubbā*	"let the two of them become great"
3fd	*tarubbā*	"let the two of them become great"
2cd	*tarubbā*	"let the two of you become great"
1cd	*narubbā*	"let the two of us become great"
3mp	*tarubbū*	"let them become great"
3fp	*tarubna* (< *tarubbna*)	"let them become great"
2mp	*tarubbū*	"may you become great"
2fp	*tarubna*	"may you become great"
1cp	*narubba*	"let us become great"

G Imperative RBB, "to be great, become great"

2ms	*rub* (< *rubb*)	"become great"
2fs	*rubbī*	"become great"

2cd	*rubbā*	"become great"
2mp	*rubbū*	"become great"
2fp	*rubbā*	"become great"

III-y Verbs in the G-Stem

G QATALA ʿNY, "to answer": *a* theme vowel

3ms	*ʿanaya* / *ʿanâ* (*aya* > *â*)
3fs	*ʿanayat* / *ʿanat* (*aya* > *â* > *a*)
2ms	*ʿanêta* (*ay* > *ê*)
2fs	*ʿanêti* (*ay* > *ê*)
1cs	*ʿanêtu* (*ay* > *ê*)
3md	*ʿanayā* / *ʿanâ* (*ayā* > *â*)
3fd	*ʿanayatā* / *ʿanâtā* (*aya* > *â*)
2cd	*ʿanêtumā* (*ay* > *ê*)
1cd	*ʿanênāyā* (*ay* > *ê*)
3mp	*ʿanayū* / *ʿanû* (*ayū* > *û*)
3fp	*ʿanayā* / *ʿanâ* (*ayā* > *â*)
2mp	*ʿanêtumu* (*ay* > *ê*)
2fp	*ʿanêtina* (*ay* > *ê*)
1cp	*ʿanênū* (*ay* > *ê*)

G QATALA ŠTY, "to drink": *i* theme vowel

3ms	*šatiya* / *šatî* (*iya* > *î*)
3fs	*šatiyat* / *šatit* (*iya* > *î* > *i*)
2ms	*šatîta* (*iy* > *î*)
2fs	*šatîti* (*iy* > *î*)
1cs	*šatîtu* (*iy* > *î*)
3md	*šatiyā* / *šatî* (*iyā* > *î*)
3fd	*šatiyatā* / *šatîtā* (*iya* > *î*)
2cd	*šatîtumā* (*iy* > *î*)
1cd	*šatînāyā* (*iy* > *î*)
3mp	*šatiyū* / *šatû* (*iyū* > *û*)
3fp	*šatiyā* / *šatî* (*iyā* > *î*)
2mp	*šatîtumu* (*iy* > *î*)

2fp *šatîtina* (*iy* > *î*)
1cp *šatînū* (*iy* > *î*)

G qatala ʾTY (ʾTW) (*a* theme vowel, *w* third radical), "to come"

3ms *ʾatawa* / *ʾatâ* (*awa* > *â*)
3fs *ʾatawat* / *ʾatat* (*awa* > *â* > *a*)
2ms *ʾatôta* (*aw* > *ô*)
2fs *ʾatôti* (*aw* > *ô*)
1cs *ʾatôtu* (*aw* > *ô*)

3md *ʾatawā* / *ʾatâ* (*awā* > *â*)
3fd *ʾatawatā* / *ʾatâtā* (*awa* > *â*)
2cd *ʾatôtumā* (*aw* > *ô*)
1cd *ʾatônāyā* (*aw* > *ô*)

3mp *ʾatawū* / *ʾatû* (*awū* > *û*)
3fp *ʾatawā* / *ʾatâ* (*awā* > *â*)
2mp *ʾatôtumu* (*aw* > *ô*)
2fp *ʾatôtina* (*aw* > *ô*)
1cp *ʾatônū* (*aw* > *ô*)

G yaqtulu ʿNY, "to answer": *i* theme vowel

3ms *yaʿniyu* / *yaʿnû* (*iyu* > *û*)
3fs *taʿniyu* / *taʿnû* (*iyu* > *û*)
2ms *taʿniyu* / *taʿnû* (*iyu* > *û*)
2fs *taʿnîna* (*iyī* > *î*)
1cs *ʾaʿniyu* / *ʾaʿnû* (*iyu* > *û*)

3md *taʿniyā(na)* / *taʿnî(na)* (*iyā* > *î*)
3fd *taʿniyā(na)* / *taʿnî(na)* (*iyā* > *î*)
2cd *taʿniyā(na)* / *taʿnî(na)* (*iyā* > *î*)
1cd *naʿniyā* / *naʿnî* (*iyā* > *î*)

3mp *taʿniyū(na)* / *taʿnû(na)* (*iyū* > *û*)
3fp *taʿnîna* (*iy* > *î*)
2mp *taʿniyū(na)* / *taʿnû(na)* (*iyū* > *û*)
2fp *taʿnîna* (*iy* > *î*)
1cp *naʿniyu* / *naʿnû* (*iyu* > *û*)

G YAQTULU BǴ, "to explain": *a* theme vowel

3ms	*yibǵayu* / *yibǵû* (*ayu* > *û*)
3fs	*tibǵayu* / *tibǵû* (*ayu* > *û*)
2ms	*tibǵayu* / *tibǵû* (*ayu* > *û*)
2fs	*tibǵayīna* / *tibǵîna* (*ayī* > *î*)
1cs	*ʾibǵayu* / *ʾibǵû* (*ayu* > *û*)
3md	*tibǵayā*(*na*) / *tibǵâ*(*na*) (*ayā* > *â*)
3fd	*tibǵayā*(*na*) / *tibǵâ*(*na*) (*ayā* > *â*)
2cd	*tibǵayā*(*na*) / *tibǵâ*(*na*) (*ayā* > *â*)
1cd	*nibǵayā* / *nibǵâ* (*ayā* > *â*)
3mp	*tibǵayū*(*na*) / *tibǵû*(*na*) (*ayū* > *û*)
3fp	*tibǵêna* (*ay* > *ê*)
2mp	*tibǵayū*(*na*) / *tibǵû*(*na*) (*ayū* > *û*)
2fp	*tibǵêna* (*ay* > *ê*)
1cp	*nibǵayu* / *nibǵû* (*ayu* > *û*)

G Jussive ʿNY, "to answer": *i* theme vowel

3ms	*yaʿni* (< *yaʿniy*)
3fs	*taʿni* (< *taʿniy*)
2ms	*taʿni* (< *taʿniy*)
2fs	*taʿnî* (< *taʿniyī*)
1cs	*ʾaʿni* (< *ʾaʿniy*)
3md	*taʿniyā* / *taʿnî* (*iyā* > *î*)
3fd	*taʿniyā* / *taʿnî* (*iyā* > *î*)
2cd	*taʿniyā* / *taʿnî* (*iyā* > *î*)
1cd	*naʿniyā* / *naʿnî* (*iyā* > *î*)
3mp	*taʿniyū* / *taʿnû* (*iyū* > *û*)
3fp	*taʿnîna* (*iy* > *î*)
2mp	*taʿniyū* / *taʿnû* (*iyū* > *û*)
2fp	*taʿnîna* (*iy* > *î*)
1cp	*naʿni* (< *naʿniy*)

G Jussive BǴY, "to explain": *a* theme vowel

3ms	*yibǵa* (< *yibǵay*)
3fs	*tibǵa* (< *tibǵay*)

2ms	*tibǵa* (< *tibǵay*)
2fs	*tibǵayī* / *tibǵî* (*ayī* > *î*)
1cs	*ʾibǵa* (< *ʾibǵay*)
3md	*tibǵayā* / *tibǵâ* (*ayā* > *â*)
3fd	*tibǵayā* / *tibǵâ* (*ayā* > *â*)
2cd	*tibǵayā* / *tibǵâ* (*ayā* > *â*)
1cd	*nibǵayā* / *nibǵâ* (*ayā* > *â*)
3mp	*tibǵayū* / *tibǵû* (*ayū* > *û*)
3fp	*tibǵêna* (*ay* > *ê*)
2mp	*tibǵayū* / *tibǵû* (*ayū* > *û*)
2fp	*tibǵêna* (*ay* > *ê*)
1cp	*nibǵa* (< *nibǵay*)

G Volitive ʿNY, "to answer": *i* theme vowel

3ms	*yaʿniya* / *yaʿnî* (*iya* > *î*)
3fs	*taʿniya* / *taʿnî* (*iya* > *î*)
2ms	*taʿniya* / *taʿnî* (*iya* > *î*)
2fs	*taʿnî* (< *taʿniyī*)
1cs	*ʾaʿniya* / *ʾaʿnî* (*iya* > *î*)
3md	*taʿniyā* / *taʿnî* (*iyā* > *î*)
3fd	*taʿniyā* / *taʿnî* (*iyā* > *î*)
2cd	*taʿniyā* / *taʿnî* (*iyā* > *î*)
1cd	*naʿniyā* / *naʿnî* (*iyā* > *î*)
3mp	*taʿniyū* / *taʿnû* (*iyū* > *û*)
3fp	*taʿnîna* (*iy* > *î*)
2mp	*taʿniyū* / *taʿnû* (*iyū* > *û*)
2fp	*taʿnîna* (*iy* > *î*)
1cp	*naʿniya* / *naʿnî* (*iya* > *î*)

G Volitive BǴY, "to explain": *a* theme vowel

3ms	*yibǵaya* / *yibǵâ* (*aya* > *â*)
3fs	*tibǵaya* / *tibǵâ* (*aya* > *â*)
2ms	*tibǵaya* / *tibǵâ* (*aya* > *â*)
2fs	*tibǵayī* / *tibǵî* (*ayī* > *î*)
1cs	*ʾibǵaya* / *ʾibǵâ* (*aya* > *â*)

3md *tibǵayā* / *tibǵâ* (*ayā* > *â*)
3fd *tibǵayā* / *tibǵâ* (*ayā* > *â*)
2cd *tibǵayā* / *tibǵâ* (*ayā* > *â*)
1cd *nibǵayā* / *nibǵâ* (*ayā* > *â*)

3mp *tibǵayū* / *tibǵû* (*ayū* > *û*)
3fp *tibǵêna* (*ay* > *ê*)
2mp *tibǵayū* / *tibǵû* (*ayū* > *û*)
2fp *tibǵêna* (*ay* > *ê*)
1cp *nibǵaya* / *nibǵû* (*ayu* > *û*)

G Imperative ʿNY, "to answer": *i* theme vowel
2ms *ʿini* (< *ʿiniy*)
2fs *ʿinî* (< *ʿiniyī*)
2cd *ʿiniyā* / *ʿinî* (*iyā* > *î*)
2mp *ʿiniyū* / *ʿinû* (*iyū* > *û*)
2fp *ʿiniyā* / *ʿinî* (*iyā* > *î*)

G Imperative BǴY, "to explain": *a* theme vowel
2ms *baǵa* (< *baǵay*)
2fs *baǵayī* / *baǵî* (*ayī* > *î*)
2cd *baǵayā* / *baǵâ* (*ayā* > *â*)
2mp *baǵayū* / *baǵû* (*ayū* > *û*)
2fp *baǵayā* / *baǵâ* (*ayā* > *â*)

G Participle ŠTY, "to drink"

		Masculine	Feminine
Sg	Nom	*šātiyu* / *šātû*	*šātiyatu* / *šātîtu*
	Gen/Voc	*šātî* (< *šātiyi*)	*šātiyati* / *šātîti*
	Acc	*šātiya* / *šātî*	*šātiyata* / *šātîta*
Dual	Nom	*šātiyāma* / *šātîma*	*šātiyatāma* / *šātîtāma*
		bound: *šātiyā* / *šātî*	bound: *šātiyatā* / *šātîtā*
	Acc/Gen/Voc (Obl)	*šātiyêma* / *šātêma*	*šātiyatêma* / *šātîtêma*
		bound: *šātiyê* / *šātê*	bound: *šātiyatê* / *šātîtê*

Pl	Nom	*šātiyūma* / *šātûma* bound: *šātiyū* / *šātû*	*šātiyātu* / *šātîtu*
	Acc/Gen/Voc (Obl)	*šātîma* (< *šātiyīma*) bound: *šātî* (< *šātiyī*)	*šātiyāti* / *šātîti*

G Infinitive ŠTY, "to drink"

Free use *šatāyu* / *šatû* "to drink"
Nom *šatāyu* / *šatû* "to drink," "drinking"
Gen *šatāyi* / *šatî* "to drink," "drinking"
Acc *šatāya* / *šatâ* "to drink," "drinking"

III-y Verbs in the N-Stem

N QATALA ŠTY, "to be drunk (imbibed)"

3ms *naštaya* / *naštâ* (*aya* > *â*)
3fs *naštayat* / *naštat* (*aya* > *â* > *a*)
2ms *naštêta* (*ay* > *ê*)
2fs *naštêti* (*ay* > *ê*)
1cs *naštêtu* (*ay* > *ê*)

3md *naštayā* / *naštâ* (*ayā* > *â*)
3fd *naštayatā* / *naštâtā* (*aya* > *â*)
2cd *naštêtumā* (*ay* > *ê*)
1cd *naštênāyā* (*ay* > *ê*)

3mp *naštayū* / *naštû* (*ayū* > *û*)
3fp *naštayā* / *naštâ* (*ayā* > *â*)
2mp *naštêtumu* (*ay* > *ê*)
2fp *naštêtina* (*ay* > *ê*)
1cp *naštênū* (*ay* > *ê*)

N YAQTULU ŠTY, "to be drunk (imbibed)"

3ms *yiššatiyu* / *yiššatû* (*iyu* > *û*)
3fs *tiššatiyu* / *tiššatû* (*iyu* > *û*)
2ms *tiššatiyu* / *tiššatû* (*iyu* > *û*)
2fs *tiššatîna* (*iyī* > *î*)
1cs *ʾiššatiyu* / *ʾiššatû* (*iyu* > *û*)

3md	*tiššatiyā(na) / tiššatî(na) (iyā > î)*
3fd	*tiššatiyā(na) / tiššatî(na) (iyā > î)*
2cd	*tiššatiyā(na) / tiššatî(na) (iyā > î)*
1cd	*niššatiyā / niššatî (iyā > î)*
3mp	*tiššatiyū(na) / tiššatû(na) (iyū > û)*
3fp	*tiššatîna (iy > î)*
2mp	*tiššatiyū(na) / tiššatû(na) (iyū > û)*
2fp	*tiššatîna (iy > î)*
1cp	*niššatiyu / niššatû (iyu > û)*

N Jussive ŠTY, “to be drunk (imbibed)”

3ms	*yiššati (< yiššatiy)*
3fs	*tiššati (< tiššatiy)*
2ms	*tiššati (< tiššatiy)*
2fs	*tiššatî (< tiššatiyī)*
1cs	*ʾiššati (< ʾiššatiy)*
3md	*tiššatiyā / tiššatî (iyā > î)*
3fd	*tiššatiyā / tiššatî (iyā > î)*
2cd	*tiššatiyā / tiššatî (iyā > î)*
1cd	*niššatiyā / niššatî (iyā > î)*
3mp	*tiššatiyū / tiššatû (iyū > û)*
3fp	*tiššatîna (iy > î)*
2mp	*tiššatiyū / tiššatû (iyū > û)*
2fp	*tiššatîna (iy > î)*
1cp	*niššati (< niššatiy)*

N Volitive ŠTY, “to be drunk (imbibed)”

3ms	*yiššatiya / yiššatî (iya > î)*
3fs	*tiššatiya / tiššatî (iya > î)*
2ms	*tiššatiya / tiššatî (iya > î)*
2fs	*tiššatî (< tiššatiyī)*
1cs	*ʾiššatiya / ʾiššatî (iya > î)*
3md	*tiššatiyā / tiššatî (iyā > î)*
3fd	*tiššatiyā / tiššatî (iyā > î)*
2cd	*tiššatiyā / tiššatî (iyā > î)*

1cd	*niššatiyā* / *niššatî* (*iyā* > *î*)
3mp	*tiššatiyū* / *tiššatû* (*iyū* > *û*)
3fp	*tiššatîna* (*iy* > *î*)
2mp	*tiššatiyū* / *tiššatû* (*iyū* > *û*)
2fp	*tiššatîna* (*iy* > *î*)
1cp	*niššatiya* / *niššatî* (*iya* > *î*)

N Imperative ŠTY, "to be drunk (imbibed)"

2ms	*ʾiššati* (< *ʾiššatiy*)
2fs	*ʾiššatî* (< *ʾiššatiyī*)
2cd	*ʾiššatiyā* / *ʾiššatî* (*iyā* > *î*)
2mp	*ʾiššatiyū* / *ʾiššatû* (*iyū* > *û*)
2fp	*ʾiššatiyā* / *ʾiššatî* (*iyā* > *î*)

III-y Verbs in the D-Stem

D QATALA ŠQY, "to give drink"

3ms	*šiqqaya* / *šiqqâ* (*aya* > *â*)
3fs	*šiqqayat* / *šiqqat* (*aya* > *â* > *a*)
2ms	*šiqqêta* (*ay* > *ê*)
2fs	*šiqqêti* (*ay* > *ê*)
1cs	*šiqqêtu* (*ay* > *ê*)
3md	*šiqqayā* / *šiqqâ* (*ayā* > *â*)
3fd	*šiqqayatā* / *šiqqâtā* (*aya* > *â*)
2cd	*šiqqêtumā* (*ay* > *ê*)
1cd	*šiqqênāyā* (*ay* > *ê*)
3mp	*šiqqayū* / *šiqqû* (*ayū* > *û*)
3fp	*šiqqayā* / *šiqqâ* (*ayā* > *â*)
2mp	*šiqqêtumu* (*ay* > *ê*)
2fp	*šiqqêtina* (*ay* > *ê*)
1cp	*šiqqênū* (*ay* > *ê*)

D YAQTULU ŠQY, "to give drink"

3ms	*yašaqqiyu* / *yašaqqû* (*iyu* > *û*)
3fs	*tašaqqiyu* / *tašaqqû* (*iyu* > *û*)
2ms	*tašaqqiyu* / *tašaqqû* (*iyu* > *û*)

2fs	*tašaqqîna (iyī > î)*
1cs	*ʾašaqqiyu / ʾašaqqû (iyu > û)*
3md	*tašaqqiyā(na) / tašaqqî(na) (iyā > î)*
3fd	*tašaqqiyā(na) / tašaqqî(na) (iyā > î)*
2cd	*tašaqqiyā(na) / tašaqqî(na) (iyā > î)*
1cd	*našaqqiyā / našaqqî (iyā > î)*
3mp	*tašaqqiyū(na) / tašaqqû(na) (iyū > û)*
3fp	*tašaqqîna (iy > î)*
2mp	*tašaqqiyū(na) / tašaqqû(na) (iyū > û)*
2fp	*tašaqqîna (iy > î)*
1cp	*našaqqiyu / našaqqû (iyu > û)*

D Jussive ŠQY, "to give drink"

3ms	*yašaqqi (< yašaqqiy)*
3fs	*tašaqqi (< tašaqqiy)*
2ms	*tašaqqi (< tašaqqiy)*
2fs	*tašaqqî (< tašaqqiyī)*
1cs	*ʾašaqqi (< ʾašaqqiy)*
3md	*tašaqqiyā / tašaqqî (iyā > î)*
3fd	*tašaqqiyā / tašaqqî (iyā > î)*
2cd	*tašaqqiyā / tašaqqî (iyā > î)*
1cd	*našaqqiyā / našaqqî (iyā > î)*
3mp	*tašaqqiyū / tašaqqû (iyū > û)*
3fp	*tašaqqîna (iy > î)*
2mp	*tašaqqiyū / tašaqqû (iyū > û)*
2fp	*tašaqqîna (iy > î)*
1cp	*našaqqi (< našaqqiy)*

D Volitive ŠQY, "to give drink"

3ms	*yašaqqiya / yašaqqî (iya > î)*
3fs	*tašaqqiya / tašaqqî (iya > î)*
2ms	*tašaqqiya / tašaqqî (iya > î)*
2fs	*tašaqqî (< tašaqqiyī)*
1cs	*ʾašaqqiya / ʾašaqqî (iya > î)*

3md	*tašaqqiyā* / *tašaqqî* (*iyā* > *î*)
3fd	*tašaqqiyā* / *tašaqqî* (*iyā* > *î*)
2cd	*tašaqqiyā* / *tašaqqî* (*iyā* > *î*)
1cd	*našaqqiyā* / *našaqqî* (*iyā* > *î*)
3mp	*tašaqqiyū* / *tašaqqû* (*iyū* > *û*)
3fp	*tašaqqîna* (*iy* > *î*)
2mp	*tašaqqiyū* / *tašaqqû* (*iyū* > *û*)
2fp	*tašaqqîna* (*iy* > *î*)
1cp	*našaqqiya* / *našaqqî* (*iya* > *î*)

D Imperative ŠQY, "to give drink"

2ms	*šaqqi* (< *šaqqiy*)
2fs	*šaqqî* (< *šaqqiyī*)
2cd	*šaqqiyā* / *šaqqî* (*iyā* > *î*)
2mp	*šaqqiyū* / *šaqqû* (*iyū* > *û*)
2fp	*šaqqiyā* / *šaqqî* (*iyā* > *î*)

III-y Verbs in the Š-Stem

ʿLY, "to cause to go up"

QATALA	*šaʿliya* or *šaʿlî*, "he caused [someone/thing] to go up"
YAQTULU	*yašaʿliyu* or *yašaʿlû*, "he causes [someone/thing] to go up"
Imperative	*šaʿli*, "cause [someone/thing] to go up" (2ms)
	šaʿlî (< *šaʿliyī*) "cause [someone/thing] to go up" (2fs)
Participle	*mušaʿliyu* or *mušaʿlû*, "one who causes to go up" (nom ms)
Infinitive	*šaʿlāyu* or *šaʿlû*, "to cause to go

Bibliography

Bordreuil, Pierre, and Dennis Pardee. "Un abécédaire du type sud-sémitique découvert en 1988 dans les fouilles archéologiques françaises de Ras Shamra-Ougarit." *Comptes rendus des séances de l'Académie des Inscriptions et Belles-Lettres* 139 (1995): 855–60.

———. *A Manual of Ugaritic*. LSAWS 3. Winona Lake, IN: Eisenbrauns, 2009.

———. *Manuel d'ougaritique*. Paris: Paul Geuthner, 2004.

Boyes, Philip J. *Script and Society: The Social Context of Writing Practices in Late Bronze Age Ugarit*. Oxford: Oxbow, 2021.

Cline, Eric H. *1177 B.C.: The Year Civilization Collapsed*. Princeton: Princeton University Press, 2014.

Cunchillos, Jesús-Luis, Juan-Pablo Vita, and José-Ángel Zamora. *A Concordance of Ugaritic Words*. Piscataway, NJ: Gorgias, 2003.

Dietrich, Manfried, et al. *The Cuneiform Alphabetic Texts from Ugarit, Ras Ibn Hani, and Other Places*. Münster: Ugarit-Verlag, 2013.

Ellison, John L. "A Paleographic Study of the Alphabetic Cuneiform Texts from Ras Shamra-Ugarit." PhD diss., Harvard University, 2002.

———. "The Scribal Art at Ugarit." Pages 157–90 in *Epigraphy, Philology, and the Hebrew Bible: Methodological Perspectives on Philological and Comparative Study of the Hebrew Bible in Honor of Jo Ann Hackett*. Edited by Jeremy M. Hutton and Aaron D. Rubin. ANEM 12. Atlanta: SBL Press, 2015.

Greenstein, Edward. "Forms and Functions of the Finite Verb in Ugaritic Narrative Verse." Pages 75–102 in *Biblical Hebrew in Its Northwest Semitic Setting: Typological and Historical Perspectives*. Edited by Steven E. Fassberg and Avi Hurvitz. Winona Lake, IN: Eisenbrauns, 2006.

Gzella, Holger. "Some Penciled Notes on Ugaritic Lexicography." *BibOr* 64 (2007): 527–68.

Hackett, Jo Ann. "*Yaqtul* and a Ugaritic Incantation." Pages 111–17 in *Language and Nature: Papers Presented to John Huehnergard on the Occasion of His Sixtieth Birthday*. Edited by Rebecca Hasselbach and Na'ama Pat-El. SAOC 67. Chicago: Oriental Institute, 2012.

Hawley, Robert, Dennis Pardee, and Carole Roche-Hawley. "The Scribal Culture of Ugarit." *Journal of Ancient Near Eastern History* 2 (2015): 229–67.

Holmstedt, Robert. *The Relative Clause in Biblical Hebrew*. LSAWS 10.

———. "The Relative Clause in Canaanite Epigraphic Texts." *JNSL* 34 (2008): 1–34.

Huehnergard, John. *An Introduction to Ugaritic*. Peabody, MA: Hendrickson, 2012.

———. *Ugaritic Vocabulary in Syllabic Transcription*. HSS 32. Atlanta: Scholars Press, 1987.

Joosten, Jan. "The Functions of the Semitic D Stem: Biblical Hebrew Materials for a Comparative-Historical Approach." *Or* 67 (1998): 209–12.

Loundine, A. G. "L'abécédaire de Beth Shemesh." *Le Muséon* 100 (1987): 243–50.

Nougayrol, Jean. Emmanuel Laroche, Charles Virolleaud, and Claude F. A. Schaeffer. *Ugaritica V: Nouveaux textes accadiens, hourrites et ugaritiques des archives et bibliothèques privées d'Ugarit*. Paris: Geuthner, 1968.

Olmo Lete, Gregorio del, and Joaquín Sanmartín. *A Dictionary of the Ugaritic Language in the Alphabetic Tradition*. 3rd rev. ed. HdO 112. Leiden: Brill, 2015.

Pardee, Dennis. *Ugaritisch: Kurzgefasste Grammatik mit Übungstexten und Glossar (Elementa Linguarum Orientis 1)*, by Josef Tropper. *AfO* 50 (2003–2004): 412–17.

Parker, Simon B. "Studies in the Grammar of Ugaritic Prose Texts." PhD diss., The Johns Hopkins University, 1967.

Riley, Jason A. "'Why, O -y?' The 1cs Suffix in Ugaritic and Its Bearing on the Case of the Vocative." *UF* 44 (2013): 261–84.

Rubin, Aaron D. *Studies in Semitic Grammaticalization*. Winona Lake, IN: Eisenbrauns, 2005.

Schaeffer, Claude F. A. *Ugaritica III: Sceaux et cylindres hittites, épée gravée du cartouche de Mineptah, tablettes chypro-minoennes et autres découvertes nouvelles de Ras Shamra*. Paris: Geuthner, 1956.

Schniedewind, William M., and Joel H. Hunt. *A Primer on Ugaritic*. Cambridge: Cambridge University Press, 2007.

Singer, Itamar. *The Calm before the Storm: Selected Writings of Itamar Singer on the Late Bronze Age in Anatolia and the Levant*. WAWSup 1. Atlanta: Society of Biblical Literature, 2011.

Sivan, Daniel. *A Grammar of the Ugaritic Language*. Leiden: Brill, 2001.

Smith, Mark S. *The Ugaritic Baal Cycle*. Vol. 1. Leiden: Brill, 1994.

Smith, Mark S., and Wayne T. Pitard. *The Ugaritic Baal Cycle*. Vol. 2. Leiden: Brill, 2009.

Tropper, Josef. *Ugaritische Grammatik*. 2nd ed. AOAT 273. Münster: Ugarit-Verlag, 2012.

Tropper, Josef, and Juan-Pablo Vita. *Lehrbuch der ugaritischen Sprache*. Münster: Zaphon, 2020.

Watson, Wilfred, and Nicolas Wyatt. *Handbook of Ugaritic Studies*. Leiden: Brill, 1999.

Yon, Marguerite. *The City of Ugarit at Tell Ras Shamra*. Winona Lake, IN: Eisenbrauns, 2006.

www.ingramcontent.com/pod-product-compliance
Lightning Source LLC
Chambersburg PA
CBHW030825230426
43667CB00008B/1380
9781628374513